W9-BKR-132

THE MIDDLE SCHOOL CURRICULUM

A Practitioner's Handbook, Second Edition

Leslie W. Kindred, *Temple University*

Rita J. Wolotkiewicz, *Temple University*

John M. Mickelson, *Temple University*

Leonard E. Coplein, *Haddon Township Public Schools*

Allyn and Bacon, Inc.

Boston, London, Sydney, Toronto

Library of Congress Cataloging in Publication Data
Main entry under title:

The Middle school curriculum.

Bibliography: p.
Includes index.
1. Middle schools. I. Kindred, Leslie Withrow, 1905–
LB1623.M52 1976 373.2'36 80-12033
ISBN 0-205-06993-2

Managing Editor: Robert Roen
Series Editor: David Pallai

Printed in the United States of America.

Contents

Preface

A strong movement has been underway during the last fifteen years to replace the junior high school with the middle school. The motivations behind this movement are varied, but the one that seems most universal is the desire to bring a more functional type of education to youngsters between ten and fourteen years of age. This desire is predicated upon recent studies of growth characteristics and needs of young people in their prepubescent and early adolescent stages of development.

Unfortunately, too many middle schools have been organized along precisely the same lines as the junior high schools they replaced. Almost identical programs of study are offered, based upon similar philosophical and psychological approaches to the learning process. Such schools have missed the real essence of middle school education.

It was for these reasons that *The Middle School Curriculum: A Practitioner's Handbook* was designed and published in 1976. The present edition updates the previous one, incorporating new developments and concepts regarding middle school education. As a result, it represents a more comprehensive treatment as well as a more useful reference while retaining the better qualities of the original text.

The reader has an opportunity to gain a sound overview of the curriculum-building process and the avenues through which learning takes place. He or she is introduced to modern technology in the middle school and how it may be used for individualizing instruction and facilitating the instructional process. Attention is given to ways of organizing and utilizing personnel in order to realize more fully the objectives of the school. The place of student activities in the curriculum and the means available for evaluating various phases of student performance are also discussed.

Like its predecessor, this edition is aimed at helping students who are taking courses in elementary and secondary school curriculum, curriculum development, the junior high school, or the middle school. It should also be most useful in the in-service preparation of teachers for the middle school. And it can become an important reference book for conferences, workshops, and study committees concerned with the improvement of middle school education.

The authors appreciate the assistance given by colleagues and friends during the revision of the manuscript and the permission given by publishers and writers to use copyrighted materials.

L. W. Kindred
R. J. Wolotkiewicz
J. M. Mickelson
L. E. Coplein

Chapter 1

The Rationale

A major question facing schools is how to provide children with an education that not only will meet each one's personal needs, but also will incorporate social realities, including the perpetuation and realistic interpretation of democratic values. How can we liberate each individual in order to enable him or her to function at the highest possible level as a member of our rapidly changing society?

Many people believe that the middle school is a partial solution to these problems. Accordingly, this chapter provides the reader with an understanding of the factors leading to the middle school's development, a progress report on that development, and an idea of what should be expected of this relative newcomer to the educational scene. Subsequent chapters describe the philosophy and process of curriculum development and present a comprehensive description of varied means of individualizing instruction, as well as a summary of the most appropriate technological innovations. Activity programs, staff utilization, and assessment of performance are discussed in the final chapters.

THE MIDDLE SCHOOL MOVEMENT

Strong advocates of the middle school regard this comparatively recent development in American education more as an educational program resulting from a variety of forces than as a rearrangement of the traditional grade organization. In many instances, the junior high schools failed to meet the needs and interests of the "in-between-agers." Insufficient consideration was given to the extreme variabilities found within the age group as well as to the need for learning experiences that expedite the transition from the skill development and general education orientation of the elementary school to the specialized educational functions of the senior high. Increased attention to the social and cultural influences affecting the learner, to changing maturation patterns, and to new concepts about the learning process was needed.

GROWTH OF THE MOVEMENT The current concept of the middle school began developing in the late 1950s. The common organizational patterns we know today came into existence by 1963. A study by Zdanowicz in 1965 showed that, of the intermediate school units in his sample, 3.8 percent were organized to include a unit consisting of grades five through eight or six through eight.[1] His population consisted of a random sample of 414 middle and junior high schools located in the northeastern United States.

Cuff, for purposes of his survey, defined a middle school as a school that included grades seven and eight in its organization and that did not extend below grade four or above grade eight. In twenty-nine states, he found 446 school districts operating 499 middle schools fitting this description.[2] Alexander's survey of the number of such middle schools in the United States in 1967–68 indicated that there were about 1,100.[3] Gross found 960 middle schools in forty-seven states and the District of Columbia. Nearly two-thirds of the schools were located in the states of Texas, California, Illinois, Michigan, New Jersey, and Ohio.[4] His information was obtained during the first quarter of the year 1967.

In a more recent study, Raymer found 1,906 middle schools in the United States during the 1973–74 school year.[5] There were 521 middle schools housing grades five through eight; 1,092 schools housed grades six through eight. The remainder housed various grade combinations from grade four to grade nine.

1. Paul J. Zdanowicz, "A Study of the Changes That Have Taken Place in the Junior High Schools of Northeastern United States During the Last Decade and the Reasons for Some of These Changes," doctoral dissertation, Temple University, 1965, p. 117.

2. William A. Cuff, "Middle Schools on the March," *The Bulletin of the National Association of Secondary School Principals*, Vol. 51, February, 1967, p. 83.

3. William M. Alexander et al., *The Emergent Middle School*, 2nd ed. (New York: Holt, Rinehart and Winston, Inc., 1969), p. 9.

4. Bernard M. Gross, "An Analysis of the Present and Perceived Purposes, Functions, and Characteristics of the Middle School," doctoral dissertation, Temple University, 1972.

5. Joe T. Raymer, "A Study to Identify Middle Schools and to Determine the Current Level of Implementation of Eighteen Basic Middle School Characteristics in Selected United States and Michigan Schools," doctoral dissertation, Michigan State University, 1974.

Brooks completed a project in 1977 that identified 4,060 middle schools serving at least three grades, no more than five grades, and including at least grades six and seven.[6] The number of middle schools had quadrupled since 1967. It must be noted that the definition used was organizational rather than programmatic.

Another example of the growth of the movement is provided by a survey, the third in a series, completed in early 1977. A total of 221 middle schools were identified in the states of Illinois, Indiana, Iowa, Minnesota, and Wisconsin. By the 1973–74 school year, the number had increased to 487, and by 1976–77, 757 middle schools had been established.[7]

Grade-level organization was examined as part of the same study. Of the 557 schools responding, 356 (or 64 percent) included grades six through eight, while 122 (or 22 percent) included grades five through eight. These percentages are very similar to the 66 percent and 23 percent, respectively, found by Brooks in his larger study.

THE LEARNERS An important factor in the movement toward the middle school has been the changing nature of the development of today's young people. Due to better nutrition and improved medical care, boys and girls are maturing physically sooner than their parents did.

Along with accelerated physical maturation we find accelerated social maturation. Mass communications media and other cultural influences are making their mark. Youth between the ages of ten and fifteen possess much more knowledge of the world than their parents, or even their older brothers and sisters, had at a corresponding age. It is for these reasons that some educators advocate the inclusion of the sixth and sometimes the fifth grade in this intermediate unit called the middle school. Proponents of these five-three-four and four-four-four grade-grouping patterns also favor them because they keep the four-year senior high school organization intact.

While the six through eight and five through eight grade organizations are most common for middle schools, inclusion of the fifth grade has been questioned. For example, Moss, Jackson, and Jackson concluded in their study that fifth graders do not belong in a middle school. They based their conclusion on the known physical, intellectual, and

6. Kenneth Brooks, "The Middle School—A National Survey," *Middle School Journal*, Vol. 9, May, 1978, p. 6.

7. Thomas A. Sinks et al., "What's Happening to Middle Schools in the Upper Midwest?" *Clearing House*, Vol. 51, No. 9 (May, 1978), p. 6.

social characteristics of ten-year-olds and on a New York State study in which a number of administrators indicated that the major disadvantages of including grade five in the middle school are related to the physical and social immaturity of the age group.[8] It appears that school districts establish grade organizations that they believe to be most appropriate to their particular circumstances. Unfortunately, the decisions are sometimes based on administrative grounds rather than consideration of the characteristics and needs of the children to be served.

In order to design a curriculum that will provide an opportunity for meaningful experiences resulting in desirable learning, one must take into account the developmental stage of the learner. That is what the middle school is all about! Little good is accomplished and harm may even result if new learnings are introduced before the appropriate level of maturation has been reached.

Learning is affected by the environmental circumstances surrounding an individual. Home, school, social environment, and geographical location all have effects upon what each learns and, as Gagné indicates, upon the kind of person each becomes.[9] We still do not know the exact extent of these effects. However, each human being does develop his or her own ideas about the world, and each one's behavior is adjusted accordingly. On the basis of individual experiences, each moves constantly toward higher levels of maturation.

Related to maturity is the concept of readiness. Mastery of simple skills enables the individual to move on to development of higher-level skills. Concepts are developed in a hierarchical fashion, particularly during adolescence, when language becomes more and more important as a medium of expression. Readiness also implies that the student actively wants to learn. What a student wants to learn, of course, is that which each believes will satisfy his or her own needs. The most effective learning experiences help each student to recognize needs and to find means to fulfill them, thus fostering faster learning and greater gains in achievement. This, in turn, will lead to the development of a new set of needs to be met. (See Figure 1–1.)

Another important relationship is that between learning experiences and the ability of the learner. As students advance through the various levels or grades in school, individual differences in ability become more obvious. Each pupil's level of aspiration should be raised, but the extent of the individual's mental and physical abilities must not

---

8. Theodore C. Moss, Diane J. Jackson, and Richard G. Jackson, "Do Fifth Graders Belong in the Middle School?" *Middle School Journal*, Vol. 10, No. 2 (May, 1979), p. 3.

9. Robert M. Gagné, *Conditions of Learning*, 2nd ed. (New York: Holt, Rinehart and Winston, Inc., 1970), p. 2.

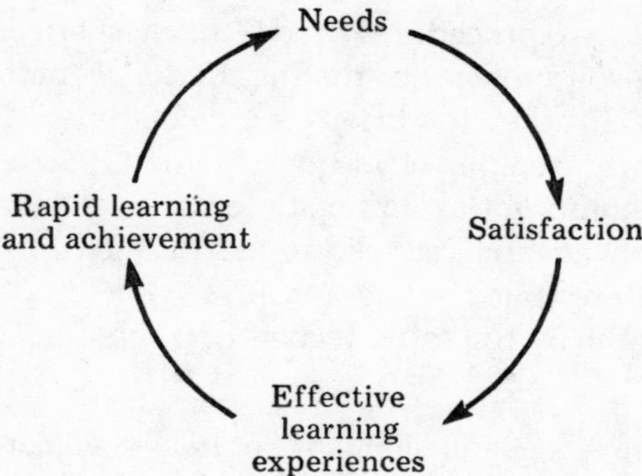

Figure 1–1. Readiness and Learning

be ignored. There is a point beyond which further additions to the quantity of the experiences could be detrimental to the quality of learning, or even to the student's health.

Additional impetus to individualization has been provided by Benjamin Bloom's concept of mastery learning. Bloom tells us that if we provide the needed time and appropriate methods, each individual can achieve the optimum level. Implicit in the approach is the need to break down each task into manageable parts. The learner moves on to the next step only after mastery of the previous one has been achieved. Bloom believes that, with favorable learning conditions, it is possible for 95 percent of the students to learn, at or near the same mastery level, all that the school has to teach. The kind and quality of instruction and the amount of time must vary according to the characteristics of the individual learner.[10] The implications for individualized learning approaches are obvious.

In his paper, "The Development of Talents," Benjamin Bloom points out that one problem he confronted in his studies was how to get the students to work toward a higher standard of excellence.[11] He reports:

> An effective solution was to provide periodic *feedback* to each student on what he had learned well and what he still needed to learn, supplemented by *corrective support and extra time* for him to correct his difficulties.

10. Benjamin S. Bloom, *Human Characteristics and School Learning* (New York: McGraw-Hill Book Co., 1976).

11. Benjamin S. Bloom, "The Development of Talents," unpublished paper.

Of the corrective procedures tried, "the most effective were to refer the student to specific places in the instructional material and to have students help each other for brief periods of time." Most of this was done outside of the regular class time. At first, some students needed five times the amount of time other students did to reach the same standard. This ratio was later reduced to less than two to one.

Another interesting finding resulted when mastery and control classes were taught by the same teacher. In these instances,

> . . . typical results on the summative or final examinations were that about 80% of the mastery students reached the same level as the top 20% of the control students. The achievement of the control students was highly predictable from aptitude tests, intelligence tests, or previous achievement tests. In contrast, the achievement of the mastery students was, in general, not predictable from these earlier measures.

Under mastery conditions, it was found that students tended to improve in their learning on each subsequent learning task, while the control group of students tended to remain the same or decline over the subsequent learning tasks. In addition, during one phase of Bloom's studies, mastery students increased the proportion of course time spent actively learning from about 60 percent of the classroom hour to about 85 percent, while the control students decreased their active learning period from the same 60 percent to about 45 percent on the average. The researchers attributed the changes "to the fact that most of the mastery students were helped to master the cognitive *prerequisites* for each subsequent learning task while many of the control students lacked these prerequisites." It also appeared that mastery students developed increased confidence in their ability to learn as they observed their own high level of achievement, while many of the control students who saw evidence that they learned poorly became convinced they could not learn the subject.

As the result of his work, Bloom has identified four processes that seem to have the most general applicability in education, human development, and talent development. He is using these categories in his current research on the development of talent. The four are as follows:

1. The setting of an appropriate standard of achievement and encouragement of individuals to attain it.
2. The provision of frequent feedback-corrective processes which enable most individuals to meet the standard for each learning task in a long series of such tasks.

3. The availability of some technique for individualization of the time and help needed by the individual in both the learning and the corrective process.
4. Increasing the amount of active learning time for the individual in and outside of the classroom.

INNOVATIONS IN METHODS AND MATERIALS The comparatively recent development of the middle school makes it an ideal place for innovation and change, since it has no traditions to uphold or break.

Much has yet to be learned about how to bring about optimum learning, but technology is doing its part to improve the learning process. The use of data processing for administrative purposes such as rostering and issuing grade reports is only the beginning. One hears the terms hardware and software applied to educational materials—the former being the physical computer equipment itself, and the latter being the programs, the data base, and various materials needed by the educational organization. The application of technology to education need not be accompanied by dehumanization. The interaction between students or between students and teachers makes for humanization. An appropriate use of technology can free teachers to be more available to learners who need special, personalized attention.

Another innovation is the development of open classrooms, with their completely student-centered approach. Flexibility in the use of space, furniture, and equipment leads to more informal teaching and learning situations. The importance of the individual becomes more apparent in an open classroom, where the personal freedom of the student is tempered by the necessity for intelligent student decision making.

Innovations in methods, materials, and educational settings will be successful only to the extent that they are related to the objectives of the teachers. Adaptation of any new approaches must be based on the teacher's decision that such approaches will improve the effectiveness of the teaching-learning situation, but fads must be avoided if the middle school is to be an effective institution.

RECENT INFLUENCES

Several influences that might be characterized as movements have exerted new pressures upon schools. While these pressures are directed at all levels of basic education, their implications for middle schools cannot be ignored. In addition, a changing society makes it mandatory that educational institutions be responsive. A well-conceived, flexible middle school curriculum is one means for responding.

BACK-TO-BASICS AND ASSESSMENT PROGRAMS Demands for accountability are being heard from community groups, school boards, state departments of education, and legislators. State legislation requiring specific minimum competencies for acquiring a high school diploma has become common. These demands, along with the clamor for a back-to-basics movement, have opened up a discussion of the meaning of "basics." Are reading, writing, and computation the only basics? Should the appreciation of aesthetics, personal and career development, development of warm interpersonal relationships, and pride in the quality of one's work be considered basics? Are the needs to learn to direct one's behavior and to learn to make wise decisions basics? Are not the basics, in fact, those learnings that will help youngsters move toward self-actualization?

There are many additional related questions: What competencies and levels of achievement are important? How are competencies to be assessed? What should follow after obtaining the results of assessments? How does one evaluate the affective aspects of an educational situation? Teachers need to be familiar not only with standardized measures of cognitive achievement but with measures in the affective domain, such as those mentioned by Swick and Gatewood: *Improving Education Assessment and an Inventory of Measures of Affective Behavior* (Washington, D.C.: ASCD); *Measures of Social Psychological Attitudes* (Ann Arbor, Mich.: Institute for Social Research, University of Michigan), and *Tests in Print: A Collection of Unpublished Research Instruments* (Princeton, N.J.: Educational Testing Service).[12] If the middle school is to be a credible institution, it must provide an educational program based on a broad definition of basics and competencies and accompanied by evaluation and research.

BEHAVIORISM VS HUMANISM The accountability movement has been strongly supported by scientific behaviorists. To disagree with their research designs, statistical approaches, and findings is difficult. The use of behavioral objectives does require identification of more precise and measurable pupil behaviors in place of traditionally vague

12. Kevin Swick and Thomas Gatewood, "Developing a Learning Climate Which Is Both Affective and Accountable," *Middle School Journal*, Vol. 9, May, 1978, pp. 10–11.

statements. An examination of instructional efforts is a necessary part of the approach.

On the other hand, some strong proponents of the humanistic approach argue that behavioristic approaches are mechanical and dehumanizing. They need not be, but behavioral approaches alone are not adequate to satisfy the developmental needs of students, and particularly the special needs of middle school students. Combs defines humanistic objectives as "broad, holistic goals of education." He goes on to say that

> they have to do with such objectives as self-understanding, self-fulfillment, good citizenship, responsibility, emotional well-being, worthy home membership, creativity, commitment to democratic ideals, adaptability to change, and intelligent behavior.[13]

Both behavioral and humanistic objectives are needed for accomplishing educational goals. They should be looked upon as alternatives with different purposes and different uses.

LEARNING AND TEACHING STYLES Increasing emphasis upon individualization has led to a developing body of research on learning styles. It has become more apparent that different students learn in different ways. Some need highly structured approaches, while others are motivated by less structured approaches. Preferences may be attributed to variations in the way individuals have learned to think. Individual interests, needs, and values also play a part.

> Different pupils utilize different learning modes of thinking and styles of learning to achieve different objectives depending upon different purposes. Many modes of thinking and learning are present. Most objectives are achieved through a type of rote learning which is relatively ineffective. Learning modes must be utilized in a practical operation in which students are presented with alternatives rather than a single question with a single right answer. Some individuals will learn by programmed textbooks utilizing stimulus-response theory; others will learn best in a concrete operational procedure; and yet others will learn best in a very theoretical framework in which abstract thinking is most utilized. All modes need to be encouraged so that the high school and college pupils will be able to employ whatever mode of learning is most effective within a particular situation.[14]

---

13. Arthur W. Combs, W. James Popham, and Philip L. Hosford, "Behaviorism and Humanism: A Synthesis?" *Educational Leadership,* Vol. 35, October, 1977, p. 55.

14. Thomas E. Curtis and Wilma W. Bidwell, *Curriculum and Instruction for Emerging Adolescents* (Reading, Mass.: Addison-Wesley Publishing Co., 1977), pp. 14–15.

The complexity of the whole concept of learning styles and of the accompanying one of teaching styles is demonstrated in the writings of the Dunns and the Fischers. The former have identified eighteen elements of learning style involving the environmental, sociological, and physical.[15] The latter have suggested ten learning styles as follows:

1. incremental learner
2. intuitive learner
3. sensory specialist
4. sensory generalist
5. emotionally involved
6. emotionally neutral
7. explicity structured
8. open-ended structured
9. damaged learner
10. eclectic learner[16]

The Fischers have at the same time identified six teaching styles, which are as follows:

1. task-oriented
2. cooperative planner
3. child-centered
4. subject-centered
5. learning-centered
6. emotionally exciting and its counterpart

In accord with the above, the teacher's role becomes one of matching teaching styles with learning styles. The total classroom climate as well as methods and materials must facilitate fitting that which is to be learned to the nature and needs of individual students. Appreciation of and respect for each student's individuality are needed, as well as willingness to provide a variety of teaching approaches for that uniqueness.

---

15. Rita S. Dunn and Kenneth J. Dunn, "Learning Styles/Teaching Styles: Should They . . . Can They . . . Be Matched" *Educational Leadership*, Vol. 36, No. 4 (January, 1979) pp. 239–240.

16. Barbara Bree Fischer and Louis Fischer, "Styles in Teaching and Learning," *Educational Leadership*, Vol. 36, No. 4 (January, 1979) pp. 245–254.

While much has been done in the area of learning and teaching styles, from the earlier work of Farr[17] and Domino[18] to the more recent attempts of Rita and Kenneth Dunn to diagnose learning styles, it must be conceded that the concept of learning style is relatively new and that much more research is needed to assess the many related variables.

READINGS FOR TEACHERS

Dunn, Rita, and Kenneth Dunn, *Teaching Students Through Their Individual Learning Styles: A Practical Approach*. Reston, Va.: Reston Publishing Co., 1978.

Joyce, Bruce, *Selecting Learning Experiences: Linking Theory and Practice*. Washington, D.C.: Association for Supervision and Curriculum Development, 1978.

Joyce, Bruce, and Marsha Weil, *Models of Teaching*. Englewood Cliffs, N.J.: Prentice-Hall, Inc., 1979.

PUBLIC LAW 94-142 In December, 1975, President Ford signed the Education for All Handicapped Children Act, known as Public Law 94-142. Delivery of education to the handicapped requires due process, free appropriate public education, individualized education programs, provision of the least restricted environment, and non-discriminatory testing. The law's provisions have led to:

1. Development of individualized instructional programs
2. Placement of handicapped students in regular educational settings to the maximum extent appropriate (mainstreaming)
3. In-service training for regular and special education teachers
4. Participation in the curriculum development process by parents, teachers, specialists, etc.

The handicapped must function in society, supporting themselves and participating in community life. For this reason, they need to participate in typical school situations to the extent possible. The implications for teachers and classroom procedures are obviously enormous.

---

17. Beatrice J. Farr, *Individual Differences in Learning: Predicting One's More Effective Learning Modality*, (Ann Arbor, Mich.: University Microfilms 1332A, July, 1971).

18. George Domino, "Interactive Effects of Achievement Orientation and Teaching Style on Academic Achievement," ACT Research Report 39:1–9, 1970.

ENROLLMENT SHIFTS School districts are contending with shifting patterns of enrollment as well as decreasing numbers of pupils. Some buildings are being closed, and teachers are being "pink-slipped." Students are being transferred from one building to another. Others who previously attended schools close to home are being bussed. As the economic situation continues to tighten, school boards, parents, and citizen groups are asking hard questions. Efforts of educators at the middle school level are being diverted from curricular and instructional program improvements to defending and justifying middle school programs. If middle schools are to survive, educators must become accountable without losing sight of the humanistic basis for the existence of middle schools.

A CHANGING SOCIETY A changing society places new burdens on education. Education must respond by becoming a promoter of change and an agent for synthesizing interacting forces. It must provide a basis for participation in decision making, particularly as it affects public policy. Processes for resolving value conflicts must be developed and taught.

Education was once looked upon as a means for transmitting culture, but its function today is much broader and more complex. Emphasis on process is apparent. Processes for selection of goals and activities become important; equally important is the process for selecting, with understanding and appreciation, the appropriate responses to an increasing range of phenomena.

Young people are challenging traditions. They are not as concerned as previous generations were with financial security. The influence of television and other mass media upon the preadolescent and early adolescent makes them aware that change is taking place. The school must help them to understand reasons for and outcomes of change. Many Americans are dissatisfied with what exists and are clamoring for change, but unfortunately they have no notion of what the results of change should be or how to go about accomplishing worthwhile, lasting change. No one can deny that continuous change for the better is a desirable goal. However, it should be steady and gradual. Precipitate change produces upheavals—change just for the sake of change is not desirable.

By the time the child reaches pubescence, he or she should be ready to discover relationships, seek answers to questions, determine where and how to find the information needed, and figure out how to organize and evaluate that information. Students should become active participants in the learning process, make choices, and learn to work independently. They should be able to go beyond content to the processes by which they can attain new knowledge when the need arises. This is the ideal time to emphasize the inquiry approach to learning, which develops the self-activated individual who is able to think objectively and reasonably, and to seek new and better solutions to personal and social problems. The task of the teacher becomes more difficult but also more rewarding as he or she arranges or constructs situations that are challenging to the learners, that help them to find meaning in their experiences, and that facilitate the development of the skills and independence that will enable them to further their own learning.

The fundamental changes taking place in society must be accompanied by a reexamination and reconstruction of its institutions. In the past, the adaptation of social institutions to new needs has been painfully slow; school organization has been particularly resistant to change. The rapidity of today's societal changes calls for equally rapid changes in the organization and administration of the entire educational structure. Applicable knowledge and new techniques must be applied to curricular content and organization and to the methods and materials of instruction. The middle school, with its unique philosophy, can play a very important role in society, for it can assist young persons in making their way in a rapidly changing world. They must be prepared to deal with changing family and community relationships. The development of rational thinking, with its methods for comparing sets of alternatives, should be a major goal of the middle school. It should prepare its students for the growing trend toward a systems-analysis approach to decision making.

The prepubescent child cannot help but be more aware of the rapidly changing world. Children today have a greater talent for dealing with the problems of accelerating knowledge and a better perspective on the social scene than their counterparts had a generation ago. Every available resource is needed to help develop the ability to cope with change. New concepts and new uses of technology are required. New materials must be developed and old ones modified. Imaginative applications of a multiplicity of media are essential, as are new methods of instruction. There is a basic interdependence among students, materials, and teachers that cannot be denied. A program for self-actualization is essential if middle school pupils are to possess the capability to cope with an ever-changing world. Such a program must motivate them to think both critically and creatively about themselves, society, and the universe.

Unfortunately, society in the past demanded compliance of the individual rather than self-fulfillment. People anxiously sought the approval of their peers; people tended to conform, with the result that the individual and his or her influence were lost. The educational system needs to be an instrument in shifting the emphasis from this bureaucratic and depersonalized condition to a more productive way of life.

CHARACTERISTICS OF A MIDDLE SCHOOL

The middle school must be not only a rearrangement of grades but also a definite attempt to provide for that period in a child's life referred to by Eichhorn in his book *The Middle School* as *transescence.*[19] This is a transitional period involving late childhood and early adolescence. The psychological and social-cultural aspects of development must be taken into account, as well as the physical aspects. Child-centeredness and humaneness are essential. To harmonize with this developmental stage, the school must be transitional. The school must make it possible for students to work on the developmental tasks associated with their particular stage of life at a particular point in time. A true middle school is student-centered, not subject-centered.

ARTICULATION Everything that is now known about human development emphasizes the fact that it is a continuous, unbroken process moving from one stage to the next. A predictable pattern can be found in physical, mental, and social development. Just as human development is a continuous process, the school curriculum should reflect a continuous unity. This is what is meant by vertical articulation. The middle school can best reflect this by emphasizing the continuation of basic education in the fundamentals while, at the same time, beginning to pave the way for entrance into the senior high school. It should provide a smooth transition from elementary school methods and materials to those of the senior high school. To achieve this, communication within grade levels, across grade levels, and across disciplines is needed.

EMPHASIS ON SELF-ACTUALIZATION Our society has discovered that the individual can become more than he or she ever dreamed. We are gaining understandings of the almost infinite adaptability of humans and of the importance of becoming a self-actualizing individual. Self-actualization is the capacity to reach the fullest extent of one's potential. It can be achieved only through individual psychological

---

19. Donald H. Eichhorn, *The Middle School,* (New York: The Center for Applied Research in Education, 1966).

freedom. True self-actualization can be realized only by the "supremely healthy, fully-functioning person."[20] A. H. Maslow views the need for self-actualization, defined as the capacity to become everything that one is capable of becoming, as uppermost in the hierarchy of human needs. Below self-actualization in this hierarchy are physiological security, safety, love and affection, and belonging. These concepts are developed quite extensively in Maslow's *Motivation and Personality*.[21]

It has become obvious that more emphasis is needed on providing each individual learner with every possible means of self-development through a student-centered curriculum. A whole new approach to education dealing with self-actualization has appeared. It is recognized that the uniqueness of each individual is of prime importance and must be preserved. The learner is looked upon as a whole person who is in a state of developing or becoming. He or she is a complex person and must be recognized as such by the developers of a curriculum. All children must be accepted for what they are and where they are, and an attempt must be made to help them become what they might be—that is, to enable each to develop to his or her fullest potential. Finally, the truly self-actualizing person has a strong positive self-image which, in turn, influences his or her perceptions of others.

The middle school must provide its pupils with opportunities to explore some of their own interests and ideas, encourage them to work independently, and assist them in discovering that learning within the formalized structure of a school can be exciting. A psychologically supportive environment is essential.

The following quotation focuses on several directions the middle school can take in its efforts to help its students work toward the goal of self-actualization:

> Our society now calls for each person to achieve a kind of maturity and depth of understanding that is not commonly achieved—self-actualization. Facilitating self-actualization in pupils is a task of the schools through curriculum content and teacher-pupil relations. In order to accomplish this, creative planning for educational reconstruction is imperative.
>
> We can make possible "fulfillment" education for all pupils. While curriculum revolution may be underway in mathematics and science, one of the most significant human needs has been neglected or overlooked. This need is related to self and the human condition. Only

---

20. Association for Supervision and Curriculum Development, *Perceiving, Behaving, Becoming*, 1962 Yearbook (Washington, D.C.: National Education Association, 1962), p. 2.

21. A. H. Maslow, ed., *Motivation and Personality*, 2nd ed. (New York: Harper and Row Pubishers, Inc., 1970).

when this need occupies a central position in the curriculum will fulfillment education become a reality. To achieve this kind of education, pupils must come to explore and learn independently. Equally important, they must be introduced to ethics and values.

Specifically, these new directions in education must occur for pupils to become self-actualizing persons.

1. Pupils must select areas of learning or problems which are significant for them.
2. Pupils must learn how to think creatively and flexibly.
3. Pupils must learn to generalize from data and to group ideas in meaningful clusters if they are to solve problems.
4. Pupils must be taught to generate models and theories to explain phenomena.
5. Pupils must learn ways to test hypotheses and make critical judgments.
6. Pupils, at some point, must arrive at a decision and take a stand.[22]

DEVELOPMENT OF SELF-DIRECTION In order to achieve self-actualization, each child must be helped through education to establish his or her values and to use those values in determining how to spend his or her energies. To accomplish this, middle school students must have knowledge of themselves and the ability to assess their needs and their powers. This assessment becomes the basis from which they work toward the optimum development of their capacities. They must be able to look back upon their past, look around at the present world, and project themselves into the future.

The development of self-direction or self-management in children has long been a major goal of American education. The two major components of this goal were summarized succinctly by Lois Barclay Murphy as follows:

1. Development of capacity for independence in meeting one's own needs and dealing with the environment.
2. Development of capacity for self-control or management of one's own impulses and drives.[23]

22. Association for Supervision and Curriculum Development, *Learning and Mental Health in the School*, 1966 Yearbook (Washington, D.C.: National Education Association, 1966), pp. 97–98. Copyright by the Association for Supervision and Curriculum Development.

23. Association for Supervision and Curriculum Development, *New Insights and the Curriculum*, 1963 Yearbook (Washington, D.C.: National Education Association, 1963), p. 107.

Children of middle school age have reached a stage in their development where it is possible to teach them to recognize and understand their needs, the reasons for their attitudes and behavior, and why one direction in which they might go is preferable to another. They can begin to make intelligent decisions about themselves and their future. The middle school must provide its students with opportunities to act independently and to do creative work, and, at the same time, ensure that they have the time to read, to discover the world about them, and, finally, to discover themselves as unique individuals.

USE OF INNOVATIVE TECHNIQUES The 60s are being looked back on as the years of innovation, while the cry in the 70s was for accountability. No one can deny the need for accountability. However, if the middle school is to continue to be a vital institution meeting the needs of its students, it must provide an environment that encourages innovative approaches to the teaching-learning situation. Professional literature abounds with phrases such as computer-assisted instruction, individually prescribed instruction, large-group and small-group instruction, simulation games, modular scheduling, and instructional media centers, all of which have become common, everyday terms in many school districts.

Major goals of the middle school should focus on the personal development of the learners, with provision for their transitional nature, and should include exploration of a wide variety of educational experiences, including work, leisure, and socializing. The program must focus on increasing the self-identity of each individual and on providing each with the skills needed for continuous learning. A flexible time schedule is essential for accomplishing these goals. Also, more individualization and personalization are needed, along with various types of grouping for various instructional purposes. An individualized instructional program that utilizes commercial and quasi-commercial instructional systems can create the motivating atmosphere and the emphasis on individual rates of progress that must be characteristic of the middle school.

Because the middle school is a comparatively recent educational unit, it provides a perfect opportunity for introducing some of these innovations. Its students are entering a new stage in their development and are becoming more receptive not only to increasingly independent work, but also to teaching methods that stimulate their motivation through inquiry and learning by doing. A middle school must provide fundamentally different settings for education. The uniqueness of its framework should encourage the development of a variety of unique educational concepts.

SPECIFIC CHARACTERISTICS OF A MIDDLE SCHOOL While it is not really possible to identify characteristics that would pertain only to a middle school, Georgiady, Riegle, and Romano have presented a comprehensive list that provides an excellent framework. These conclusions were reached following a review of the literature, discussions with educators in the field, and observations. The reader should find these characteristics helpful when evaluating an existing middle school or establishing a new one:

Continuous progress non-graded organization that allows students to progress at their own individual rate regardless of chronological age
Multi-material approach
Flexible schedules
Social experiences appropriate for transescent youth
Physical and intramural activities based solely on the needs of students
Team teaching
Planned gradualism to ease the transition from childhood dependence to adult independence
Exploratory and enrichment studies
Guidance services
Independent study
Basic skill repair and extension
Creative experiences
Security factor that meets students needs for a security group
Evaluation that is personal, positive, nonthreatening and individualized
Community relations program that is two-way
Broad spectrum of student services
Auxiliary staffing to provide individual help[24]

24. Nicholas P. Georgiady, Jack D. Riegle, and Louis G. Romano, "What Are the Characteristics of the Middle School" from *The Middle School: Selected Readings on an Emerging School Program* by Louis G. Romano, Nicholas P. Georgiady, and James E. Heald (Chicago: Nelson-Hall Co., 1973), pp. 75–84.

Chapter 2

The Child Ten to Fourteen

While middle school pupils usually only range in age from ten to fourteen years, their actual growth stages range from late childhood to early adolescence. The diversity among the students in physical maturation and in emotional, social, and intellectual characteristics makes the middle school exciting. Each child is a challenge for the teacher.

IMPORTANCE OF SELF-CONCEPT

Many factors combine to make the middle school child what he or she is. Each one's stage of growth is reflected physically and emotionally. Each must cope with a rapidly changing body and changing perceptions of self and of others.

The child of ten is entering what can be called a preadolescent stage. Preadolescence has also been termed *pubescence*, the point in a child's life when rapid physical changes begin to take place. The physical changes are accompanied by changes in intellectual functioning. When the child approaches the age of thirteen or fourteen, the period of early adolescence begins. This period, in between childhood and adulthood, is when a youth starts the search for an adult personality. Early adolescents begin to view themselves as separate from their families and to look inward in their search for an identity.

The rapid changes experienced by middle school children require a period of psychological and social reorientation. The child is very conscious of rapid bodily changes and believes that they are even more apparent to everyone else. Each child must come to understand that growth patterns are highly individualized; one's own rate of change will differ to some extent from that of one's classmates. Each must also learn to accept and handle the lack of coordination that accompanies rapid growth.

It is a well-accepted fact that negative perceptions of oneself can have a debilitating effect. To be effective, a person must have an adequate concept of self, leading to a healthy outlook on life and an acceptance of one's own limitations. Each must be satisfied with the self-view. It is the view from within that counts; it is not what you are, but what you think you are.

When an individual can accept himself or herself, he or she is better able to accept others as well. Acceptance is not an innate characteristic, but something that must be learned by experiencing acceptance and openness from others. The child builds attitudes, habits, and knowledge from an experiential background. One's self is shaped in relationship to others, and each individual's behavior changes as a result of others. Individuality is derived from a biological inheritance and the effect of all past experiences, which come from the stimuli of the environment.

The person with an adequate self-view will behave more effectively and intelligently than others and will set realistic goals. Such an individual will be a more responsible person, will have the capacity to work harmoniously with others in whatever role is required, and will not be overly concerned with conformity.

The middle school child is in the process of establishing a new self-concept while facing a number of needs. There is a need for security in personal and social relationships—relationships with members of the same sex during preadolescence and with members of the opposite sex later on. This is very well expressed by the following:

How can a person feel liked unless somebody likes him?
How can a person feel wanted unless somebody wants him?
How can a person feel acceptable unless somebody accepts him?
How can a person feel able unless somewhere he has some success?
How can a person feel important unless he is important to someone?[1]

At the same time, the individual needs to develop a personal philosophy as well as to establish a feeling of worth through achievement.

1. Arthur W. Combs, ed., "The Positive View of Self," *Perceiving, Behaving, Becoming*, 1962 Yearbook, Association for Supervision and Curriculum Development (Washington, D.C.: National Education Association, 1962), p. 101.

FACTORS INFLUENCING GROWTH

Numerous factors influence the growth of an individual. During the period of late childhood, the individual experiences the most rapid growth spurt since infancy. Each particular developmental pattern is strongly affected by heredity and environment, but it has been proven that hereditary and environmental factors have their greatest effect prior to the teenage years.

HEREDITY Certain aspects of an individual's growth pattern are the result of hereditary factors. Such characteristics as body structure and the unique timetable according to which change takes place are probably determined by genes. Many physiological capacities and latent skills that are derived from parents, grandparents, and great-grandparents will appear during adolescence.

Some inheritable traits may not appear in every generation or may be modified by the influence of opposite traits from the other parent. It is sometimes difficult for a child to understand why his or her physical build and abilities are what they are. Ability to run, the level of muscular coordination, and basic physical capacities are dependent on one's heredity, which each must learn to accept, as difficult as that may sometimes be.

Frequently a child who has inherited a small stature also inherits a metabolic imbalance that turns food into body fat at a particularly fast rate. This characteristic provides an additional handicap which makes it difficult to participate effectively in physical activities. The problem becomes more severe when the child enters the adolescent period of accelerated growth, which is usually accompanied by an increase in appetite.

In the area of mental development, the nature versus nurture debate has continued for many years. The IQ test does not measure basic inherited intelligence; it measures one's ability to handle verbal symbols and shows a positive correlation with scholastic success. IQ is not independent of the environment. However, recent studies, which are admittedly limited because of the difficulties involved in conducting them under widely different environmental conditions, indicate that the genetic component outweighs the environmental component. Genetic and physical factors combine with nutritional factors to influence mental development.

ENVIRONMENT It is expected that the current trend toward earlier physical and social maturation will continue. This trend is the result of a number of forces in the environment, including socioeconomic conditions, cultural variables, and technological developments.

Socioeconomic Conditions. A relationship exists between early growth and socioeconomic conditions. Since socioeconomic conditions have been favorable in this country in the recent past, physical growth has been accelerating. It is estimated that maturation is occurring nine months to one year earlier than it was thirty years ago. This is a direct result of better prenatal care and other advances of medical science. Increased understanding of vitamins and nutrition, immunization against childhood diseases, and reduction of infection and of the debilitating effects of disease are all making their influence felt. The normal child between ten and fourteen is extremely healthy. The greatest health problem is the possibility of injury as a result of clumsiness or awkwardness arising from rapid physical growth.

Cultural Variables. Certain cultural variables may slow down or accelerate the child's developmental rate. In the American culture, a child's experiences are very closely related to socioeconomic class. The social conditions surrounding an individual provide a framework within which each learns to act and to conceptualize. The learner's self-expectations are also culturally based; the middle school child's adjustment to the environment depends upon the relationship between his or her growth patterns and the expectations of society.

Parents have more than hereditary influence over their children's growth. Children show an accelerated intellectual growth pattern when their parents are warm and accepting. These children also tend to be less excitable, more emotionally secure, and more original. If parents actively reject their children, the children tend to be slightly decelerated in intellectual development, to use their abilities relatively poorly, and to be emotionally unstable, aggressive, and rebellious. Family patterns provide a great deal of important information relative to the growth of an individual child. It is obvious that parental attitudes toward children have a tremendous effect on their ways of thinking and behaving and their emotional and social development.

A fairly recent development is illustrated by the fact that over 50 percent of the women of working age are now employed outside the home. As a result, the family structure has changed drastically during recent years so that some feel it no longer provides the closeness and security it once did. Where school was once viewed as a supplement to the home in engendering a sense of permanence and security, the situation is now often felt to be reversed. Both boys and girls have to deal with the added dimension of the changing role of females in American society.

Prepubescent and pubescent youngsters are at a stage where they are beginning to transfer their base for security from home and parents to peers. In addition, they are achieving sophistication earlier than their parents did, so adolescent culture is closer to adult culture than it was a generation ago. This earlier sophistication poses a challenge to home and school alike.

Finally, the alternative lifestyles developing from the counterculture movement of the 1960s have created some confusion in moral standards and value development. This, added to the factors above, has led to the emergence of clearly defined youth subcultures which may take any number of forms. An academic orientation is the least likely result, while there has been an unfortunate increase in delinquent behavior. Middle school students are finding the pressures to conform to peer cultures more difficult to deal with than ever.

Technological Developments. Another important influence on growth is the current rapidity of technological change. Although civilization has always been in a state of change, the pace has been accelerating much faster. The increased emphasis on technology is influencing all aspects of life, including personal values and moral and religious beliefs.

The current period of rapid change tends to widen the gap between child and adult. Many adults were awed by the developments that made it possible not only for a man to walk on the moon, but for viewers on earth to watch while it happened. Each launch into space triggered a feeling of excitement in many adults because they remember that it once took two days to fly from New York to California. To children growing up in today's world, taking off into space does not create a great feeling of wonder because they have not lived through the slow developmental stages.

Today we can view something on the far side of the earth at the same time it is occurring. New stereophonic sound systems, popular among young people, have produced a new vocabulary including words such as "woofers" and "tweeters." The effects of technological advances on school curricula make it almost impossible for parents to assist with the mathematics and science being studied by their children in school.

The current instability of international and national affairs is exerting its pressure on the developing middle school child. International relations are strained by the possibility of a nuclear war. Today's generation is living during a period in which wars are being fought, but the horrors of an "all-out" nuclear war, which would threaten even the survival of civilization, are almost unimaginable. Add to this the internal struggles between the various subcultures in the United States and you begin to appreciate the difficulty facing students who are preparing to make their way in this world. Each individual must have an adequate personality in order to survive in a far-from-perfect social world and a rapidly changing physical environment. The more complex society and its cultural forces become, the more strain and stress are placed upon each individual.

Paradoxically, technology is also foremost among the factors aiding in the growth and development of middle school learners. Many children spend more time with the television set than with the teacher. The adverse effect of this increased viewing must be countered with responsible action by family and community. It should be recognized, however, that the various communications media do sometimes provide unparalleled opportunities for enriched intellectual experiences. Television programs such as the "Underwater Explorations of Jacques Cousteau" make their impact by presenting in a very palatable form knowledge that hitherto was unavailable to children. The positive effect of "Sesame Street" on the mental development of preschool children is being publicized. These kinds of experiences will have a long-range effect on the middle school child.

The learner can take advantage of other products of technology alone. A child between ten and fourteen years of age can manipulate the simple machines that give access to filmstrips, slides, and tape recordings. Newspapers are becoming accepted as part of the vast array of available teaching materials; in many homes boys and girls have been reading them since an early age.

We are much more closely linked with people of other lands than ever before. Advances in transportation, communication, and mass media will foster this link with increasing effectiveness. Transportation is allowing us to become a nation of globe-trotters; one finds among children in a middle school many who have lived and traveled in other parts of this nation and in other countries. And for boys and girls of middle school age who have not gone beyond their immediate neighborhoods, because of the cultural disadvantages of being born and raised in a ghetto area, mass media can be a vital link with the world.

GROWTH PATTERNS

It is essential that maturing boys and girls understand the changes taking place within themselves and accept them as part of growing up. The term *adolescence* means a period of transition, a time of many changes between childhood and full maturity. As middle schoolers approach puberty and the subsequent adolescent period, they become more aware of themselves and the ways in which they are beginning to change. This awareness causes conflicts in their thinking and in their emotions.

PHYSICAL DEVELOPMENT Increases in an individual's height and weight are related to age and to stage of pubescence. The most marked changes in height and weight occur at the onset of puberty.

Most boys reach the stage of puberty, the point at which adolescence begins, at the age of fourteen or fourteen and a half, whereas girls reach that point at about age twelve and a half or thirteen. Thus the physical development of girls is about one and a half to two years ahead of that of boys. In the approximately three years during which their bodies change most rapidly, girls gain an average of thirty pounds, while boys gain an average of forty.

One of the results of this rapid physical growth is poor motor coordination. Although adolescents have relatively few health problems, they tend to have difficulties with injuries resulting from accidents. Not only is the rapidity of growth a problem, but the unevenness characteristic of growth during this stage also produces difficulties. Arms and legs may suddenly increase in length; the awkwardness that results can be embarrassing and disconcerting.

Ten-year-olds generally have acquired the motor skills they need, but, as they reach the age of twelve, they become more self-conscious about learning new skills. And, because of their growth at this time, it is more difficult for them to develop new skills. During later adolescence (when girls are fourteen to eighteen years of age and boys range in age from sixteen to twenty), increased muscle growth and decreased growth in height and weight make the acquisition of new motor skills easier again.

The period of most rapid growth not only produces poor motor coordination, but also a low tolerance for fatigue. In addition, both boys and girls begin to develop anxieties about their personal grooming, accompanied by feelings of restlessness and irritability. Physical development is the base for other kinds of development, which can be seriously affected if one is dissatisfied with his or her physical development.

MENTAL DEVELOPMENT Two of the more important areas in which mental development takes place are problem solving and creativity. Rapid physiological development at an early age will be accompanied by a correspondingly rapid rate of mental growth. If physiological development occurs later, mental development will occur at a slower rate. Among children between the ages of ten and fourteen, one will find a wide range in mental abilities because of the irregularities of physical, social, and psychological growth. The home, the school, and the influence of society are additional factors.

The noted learning theorist Jean Piaget identified several hierarchical stages in the intellectual development of the child. The final two of these stages are pertinent to the middle school child: the stage of concrete operations, which takes place between the ages of seven and eleven, and the stage of formal operations, which occurs between eleven and fifteen years of age. In the stage of concrete operations, the learner can manipulate ideas only in the presence of actual things and immediate experiences. In the stage of formal operations, the individual can develop ideas about ideas and handle relationships in the absence of the concrete. It is believed that most boys and girls enter the formal operations stage during transescence. How an individual student functions depends upon how he or she is taught. Mentally, the child of middle school age should be ready to move from an understanding of the real and the concrete to an understanding of the theoretical and the hypothetical. However, there are individual differences as to when the stages begin, so one finds middle school students functioning at different Piagetian stages. While some are in the concrete-operations stage, others are dealing with the abstract, and still others are at various stages in between. At the same time, there are differences in the accomplishments of the same individuals in various fields of subject matter.

An extensive analysis of the Harvard Growth Data by Ethel Cornell and Charles Armstrong indicates that a variance in mental growth occurs between the end of the childhood cycle and the beginning of the adolescent cycle. This suggests the existence of a plateau or period of no growth in early adolescence, and hence the possibility that it might be more logical to classify pupils according to growth patterns rather than chronological age.[2]

Epstein has brought this concept of brain growth periodization during early adolescence to the attention of educators. He states that in perhaps 85 percent of all youngsters between ages twelve and fourteen, the brain virtually ceases to grow, and that in a large number of cases, "this slow brain growth period parallels the transescent's pubertal metamorphosis . . . ."[3] Brain growth spurts appear in five age-intervals, with those between ten to twelve years and fourteen to sixteen years being most significant for middle school educators. These spurts are also somewhat related in time to Piaget's developmental stages. Because the ages twelve to fourteen correspond roughly with grades seven and eight,

2. Ethel L. Cornell and Charles M. Armstrong, "Forms of Mental Growth Patterns Revealed by Reanalysis of the Harvard Growth Data," *Child Development*, Vol. 26, September, 1955, pp. 200–202.

3. Herman T. Epstein and Conrad F. Toepfer, Jr., "A Neuroscience Basis for Reorganizing Middle Grades Education," *Educational Leadership*, Vol. 35, May, 1978, p. 657.

> the prediction here would be that it is relatively more difficult to initiate novel intellectual processes in the middle grades years than in periods both preceding and following this period. Another aspect of this prediction is that it should be characterized far more by maturation in already initiated and learned cognitive skills than in the acquisition of new skills. . . . Emphasis on affective and psychomotor aspects of learning might well receive increased attention and opportunity during this slow brain growth period.[4]

Other recent research has established new insights into the basic functions of the two hemispheres of the brain. Experiments were initially conducted with severe epileptics and accident patients by California neurosurgeons Roger Sperry, Joseph E. Bogan, and Phillip Vogel. Further experiments on normal people by a psychologist, Dr. Robert Ornstein, and his colleagues established the concept of the "bifunctional" brain in man.

> The researchers found that the left hemisphere controls functions of language, logical thought, and sense of time. It is analytical in that it breaks things down and logical in that it puts things in order. Oral and written language are good examples of functions of the left brain.
>
> The right hemisphere, on the other hand, specialized in intuition, creativity, spatial abilities, and simultaneous understanding. It sees interrelated patterns, perceives things as a whole, and has a comprehensive sense of time and space. It can encompass many thoughts and actions at the same time. The right brain is less verbal. Painting, sculpting, and dancing are examples of activities of the right brain.[5]

The implications of the research described are that different students may approach problems in different ways, since they may be predisposed toward one hemisphere or the other, as shown in Figure 2-1. Max R. Rennels emphasizes another important concern when he says: "In emphasizing linear thought, educators have neglected the brain's right hemisphere. By encouraging imagination, visualization, and attention to sensory stimuli, the balance can be corrected."[6] Rennels also discusses the importance of unifying the neural functions residing in both hemispheres of the brain.

---

4. Ibid., pp. 657–658.

5. Leanna Landsmann, "The Brain's Division of Labor," *New York Times*, 30 April 1978, Section 12, p. 24. © 1978 by The New York Times Company. Reprinted by permission.

6. Max R. Rennels, "Cerebral Symmetry: An Urgent Concern for Education," *Phi Delta Kappan*, Vol. 57, March, 1976, p. 472.

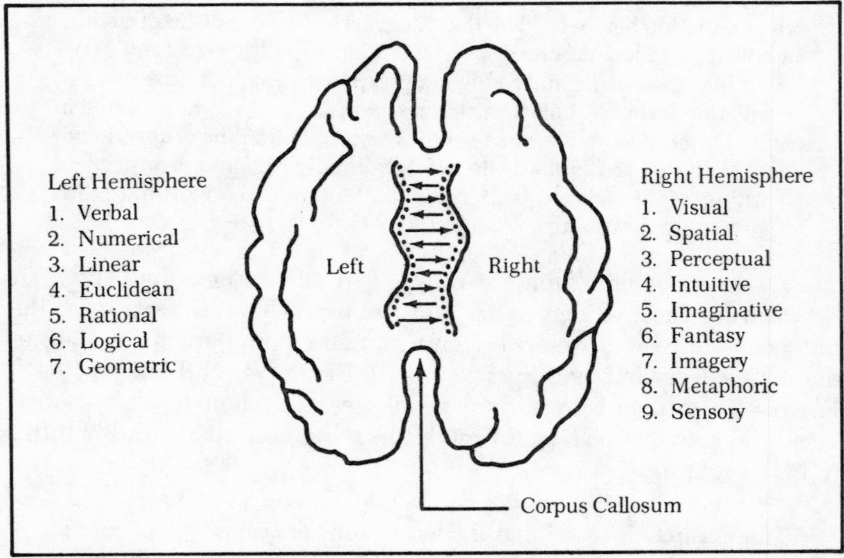

Figure 2–1. Resident Functions of Left and Right Hemispheres (Source: Max R. Rennels, "Cerebral Symmetry: An Urgent Concern for Education," *Phi Delta Kappan*, Vol. 57, March, 1976, p. 472.)

Everyone is born with some potential for creativity. Encouragement and nurture are essential to its development; otherwise the potential may be lost because of the self-consciousness of the individual child. As youth and adults advance in years, the use of creative power seems to diminish, although it is believed that a positive relationship exists between general intellectual ability and creative abilities. Children of ten or eleven entering the middle school should not yet have been stifled in utilizing their creative abilities, and development of these abilities should be encouraged with the appropriate school atmosphere.

After a young child in his first years in school watched a garden worm for a while, he came up with the following:

HOW WORMS WALK

Some worms don't have any feet.
They pull themselves out,
And they pull themselves in,
And they pull themselves out,
And they pull themselves in;

And that's the way they get along—
Because they don't have any feet.[7]

Education should continually nurture in children their ability to express themselves. If experiences are capitalized on, we will find poems of the caliber of the one below, which was written by a sixth-grade boy.

THE KING

It grew from a thought
And there it stands,
Tall and graceful,
King of steel and cement
Looking down loftily from the high perch
At its far-flung realm.
There, look above you;
In a heaven of blue mist
Waiting to be praised
Stands the finished skyscraper.
It grew from a thought
And there it stands![8]

Simple short stories, skits, playlets, and songs are among the wide variety of opportunities for self-expression. Many delightful songs have resulted from class efforts when individuals contributed single lines of the final whole.

The opportunities presented by the many art media from pencil and charcoal to oil paints are endless. Burlap, noodles, rice, and odd beads can be made available as additional materials for self-expression and creative effort. Creative efforts give children an opportunity to view with pleasure and satisfaction what they have wrought. They need constant encouragement to be freely creative; they must not be bound by endless rules of proportion, balance, use of color, and perspective. These rules have their place in instruction, but they must not be emphasized to the point of inhibiting children's freedom of expression.

Some teachers prefer quiet, complacent conformists for students. However, the most creative youngsters often do not fit this mold. They are inclined to act quickly without considering all possible outcomes, and they tend to be less concerned about how others regard them. With

7. Hughes Mearns, *Creative Power: The Education of Youth in the Creative Arts* (New York: Dover Publications, Inc., 1958), p. 108.

8. Ibid., p. 111.

the rapid increase in knowledge, there is a need for divergence and new ways to cope with new circumstances. The creative individual who possesses abilities such as fluency, originality, and flexibility is just the kind of person needed to meet these new situations. Boys and girls must learn to question tradition without being lawbreakers.

SOCIAL DEVELOPMENT The development of individuals may be affected positively or negatively by the group to which they belong. They learn about themselves through interaction with others, including their peers. While the social growth patterns of the early adolescent are characterized by many and varied changes, and those of early childhood by stability, the preadolescent period appears to be quite unique.

During the preadolescent stage, boys are most likely to relate to closely organized gangs. They are boisterous, noisy, aggressive, and often just plain sloppy. Girls present an opposite picture. They are more friendly, neat, shy with their peers, and less likely to have tight gangs. They gradually become more talkative and develop an aggressiveness toward boys taking the form of teasing to gain their attention. Also, girls are usually more interested in making good grades than boys.

During the early middle school years, boys find relationships with the same sex satisfying, but by the time they complete eighth grade, boys are beginning to be attracted to girls. The girls, in many instances, have been attracted to boys for a whole year already.

Ten-year-olds learn a great deal from the "gang" or group to which they belong. They feel the pressures of its demands to conform for social acceptance. It is from this relationship that they develop social attitudes and the ability to participate in and enjoy social and group activities. At the age of ten, boys and girls tend to belong to a gang whose members are of the same sex. With maturity, heterosexual interests, activities, and relationships increase in importance. By the age of fourteen, boys and girls are beginning to become more interested in themselves as individuals and less interested in conformity. They must develop the skills required to conform to the peer culture, but continue their development as individuals with distinct abilities and characteristics.

Early adolescents are on the threshold of maturity, physically and psychologically. As children, they were protected by adults. Now they are vulnerable. They try to cover up what they feel to be their inadequacies. They cannot meet adult standards, so they learn heavily on their peers; peer standards become extremely important to them. They try to meet the group's expectations in order not to feel inferior and, most important of all, to be accepted by them. They make every effort to be like other members of their own particular group.

Peer groups can provide opportunities boys and girls need to get along with others of their own age; these are the people they will later work with, play with, and marry. The peer group also provides an opportunity to have fun. Children need to be part of a group that will exert pressure on them to conform. It is a place to escape from family influences.

As children approach the ages of twelve, thirteen, or fourteen, they begin to view their parents objectively and sometimes see them as authoritarian and demanding. Early adolescents believe their parents to be totally oblivious of their deep feelings and yearnings; bickering and quarreling with parents are not uncommon. Young boys and girls try in every way to express their new independence and their desire to be less helpless than they feel. In order to conform to demands from outside the home, such as those of the peer group, they may abandon a pattern of complete loyalty to their parents.

Middle school children have a world of their own which is reflected in their interests and values. The characteristics of this world are circumscribed by their family relationships, by the influences of school and the world in general, and, as family influence diminishes, by the values of their peer group.

A rather recent change in American society which has had an additional impact upon social development is the increased awareness of ethnic identity. Children come from diverse ethnic and social backgrounds. Once looked upon as an "Americanizing" agent, the school has since become an instrument for preserving ethnic consciousness and developing multicultural understanding. Students have been encouraged to become more aware of their ethnic background and to retain this awareness. An unfortunate result has been the polarization of students with similar backgrounds, producing an adverse effect upon their overall social development.

EMOTIONAL DEVELOPMENT At the age of ten or eleven, children are on the threshold of a number of emotional changes. As their bodies begin to change and it becomes necessary for them to deal with the changes, they become extremely sensitive. Their own assets are not quite adequate to meet the demands on them. They must learn how to control their emotions and refrain from relieving tension through an outward expression such as boisterousness, which, in many instances, is considered inappropriate to the situation.

The transition from preadolescence into early adolescence may be accompanied by increasing emotional instability. Curtis and Bidwell list the characteristics of this period as:

1. tension due to developmental characteristics
2. ambivalence
3. sex-role conflicts
4. restlessness
5. introspection
6. idealism
7. enthusiasm
8. negative attitudes[9]

Blount and Klausmeier summarize the particular needs of children during this stage as follows:

1. Understanding socially approved methods for relieving emotional tensions and substituting these for childish or otherwise disapproved methods.
2. Analyzing emotional situations objectively.
3. Obtaining a broader understanding of situations in which disruptive emotions are produced.
4. Acquiring many social skills to meet new situations.
5. Eliminating fears and emotionalized patterns of response that are already firmly established.[10]

Gertrude Noar sees the following as "needs all children experience as they strive to lead emotionally comfortable lives in which they can make normal progress toward maturity":

1. The need for affection and security, which create feelings of being wanted and a sense of belongingness.
2. The need for recognition and reward.
3. The need for achievement and success, which help to create feelings of adequacy.
4. The need for fun and adventure: new experience.[11]

9. Thomas E. Curtis and Wilma W. Bidwell, *Curriculum and Instruction for Emerging Adolescents* (Reading, Mass.: Addison-Wesley Publishing Co., 1977), p. 33.

10. Nathan S. Blount and H. J. Klausmeier, *Teaching in the Secondary School*, 3rd ed. (New York: Harper and Row Publishers, Inc., 1968), p. 45.

11. Gertrude Noar, *The Junior High School: Today and Tomorrow*, 2nd ed. (Englewood Cliffs, N. J.: Prentice-Hall, Inc., 1961), p. 32.

As they meet the needs above, children gain an insight into their own behavior that enables them to deal with problem situations without tremendous stress and strain. Thus, they move toward emotional stability. If they are to develop and mature in the school situation, they must be free from anxiety and preoccupation with personal problems; otherwise their achievement can be seriously affected by their emotional disorganization.

GROWTH AND THE CURRICULUM

Human development is a continuous, predictable process. At every stage, an individual is capable of achieving certain competencies, both mental and physical. In other words, one can expect that certain developmental tasks will be acquired within the framework of specific chronological periods.

DEVELOPMENTAL TASKS One of the best-known contributors to the concept of developmental tasks is Robert J. Havighurst. He has specifically defined what it is the child needs to accomplish at each developmental stage in order to be ready to move on to the next stage. He has even extended this concept to include the various stages of adulthood. The tasks of later childhood and adolescence might comprise one base for developing a curriculum appropriate for the middle school. Developmental tasks are defined as follows:

> The tasks the individual must learn—the developmental tasks of life—are those things that constitute healthy and satisfactory growth in our society. They are the things a person must learn if he is to be judged and to judge himself to be a reasonably happy and successful person. A developmental task is a task which arises at or about a certain period in the life of the individual, successful achievement of which leads to his happiness and success with later tasks, while failure leads to unhappiness in the individual, disapproval by the society, and difficulty with later tasks.[12]

Three sources of developmental tasks are physical maturation, cultural pressure of the society, and the personal values and aspirations of the individual that are part of his personality. Havighurst gives two reasons why developmental tasks are important to educators: (1) they help

---

12. Robert J. Havighurst, *Human Development and Education* (New York: Longman, Inc., 1953), p. 2.

in discovering and stating the purposes of education in schools, i.e., to help the individual to achieve certain of the tasks; and (2) they affect the timing of educational efforts by determining the teachable moment when conditions are most favorable for learning the tasks.

As previously mentioned, two developmental periods, later childhood and adolescence, are very important to the middle school. The developmental tasks of later childhood cover three areas. The first is the child's movement away from the home influence to that of the peer group. The second is the development of neuromuscular skills, and the third is the introduction to adult concepts. These are then broken down more specifically into the following areas:

1. Learning physical skills necessary for ordinary games.
2. Building wholesome attitudes toward oneself as a growing organism.
3. Learning to get along with age-mates.
4. Learning an appropriate social role.
5. Developing fundamental skills in reading, writing, and calculating.
6. Developing concepts necessary for everyday living.
7. Developing conscience, morality, and a scale of values.
8. Achieving personal independence.
9. Developing attitudes toward social groups and institutions.

The developmental tasks of adolescence cover particularly the areas of physical and emotional maturity. They include the following:

1. Achieving new and more mature relations with age-mates of both sexes.
2. Achieving an appropriate social role.
3. Accepting one's physique and using the body effectively.
4. Achieving emotional independence of parents and other adults.
5. Achieving assurance of economic independence.
6. Selecting and preparing for an occupation.
7. Preparing for marriage and family life.
8. Developing intellectual skills and concepts necessary for civic competence.
9. Desiring and achieving socially responsible behavior.
10. Acquiring a set of values and an ethical system as a guide to behavior.

As can be seen from the above, life tasks are also expectancies. They represent not only what is expected of a human being at each stage of development, but also what each person expects of himself or herself. These tasks help to give direction to one's life. They must be taken into consideration when structuring the curriculum so that the learning expected is at a level appropriate to the maturity and ability of the learners.

PERSONAL AND SOCIAL NEEDS An individual's needs fall into two classes: personal and social. A personal need is an individual want or wish that may be long range or immediate. Personal needs may arise as a result of the demands of society upon an individual. A social demand may be one an individual recognizes and accepts, and even personally feels, or it may be a demand placed upon the individual by some outside force which one does not accept or personally feel.

As rapidly changing and developing personalities, middle school children need moral support and advice. They must be made to feel like intelligent human beings, encouraged to find their own answers, and treated like the individuals they aspire to become. They must develop competencies to love, work, and play, and they must find healthy self-fulfillment through satisfaction of their personal needs. A positive self-view will enable each to face new situations adequately.

The middle school program must provide its pupils with experiences that will foster satisfactory relationships among peers and mature relationships with adults. Students must be able to work harmoniously with others in the role of leader or follower. If a child receives effective guidance through the early middle school experiences, social problems should decrease during the pubescent and early adolescent years. Interest and hobby groups, classroom group experiences, and activity programs all provide opportunities to achieve this goal.

Adjustment to relationships with the opposite sex is a problem that must be recognized. Boys and girls must be given opportunities to associate with one another if they are to derive maximum benefit from the academic program. Assignments that require boys and girls to work together in groups are an excellent means of achieving this goal. Five or six students may be required to plan and work together to develop and present a report in social studies. When groups of boys and girls are told to present current events in an unique manner, some very clever presentations may result.

PHYSICAL AND MENTAL DEVELOPMENT Patterns of mental development and physical growth have a definite effect on school learning and cannot be ignored in curriculum planning. Learning may decrease during periods of rapid physical growth as energy is depleted by the heavy demands upon it. The sequence and content of the curriculum and the methods of instruction must reflect the changing patterns of the child's mental development. Energies and interests characteristic of middle school pupils at each stage of their development must be considered when planning the program. As the old saying goes, "You can lead a horse to water but you can't make him drink it."

Krathwohl has defined education as "changing the behavior of a student so that he is able, when encountering a particular problem or situation, to display a behavior which he did not previously exhibit."[13] This should be the overall objective of the total school program, particularly that portion described as general education. Preadolescents begin to be aware of certain goals which become more apparent as they approach adolescence. These goals include the various aspects of maturity, from physical through social-emotional to intellectual. Education should be directed toward achievement of these goals in order to develop the desired self-actualizing, integrated personality.

Curricular provision for special interests is also influenced by growth patterns. An obvious example is a physical education activity program. Appropriate selection of sports activities will minimize the probability of students injuring themselves through clumsiness, yet provide them with a feeling of achievement as they increase the effectiveness of their coordination.

The fact that girls tend to mature earlier than boys is another consideration, particularly when determining the kinds of social activities to provide. Shop and home economics experiences, music and art, and other areas must be available for exploration to meet developing special interests and capabilities. Availability of a variety of offerings should be the keynote for an effective middle school curriculum.

INDIVIDUALIZATION Teachers must recognize students as individuals; different individuals have different experiences when participating in the same learning activities.

Conformity and individuality each have a place, and the school must provide for the balanced development of both. Each individual must have the opportunity to develop his or her potential to the fullest.

---

13. David R. Krathwohl, "Stating Objectives Appropriately for Program, for Curriculum, and for Instructional Materials Development," *Journal of Teacher Education*, 1965, p. 9.

This can be accomplished by curricular provision for both individualized and group learning situations.

The curriculum must be pupil-centered; it must provide opportunities for each child to exercise a desire for independence. Each must be able to achieve personal goals while learning. Each student must be assisted in establishing realistic goals that will help him or her to move toward self-acceptance and acceptance of others. Each must experience success as an individual, and the curriculum must lead toward self-understanding.

THE TEACHER'S ROLE

A prerequisite for development of a true middle school program is a team of teachers who are attuned to the nature of the students and who respond accordingly both in curricular planning and in their relationships with students. The teachers must observe student characteristics and behaviors, and be responsive to students' intellectual, personal, and social needs.

While it is obvious that teachers must be familiar with the characteristics of middle-school-age children, they also need some insight into the later stages of adolescence. The reader is referred to a recent National Society for the Study of Education yearbook titled *Youth*,[14] in which the authors view adolescence as basically biological and "youth" as a social state. They raise a rather interesting question when they point out that we might be overestimating the inevitability of turbulence, rebellion, and upheaval among children of adolescent age. This has important implications for middle school teachers, who could be effective in reducing the negative aspects of later adolescence through appropriate methods of instruction.

DIFFERENCES IN GROWTH PATTERNS As stated earlier, girls generally are ahead of boys in physical development by one and a half to two years. The boys, meanwhile, are gaining over the girls in physical strength. The teacher needs to realize that the growth spurts of the preadolescent and early adolescent periods consume much of the student's energy. Because boys develop at a slower rate and the changes are greater, their painful period of awkwardness seems to extend longer than it should. This requires patience on the part of the teacher. Boys'

14. Robert J. Havighurst and Philip H. Dreyer, eds., *Youth*, National Society for the Study of Education Yearbook Series, No. 74, Pt. 1 (Chicago: Univ. of Chicago Press, 1975).

clumsiness and overactivity must be tolerated. This is particularly difficult if teachers compare them to the quieter, more mature, and seemingly "settled" girls. Boys and girls should not be compared; variations in growth must be accepted and provision made in curricular activities to accommodate their differences.

HEALTH PROBLEMS Although children of middle school age are characteristically quite healthy (since childhood illnesses have been left behind), the teacher must still be alert to health problems. A seeming lack of interest could actually be the result of depleted energies stemming from very rapid growth. Lack of sleep and poor eating habits are not uncommon. Some parents tend to become less watchful when their children reach this stage, since prepubescents and pubescents become more and more independent.

Late hours can be a particular problem as late-hour television programs become more attractive to the child. Students have been known to fall asleep in school because they stayed up to watch the late show while their parents went to bed. A healthy, rested child should be able to participate actively during the entire school day; if anyone appears unable to do so, this warrants investigating. Lack of muscular coordination, a certain amount of poor posture, and sluggishness are temporary reactions to spurts in physical growth.

VARYING LEVELS OF SKILL DEVELOPMENT Each child brings to school a unique background and individual physical, mental, and social characteristics. One child may have a special aptitude for music and another for art. It is not unusual for a sixth-grade teacher to find a variation of three or four years in the reading levels of children in a particular class. Tremendous differences are apparent in other basic skills, such as mathematical skills. A truly homogeneous class does not exist.

By the time children enter the middle school, the diversity in their basic skill development is greater than it was in the lower grades. This is normal and must be accepted by the middle school teacher. Middle schools must attempt to strengthen basic skill development where needed and to encourage the child with well-developed skills to use these skills for further learning. During middle school is not the time for teachers to complain that the elementary school teachers did not do their job. Each teacher needs to determine the level of accomplishment of each child and then use it as a base from which to proceed. No child need be downgraded because his or her spelling skills leave something to be desired. Such a view weakens rather than strengthens an individual's self-concept. The middle school is a place to further development of each child's basic skills; teachers should not expect the child to have mastered all skills and be ready for secondary-school-type activities.

PEER RELATIONSHIPS Teachers can learn much about their students from observing them as a group or in groups. Some students are members of many groups, whereas others seem to belong to none. Sometimes it is desirable to modify grouping patterns to improve the distribution of children with low peer-status. The isolated child needs to be looked after carefully.

To many children, particularly as they approach adolescence, being "in the right crowd" is important. Efforts in this direction may divert too much attention from their learning activities. The teacher must recognize these situations and try to develop a positive, supportive classroom situation for all children so that they can use all their abilities.

Children of low peer-status need to be given tasks to improve their status, and all children must be encouraged to observe their own behavior in relationships with others. Teaching about individual differences and causes of behavior can be helpful. Membership in a group provides a kind of strength that must be recognized by the teacher who is on the outside of that group. The teacher must also recognize that a child's peer-status can be enhanced by open disagreement with the teacher.

THE AFFECTIVE APPROACH Attitudes toward self and toward others have an important influence upon motivation and achievement. Everyone wants to be recognized, appreciated, respected, and loved. Fully functioning, responsible individuals will demonstrate positive attitudes toward school and their fellow human beings. Stress will not take an undue toll on their abilities to respond, and there will be constant growth in their ability to cope with stress. The overanxiousness of pupils is as much of a signal to the teacher that there is a problem as apathy or boisterousness. Consistent guidance and emotional support on the part of the teacher are essential. The teacher should avoid situations from which an emotional crisis might result.

The attitudes of the teacher are important to the students, just as the attitudes of the students are important to the teachers. The teachers must reflect neutral attitudes and refrain from harsh, unnecessary judgments. If the teacher shows concern about the student, the student's attitudes will reflect this: "The teacher is interested in me." An attitude of rebellion and insubordination will be replaced by one of interest and eagerness to become involved.

Each student needs to develop an understanding of his or her self within the framework of the environment and to accept the uniqueness of self and of others. Responsibility for one's own behavior as well as that of others must also be developed. In other words, an affective approach is one that encourages socially acceptable and socially responsible behavior.

Another important area is that of values clarification. This includes experiences with formal ethical statements as well as with the processes of exploring and identifying the values one really holds as opposed to those to which lip service is given because of the opinions of others. There is also a need to become acquainted with and to develop a respect for the value systems of others. The right to express divergent opinions and ideas must be stressed.

Curtis and Bidwell discuss seven processes in the affective domain that provide direction for the development of affective process objectives. These are:

1. development of viable self-image
2. development of social skills
3. inculcation of sportsmanship
4. encouragement of creativity
5. development of leadership capabilities
6. engagement in the valuing process
7. cultivation of aesthetic skills[15]

In short, value systems, feelings, and attitudes may play an important role in how students orient themselves to learning and how they achieve in their school work. As children grow up, they want some tangible value in the tasks assigned to them by teachers and parents. They are assembling a set of values to serve as ideals and standards, which will enable them to lead healthy, happy, useful lives. Current conflicts in our society between widely divergent social, economic, and political views make the choosing of such a set of values more difficult than ever. Much discussion and a wide range of reading are essential. Through discussion the teacher can gain insight into the values held by individual students so that strategies can be determined. The teacher's goals as defined by Kimball Wiles are the following:

> Each pupil will: (1) develop a set of values that will guide his behavior; (2) acquire the skills necessary to participate effectively in the culture; (3) gain understanding of the social, economic, political and scientific heritage; and (4) become able to make a specialized contribution to the society.[16]

15. Thomas E. Curtis and Wilma W. Bidwell, *Curriculum and Instruction for Emerging Adolescents* (Reading, Mass: Addison-Wesley Publishing Co., 1977), p. 174.

16. Kimball Wiles, "Education of Adolescents: 1985," *Educational Leadership*, Vol. 18, May, 1960, p. 489.

Students must be asked questions that will help clarify their own beliefs and purposes. They must be helped to understand their own values and to evaluate the acceptability of these values to themselves, their peers, their parents, and the culture. Throughout this process, the teacher must serve as nonjudgmental facilitator as each child attempts to develop a personal system of values and resolve conflicts in values to his or her own satisfaction. The teacher who senses that students are having a particularly difficult time going through the process of value clarification can help by leading them to see themselves clearly and then to identify their individual purposes and goals. The thinking required for this clarification of values will help in development of the thinking process. The process should also lead toward achievement of improved emotional health, ethical growth, and moral development.

While the majority of young adolescents emerge from the period quite well, there are many who do have problems. As Lipsitz points out:

> Seventh graders are most likely to be the victims of violence in school. The reported incidence of gonorrhea in adolescents ages 10–14 increased 10% between 1964 and 1975, nearly twice the increase of reported cases in 15–19 year olds. Drug abuse peaks during early adolescence. Girls 15 and under are the only age group for whom the birth rate is not decreasing. The onset of alcohol abuse occurs at around age 12. The rate of running away has doubled in the past decade, and the average age of runaways is 14. Fifteen and under is the only age group experiencing an increase in the rate of first admissions to mental hospitals. Juvenile crime appears to "blossom" around age 14. The average age of children in foster care is 12.[17]

The field of early adolescence has been neglected by researchers, so little is known about the relationships among emotional, social, intellectual, and biological development. However, there is an increasing awareness of the need for social institutions to be more responsive to young adolescents; this has become even more apparent as a result of the findings of a report prepared by Lipsitz for the Ford Foundation.[18]

PARTICIPATION IN IN-SERVICE PROGRAMS Many teachers assigned to middle schools have received no specific preparation for teaching in a situation in which the unique characteristics of transescents are emphasized. Participation by all middle school teachers in high quality

17. Joan Scheff Lipsitz, "Growing Up Forgotten—Must They?" *Middle School Journal*, Vol. 10, February, 1979, pp. 3–4.

18. Joan Scheff Lipsitz, *Growing Up Forgotten; A Review of Research and Programs Concerning Early Adolescence* (Lexington, Mass.: D. C. Heath & Co., 1977).

in-service programs is needed. Those who have special training and/or skills must provide leadership for others so that all teachers will possess the competencies to:

1. understand and communicate with middle school students
2. balance the cognitive and the affective
3. provide effective instruction
4. deal with a variety of learning styles
5. allow for varying levels of skill development
6. develop appropriate teaching materials
7. work across interdisciplinary lines

The result should be truly competent teachers capable of providing the necessary environment of the intellectual, social, physical, and emotional growth of middle school students.

READINGS FOR TEACHERS

Adams, James F., ed., *Understanding Adolescence: Current Developments in Adolescent Psychology.* Boston: Allyn and Bacon, Inc., 1976.

Association for Supervision and Curriculum Development, *Feeling, Valuing, and the Art of Growing: Insights into the Affective,* 1977 Yearbook. Washington, D.C.: ASCD, 1977.

Cornell, Ethel L., and Charles M. Armstrong, "Forms of Mental Growth Patterns Revealed by Reanalysis of the Harvard Growth Data," *Child Development,* Vol. 26, September, 1955, pp. 169–204.

Epstein, Herman T., "A Neuroscience Framework for Restructuring Middle School Curricula," *Transescence: The Journal of Emerging Adolescent Education,* Vol. 5, 1977, pp. 6–11.

Epstein, Herman T., and Conrad F. Toepfer, Jr., "A Neuroscience Basis for Reorganizing Middle Grades Education," *Educational Leadership,* Vol. 35, May, 1978, pp. 656–660.

Chapter 3
Learning and Intellectual Development

It is the premise of the present volume, and of all other works that deal with the middle school, that the young person of middle school years is different from the child of the years before and the adolescent of the years to follow. If the child's overall development is unique at this stage, it follows that during this period intellectual development is also unique. Further, it is quite likely that certain learning procedures or instructional strategies are more characteristic of or appropriate to this age group than to others. The present concern, then, is the development of a rationale to undergird curriculum planning and classroom instruction.

The development of such a rationale is not an easy task. Waetjen has noted that "unfortunately, learning is not the simple act of taking over information that is made available, nor is teaching the simple act of organizing material in logical order and presenting it to learners."[1] Although it is possible to generalize about teaching groups of youngsters, each middle schooler is after all an individual. Children and young adolescents grow according to generalized patterns of development, yet within the general pattern each has a special pattern and a particular rate of growth. The complexity arising from individualized growth patterns is increased by the fact that children bring with them their own personal values, problems, drives, and incentives, most or all of which may conflict with the purposes of the school.

---

1. Walter B. Waetjen, "Curiosity and Exploration: Roles in Intellectual Development and Learning," in *Intellectual Development: Another Look*, A. H. Passow and R. R. Leeper, eds. (Washington, D.C.: Association for Supervision and Curriculum Development, 1964), p. 54.

> Basic ability and cultural differences, reflected in that which boys and girls have learned previously, result in some who are younger in age than their peers in the grade groups, while still others, encrusted with years of failure and frustration in school, are one, two or even three years older than their grademates. . . . The more successful the schools are in meeting the needs of their clientele, the larger the differences that will exist between individual students; the longer boys and girls remain in school, the greater the differences will become.[2]

The foregoing underlines the difficulties created for students when each is expected to adapt to a single curriculum. Thus, as Appel points out: "Individualization of instruction is the instructional strategy most appropriate to the promotion of cognitive development."[3]

THEORIES OF LEARNING AND INTELLECTUAL DEVELOPMENT

No theory of learning or intellectual development explains to everyone's satisfaction either the manner in which learning occurs or the conditions that are essential for intellectual development. It is possible—with due regard for consistency—to be eclectic, drawing from the theorists those of their explanations and propositions that have relevance for the design of curriculum and the planning of instruction. Space limitations prohibit a detailed examination, but it is possible to present highlights from those theories of learning and intellectual development most pertinent to the middle school.

LEARNING DEFINED A generally accepted, working definition of learning states that *learning is the modification or change of behavior.* In this usage behavior is viewed as encompassing both the cognitive and affective domains. Perhaps the preceding definition is an oversimplification, but it is useful in that it excludes those notions of learning that view the mind as a muscle to be exercised or a reservior to be filled. A more precise definition is provided by Gagné, who defines learning as

2. John M. Mickelson, "Instructional Processes," in *The Intermediate Schools,* Leslie W. Kindred, ed., (Englewood Cliffs, N.J.: Prentice-Hall, Inc., 1968), pp. 59–60.

3. Marilyn H. Appel, "The Application of Piagetian Learning Theory to a Science Curriculum Project," in *Topics in Cognitive Development,* Vol. I, The Jean Piaget Society, M. H. Appel and L. S. Goldberg, eds., (New York: Plenum Press, 1977), p. 191.

"a change in human disposition or capability, which can be retained, and which is not simply ascribable to the process of growth."[4]

Some writers concerned with learning and intellectual development in the middle school extend the foregoing definition of learning thus—learning is the modification or change of behavior *through experience.* Technically, a definition of something should not include the means by which that something is acquired, but the violation is deliberate and is intended to emphasize the importance attached to the proposition that one learns through experiencing.

If the curriculum designer, instructional planner, or classroom teacher accepts the foregoing definition of learning, major changes will be required in his or her role. The function of instruction, and instructional content and format, will be to promote desirable behavior change; so, to various degrees and in varying ways, curriculum designers, instructional planners, and classroom teachers become change agents. This modified definition of learning requires new approaches to the selection of curricular content and the organization of instruction. Teaching can no longer be equated with telling; rather, the teacher or the teaching team must actively create the type of situation in which learning can occur. This represents a major shift in the role formerly allotted the classroom teacher.

EXPERIENCING AND LEARNING Because it is basic to modern educational practice, it is important that the curriculum designer, the instructional planner, and the classroom teacher understand the relationship between experiencing and learning.

Experiencing (as contrasted with experience) is an active process which is often poorly understood. At any given time the learner is an integral element of some situation. The situation may be the classroom, the playground, the home, or the community. In any event, the learner is bombarded by stimuli. His or her responses are selective; that is, he or she responds to some stimuli and not to others. The learner acts or reacts to the stimuli in terms of the situation. This interaction constitutes the process of experiencing. Experiencing may, in some circumstances, be a relatively simple thing; in other situations, it may be extremely complex. In any event, the learner is acting and reacting (interacting) in some sort of stimulating situation.[5]

---

4. Robert Gagné, *The Conditions of Learning*, 2nd ed. (New York: Holt, Rinehart and Winston, Inc., 1970), p. 5.

5. Thomas E. Clayton, *Teaching & Learning: A Psychological Perspective* (Englewood Cliffs, N.J.: Prentice-Hall, Inc., 1965), pp. 35–36.

For the purposes of designing the curriculum and planning instruction for the classroom, experiences may be equated with the opportunities for learning available to the learner. It is through the process of acting and reacting in response to situations—experiencing—that behavior change occurs. Thus, it can be said that from experience comes learning and out of many experiences arises understanding.

The child is constantly experiencing in all types of places and under all kinds of circumstances. The circumstances under which the experiences occur may result in desirable learning or undesirable learning. It is impossible to predict which will result, since controls may be limited or absent. However, within the school environment it is possible to select and to control many of a child's experiences—that is, to limit, to complicate, to simplify, or to focus them. The task of the curriculum designer and the instructional planner is, then, to specify the content and the conditions under which opportunities for learning will be provided.

Certain aspects of learning and intellectual development theory pertinent to the design and organization of middle school programs will be examined next.

COGNITIVE DEVELOPMENT The term *cognitive processes* refers to the ways in which one perceives, interprets, forms judgments about, and reacts to the environment. From one's reactions to one's environment, the individual develops the concepts, generalizations, and principles with which to make decisions, solve problems, and discover, classify, and synthesize new data. From his or her experiences, the child obtains the data essential to the development and refinement of his or her cognitive processes.

Waetjen has compared the cognitive structure to a kind of private map which an individual gradually develops as a result of the cumulation of experiences.[6] If Waetjen is correct, then the way that cognitive structures develop, the order in which they develop, and the ways they are modified or changed are of critical importance to designing curricula and planning instruction. Knowledge of these mechanisms helps to provide a rational basis for planning curricula consistent with the developmental stage of the middle school child, while achieving the flexibility necessary if individualization is to occur.

Piaget and his colleagues at the Geneva Institute have engaged in extensive research and theory-building in the area of cognitive development. Piaget differs from many American theorists in that he substitutes for the idea

6. Waetjen, op. cit., p. 41.

> of an intelligence sufficiently fixed by heredity . . . that [a] child's position relative to his peers [remains] constant throughout the period of development, the notion of natural ordinal scale of intelligence. The position a child [has] reached on such a scale would indicate the intellectual progress he [has] already made, but prediction of development from that point forward would have to be predicated on knowledge of the experiences in store for him.[7]

Piaget does not eliminate the organism as an important factor. In fact, he states quite categorically that "mental growth is inseparable from physical growth."[8] On the other hand, there are "other, equally important factors . . . to be considered, [i.e.,] exercise or acquired experience as well as social life in general."[9] In other words, maturation alone is not enough; wide and varied experiences are necessary to permit the individual to capitalize on the structures he or she has inherited.

No matter how rich and varied a child's experiences and no matter how unique a child ultimately becomes, according to Piaget, intellectual development will proceed through four distinct but overlapping periods.[10] Thus, the problems inherent in meeting the individual needs of the child are somewhat alleviated by the facts that: (1) there is a well-defined progression through four broad stages in intellectual development, and (2) large numbers of boys and girls are at similar stages at the same time. Although Piaget delimits the stages according to chronological age, the groupings must be perceived as ranges, not definitive rubrics.

The four stages can be summarized as follows:

1. The *sensorimotor period*, which has little direct bearing on the middle school program, lasts roughly from birth through eighteen to twenty-four months of age. Initial cognitive development is obviously dependent upon whatever sensorimotor schemata exist at birth. During this period, the elemental intellectual processes are developed as the infant interacts with the environment.

---

7. Millie Almy, "New Views on Intellectual Development in Early Childhood Education," in *Intellectual Development: Another Look*, A. H. Passow and R. R. Leeper, eds. (Washington, D.C.: Association for Supervision and Curriculum Development, 1964), p. 21.

8. Jean Piaget and Barbel Inhelder, *The Psychology of the Child* (New York: Basic Books, Inc., 1969), p. vii.

9. Ibid., p. viii.

10. Piaget specifies three broad stages or periods. However, for convenience in description, the first half of the period of operations here has been designated the preoperational period. See Jean Piaget and Barbel Inhelder, *The Psychology of the Child* (New York: Basic Books, Inc., 1969), p. 152.

2. The *preoperational period* is characterized by intuitive thinking, much of which is illogical, and by egocentricity. Logical, reversible operations have yet to emerge.[11] The preoperational stage is a sort of transitional period between the latter part of the sensorimotor stage and the earlier phases (at about ages seven or eight) of the stage of concrete operations.
3. The *period of concrete operations*, which encompasses children from age seven or eight to age eleven or twelve, is the stage during which cognitive systems of a sophisticated nature are beginning to develop, and the child becomes more autonomous as a thinker. Concrete operations based on concrete objects—such as ordering, classification, seriation, and mathematical processes—can be undertaken.
4. The *period of formal operations*, which is characterized by the development of formal operations or propositional thinking, takes place for most boys and girls between the ages of eleven or twelve and thirteen or fourteen. At this time, the individual begins to systematize the concrete operations that were the chief achievements of the previous level. He or she is now becoming able to deal with all possible combinations in any situation without being limited to the empirical. Ideally, by the end of this period, development of a system thought structures to deal with formal, abstract thought operations has been achieved.[12]

To this point, the discussion has been focused mainly upon the various stages of cognitive development and their general characteristics. Next, the way in which the individual's cognitive structures are modified will be examined.

It is in the process of experiencing that intellectual development occurs, and experiencing involves two complementary processes referred to by Piaget as *assimilation* and *accommodation*.[13] Assimilation is the process by which raw data are taken in from the environment and made a part of the cognitive structure. It is a continuing process. Cognitive structures are constantly being refined. For instance, to the possible embarrassment of his or her mother, the very small child may at first associate all men with "daddy" and address them as such. As experiences with men accrue, the child gradually comes to realize that "daddy" has a special meaning; he or she is able to distinguish between "daddy" and

11. Piaget uses the word *operations* to denote the activities of the mind as contrasted with the sensorimotor activities of the body.

12. See J. McV. Hunt, *Intelligence & Experience* (New York: The Ronald Press, 1961), p. 115.

13. Piaget uses the term *adaptation* to encompass assimilation and accommodation.

other men. Although this is an oversimplification, it can be said that cognitive patterns are developing through the process of assimilation.

Accommodation—the other side of the adaptive coin—is involved whenever one is faced with a situation for which one's previous experience is not adequate preparation, or for which one's existing cognitive map is not adequate. "It is in the process of accommodation that existing cognitive structures (concepts, generalizations, etc.) are modified, reorganized, or even discarded in the light of the new information."[14] For instance, at a family reunion the small child discovers that all men are not either daddies, nondaddies, or possibly grandpas, but that some are called uncle, cousin, brother, or even mister. A further discrepancy with the child's previous experience occurs upon the discovery that other daddies may be older or younger than his or her own. These and similar new experiences, confusing though they may be in the beginning, ultimately result in the reorganization of existing cognitive patterns and the formation of a new perceptual structure to account for "daddy." Further experiences with men will involve the process of assimilation (as opposed to accommodation) and will tend to be increasingly less demanding. The new experiences that are most readily assimilated are those most like previous experiences. Existing cognitive patterns are adequate for managing the foregoing sort of new information, but

> as the experiences confronting the individual become more and more novel, assimilation increases in difficulty until the process becomes one of accommodation. It also follows that if new experiences are too far beyond the bounds of an individual's previous experience, they may simply be rejected, since he lacks the cognitive structures with which to deal with them.[15]

It is through the interaction of assimilation and accommodation that previously developed cognitive patterns are refined, discarded, modified, or replaced by new ones.

In sum, intellectual development is a continuing process whose limits are not, for practical purposes, predetermined at birth. Development takes place gradually as the child confronts new experiences and modifies his or her cognitive structures accordingly. The child transforms data from interactions—assimilation—into existing cognitive structures.[16] It is clearly critical that the child have a wealth of carefully

14. Mickelson, op. cit., p. 65.

15. Ibid., p. 65.

16. Celia Stendler Lavatelli, "Environment, Experience and Equilibration," in *Topics in Cognitive Development,* Vol. I, The Jean Piaget Society, M. H. Appel and L. S. Goldberg, eds. (New York: Plenum Press, 1977), p. 127.

chosen experiences while developing; intellectual deficits will result from limitation of the child's experiences.

ATTITUDE AND SKILL DEVELOPMENT The emphasis of the present chapter has intentionally been on the cognitive development of the individual. Nothing has yet been said about the affective and psychomotor domains.

While much has been written concerning the development of attitudes and skills, there is no body of research and theory to compare with that available in the fields of learning and developmental psychology. Nevertheless, helpful insights can be found by those concerned with attitude formation and skill development in middle school youth.

Attitudes have been variously described as mental sets, predispositions to behavior, or acts waiting to happen. However they may be perceived, it is clear that attitudes are learned. Skills are defined as the application of intelligence to the solution of problems. Obviously, skills are also learned; they encompass many specific behaviors of a cognitive or manipulative nature.

Discussing attitudes and skills in the same paragraph may seem incongruous, but there are valid reasons for doing so.

> First, they each involve learned behavior, and as with cognitive development, the concepts and generalizations that form them are evolved from experience. Second, both skills and attitudes are difficult to define precisely, yet, despite their general fuzziness, any self-respecting list of objectives recognizes the necessity of teaching for skills and attitudes.[17]

For a long time schools apparently operated on the assumption that attitudes and nonmanipulative skills (that is, critical thinking) developed more or less spontaneously as the student gradually accumulated a storehouse of facts. Studies now show that, on the contrary, attitudes develop slowly out of shared cultural experiences. The title of a study of prejudice conducted over twenty-five years ago puts the whole matter most succinctly: *They Learn What They Live.*[18] A child develops attitudes by becoming involved in his or her culture, by experiencing. It is this factor in the acquisition of attitudes that accounts in large part for the present efforts to integrate the public schools. Attitudes must be embedded in the individual's cognitive structures.

---

17. Mickelson, op. cit., p. 85.

18. Helen G. Trager and Marian R. Yarrow, *They Learn What They Live: Prejudice in Young Children* (New York: Harper & Row Publishers, Inc., 1952).

Psychomotor skills are also embedded in the cognitive structures, as the prefix to "motor" suggests. Except for certain rote manipulative behaviors (tying one's shoelaces, for instance), skilled behavior requires competency in problem-solving and the ability to generalize.

Also of concern to educators at this period in the children's lives is the development of social skills. Just as the development of attitudes and intellectual and motor skills is rooted in experience, so too is the development of the social skills. During the middle school years nearly all boys and girls will become pubescent, with all the developmental tasks—particularly sexual adjustment—that that particular period implies. Regardless of the position the school may wish to take, young people will attempt to master these tasks. That school is well-conceived whose curricula and teachers are geared to funnel this youthful energy into creative and socially useful channels.

READINGS FOR TEACHERS

Elkind, David, *Children and Adolescents,* 2nd ed. New York: Oxford University Press, 1974 (paperback). Excellent series of essays on Piagetian theory. Particularly helpful are Chapter 6, "Cognitive Structure and Experiences in Children and Adolescents," and Chapter 7, "Piaget and Education."

Johnson, Mauritz, Jr., "The Adolescent Intellect," in *Middle School in the Making,* R. R. Leeper, ed. Washington, D.C.: Association for Supervision and Curriculum Development, 1974, pp. 60–67. A brief, thought-provoking article stressing the importance of intellectual development at the middle school level.

Piaget, Jean, and Barbel Inhelder, *The Psychology of the Child.* New York: Basic Books, Inc., 1969. A synthesis or summing-up of the author's work.

Pulaski, M. A. S., *Understanding Piaget.* New York: Harper & Row, Pubs., Inc., 1971. An excellent introduction to Piagetian thought.

IMPLICATIONS FOR THE MIDDLE SCHOOL

Throughout this summary of some of the more useful ideas concerning learning and intellectual development, the relationship of these ideas to the middle school has been kept in the forefront. Nevertheless, it seems worthwhile to summarize with a slightly different focus the implications of these ideas for curriculum and instruction in the middle school, especially since the two succeeding chapters will consider curriculum design and program implementation.

SCOPE AND SEQUENCE If one accepts the middle school as serving a population unique in terms of its developmental characteristics, it is apparent that the scope and sequence of the curriculum must follow a developmental pattern. The direction and pace of the developing curriculum must follow the direction and pace of the intellectual growth of the child, and allow also for social, physical, and emotional growth. When entering middle school, the child is probably near the end of Piaget's stage of concrete operations. While in the middle school, he or she enters the stage of formal operations.

Two implications are clear: (1) in the beginning the curriculum should emphasize the concrete, playing down highly verbal or highly abstract types of content; and (2) the scope (breadth) of the curriculum should be consistent with the child's growth stages, encompassing as many experiences of as wide a variety as can be realistically managed by the child at his or her level of development within the school milieu. The experiences should in the beginning place major emphasis on the concrete, with provisions for inferential thinking rooted in the concrete. Gradually, experiences should move to the point where the young person, now an adolescent, not only performs formal operations, but thinks about them. In other words, the student performs operations on the outcomes of previous operations.

CURRICULAR EXPERIENCES The point has been made that the child learns through personal experiences, which involve both assimilation and accommodation. The implications for both curriculum and instruction are clear: (1) school experiences must be rooted in the child's past experiences, whether these are from school, the environment, or both; (2) school experiences must stretch the child sufficiently so that accommodations in cognitive structures are required; and (3) school experiences must not be set beyond the limits of the child's experience nor be inconsistent with the current developmental stage if frustration, rejection, and alienation are to be avoided.

There is little value in introducing into the content of the curriculum concepts for which *the child is not yet ready in terms of intellectual development.* To do so can be both time-wasting and frustrating. Confronting children with concepts, ideas, principles, and information unsuited to or inconsistent with their stage of development is undoubtedly a major contributor to pupil learning difficulties, pupil failure, and pupil alienation. For example, giving the beginning middle schooler abstract concepts not rooted in the concrete and not consistent with the limitations of the child's already developed cognitive structures is, in all likelihood, going to result in rejection or rote memorization. Rote memorization of the multiplication tables is an excellent case in point; it is not unlike learning nonsense syllables.

This author recalls the illuminating experience he had in his own first year of teaching when he decided that his fifth-grade class, rather than simply reciting the "American Creed" in unison each morning, was going to understand its meaning. The whole project limped from the beginning, but foundered completely when the class came to the term "sovereign state." The coup de grace was administered by the class dictionaries, in which sovereign was defined as a gold coin. To the children this definition suggested *Treasure Island*, a far cry from the abstract notion of sovereignty. The developmental stage of those students was firmly fixed at the level of concrete operations. The concept of a sovereign state was simply beyond their stage of development and experience. They could perceive sovereign as meaning a coin, for they had previous experiences with coins, even though those might not have been gold or British; sovereign as applied to a state was another thing. The cognitive structures needed to deal with the concepts inherent in the words sovereign and state had yet to be developed in these children.

It is important, then, that the content of both the middle school curriculum and the instructional program be consistent with the prevailing stage of operations, and yet provide ever-increasing opportunities for those students moving into the next stage.

INDIVIDUALIZATION As Appel pointed out, in order to promote cognitive development, ways must be found to individualize (or even, in some cases, personalize) instruction. This can be accomplished through such programs as IPI (Individually Prescribed Instruction) or ISCS. (See the discussion of individualizing instruction in Chapter 6 and of instructional systems in Chapter 7.)

The ISCS program (Intermediate Science Curriculum Study) is an excellent example of a curriculum that attempts to provide for the shift from concrete operations to formal operations. It is designed for grades seven through nine. At the seventh- and eighth-grade levels the emphasis is on experiments in the area of the physical sciences. The kits include a wealth of objects upon which experiments are performed. These object-centered experiments permit the simple observation of what happens in given situations; they also provide opportunities for inferential thinking. Questions can be raised, such as the following: What happens when the model car runs down the inclined plane? What happens to the car when the angle of the plane is changed? What happens to the earth in the tray when water runs through it? What does this reveal about the process of erosion? What inferences can be drawn?

It must be reemphasized that not all children will be at the same developmental stages at the same time. Because of limited or different experiential backgrounds or because of lack of ability, some students will not have progressed as far as their fellows. Others will have forged ahead. The important thing is to design a curriculum that makes it possible to deal with each student at his or her stage. The ISCS program is an example of a curriculum that permits the pupil to plug in at his or her own level of development and to proceed at his or her own rate.

However, no new curriculum development projects designed for the middle school years and based upon a carefully and rigorously developed rationale have been originated and widely disseminated since the 60s.[19] This is, indeed, unfortunate, yet it presents an inviting challenge for creative and thoughtful program developers working at the middle school level.

READINGS FOR TEACHERS

Gagné, Robert M., and Leslie J. Briggs, *Principles of Instructional Design*. New York: Holt, Rinehart and Winston, Inc., 1974. Excellent discussion of instructional design. Behavioristically oriented, not a curriculum book.

McComber, Lois P., "Some Implications of Jean Piaget's Theory for the Education of Young Children," in *Topics in Cognitive Development,* Vol. I, The Jean Piaget Society, Marilyn H. Appel and Lois S. Goldberg, eds. New York: Plenum Press, 1977, pp. 151–163. Excellent in relating Piaget to schooling; describes the pre–middle school child, whom every middle school teacher should know.

Piaget, Jean, *Science of Education and the Psychology of the Child*. New York: Orion Press, 1970. Piaget looks at teaching methods.

Rogers, Carl R., *Freedom to Learn*. Columbus, Ohio: Charles E. Merrill Publishing Co., 1969. The affective approach to learning.

19. An exception is the Human Sciences Program, to be available in early 1980 from the Biological Sciences Study Committee. It is an interdisciplinary program grounded in the natural and behavioral sciences for grades six to eight. It is composed of nonlinear learning modules but is based on Piaget's stages of intellectual development. It is easily individualized and mainly based on hands-on activities.

ROLE OF THE TEACHER The role of the classroom teacher must shift dramatically in order to accommodate present views of learning and intellectual development. No longer is he or she solely the dispenser of wisdom. He or she must now function as a facilitator of behavior change. He or she must help students to grow and develop in ways consistent with their developmental patterns. In this new role he or she is diagnostician, guide, resource person, and evaluator. It is the teacher's responsibility to create a situation in which children can learn; he or she is no longer expected to beat learning into their heads.

Chapter 4
Curriculum Design

For many years the emphasis of those who designed educational programs, courses of study, curricula, or units was upon method. Educational thinkers and planners were searching for a general method by which unity and order could be brought to the planning of instructional programs.[1] They favored a consciously planned approach, as opposed to the prevailing practice of simply following a textbook. The methodological emphasis may account for the fact that many middle school curriculum planners still approach the problem of curriculum design from an instructional viewpoint. But within the last thirty years, important curriculum proposals have been characterized by a conscious rationale or framework.

Factors influencing the design of a middle school curriculum are generally the same as those influencing curriculum design at any level. Whatever differences may conceivably arise derive from the particular population to be served. Other factors affecting the design of the curriculum include the school's expressed purposes, the underlying views of the nature of subject matter and learning held by the designer, the nature of the students, and the community from which the students come.

As was implied earlier, many currently accepted definitions of curriculum emphasize the instructional element; i.e., the curriculum consists of all the planned learning activities under the aegis of the school. Such definitions confuse curriculum with instruction. For present purposes, curriculum design will be perceived as placing primary emphasis

1. John M. Mickelson, "The Evolving Concept of General Method," *Theory into Practice,* Vol. 5, No. 2, April, 1966, pp. 81–86.

on content, whereas instructional design gives first priority to the planned interaction between teachers and students. The two are interdependent. Thus, the chief difference between curriculum and instruction is derived from the purposes of the designer, the level of generality at which he or she is working, and the resultant set of problems to be faced.

Curricula cannot be designed without concern for ultimate teacher-student interaction, nor can instructional systems be developed without a concern for content. Similarly, neither curricular nor instructional systems can be designed and implemented with total disregard for goals or objectives.

A curriculum design, then, constitutes the basic plan from which instructional systems are derived. The design of the curriculum precedes the development of the instructional design. Most curriculum designs permit the development of more than one instructional system. If only one sort of instructional system—such as programmed learning—can be developed from the curriculum design, then the design is much too narrow and probably inadequate for all except extremely limited purposes. The curriculum design should represent a higher level of generalization than the design for instruction, which should be quite specific.

Any curriculum design must be concerned with the following components: objectives, content, and instructional strategies. These elements are interdependent, and are specified in the curriculum design. (See Figure 4–1.) Unless there is a carefully developed design, the curriculum becomes a series of improvisations. Improvisation leads ultimately to chaos.

The above three essential components will be examined in detail, along with the related problems of scope, sequence, articulation, and evaluation.

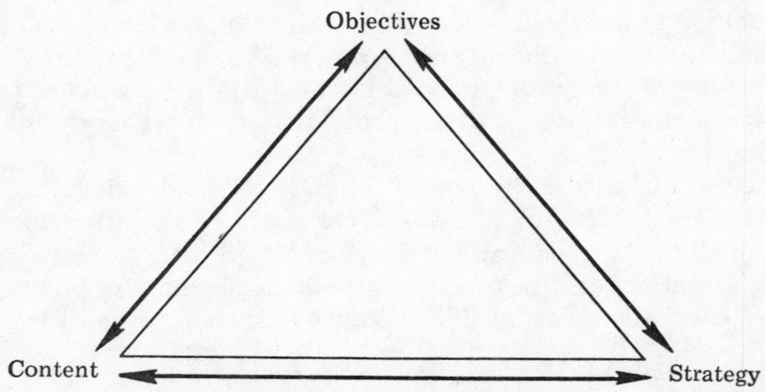

Figure 4–1. The Essential Elements of Curriculum Design

PURPOSES AND OBJECTIVES

If you are not sure where you are going you are likely to end up somplace else.[2]

Perhaps, as well as anyone, the student who produced this non sequitur in a final examination discussion of the role of objectives in curriculum planning identified their chief function—that of pointing a direction. Objectives are statements of ends or intent. As such, they are value statements. The goals and objectives of the middle school represent the educational ends to be achieved at the middle school level, and thus provide the ultimate criteria for the selection of curricular content and instructional strategies.

Little distinction was once made between the word objectives and the words purposes, goals, and aims. All were often used synonymously. But in recent years the terms goals, aims, and purposes have come to be applied to the grander, more global ends of education, whereas the word objectives is used to denote much more specific and, in some instances, much more limited statements of educational ends, particularly in the very restricted versions of behavioral objectives described by Gagné[3] and Mager.[4]

The chief function of the stated objectives of the middle school is to give direction to curriculum planning and instructional practice. Statements of objectives detail the answer to the question: Education for what? Further, "educational objectives [constitute] the criteria by which materials are selected, content is outlined, instructional procedures are developed and tests and examinations are prepared."[5] Ends must be specified if an appropriate choice is to be made of the means to achieve those ends. So, the question to ask first is not "How?" but "What?" Further, we must not ask "What are the means?" but "What are the ends?" When the ends are clarified, so are potential means to those ends.

PURPOSES The purposes of the middle school have already been discussed in Chapter 1. However, it seems wise to review them, since the

2. Robert F. Mager, *Preparing Instructional Objectives*, 2nd ed. (Belmont, Calif.: Fearon Pitman Publishers, 1975), preface.

3. Robert M. Gagné, "Curriculum Research and the Promotion of Learning," in *Perspectives of Curriculum Evaluation*, AERA Monograph Series on Curriculum Evaluation, No. 1 (Chicago: Rand McNally & Co., 1967), pp. 19–38.

4. Mager, op. cit.

5. Ralph W. Tyler, *Basic Principles of Curriculum and Instruction* (Chicago: University of Chicago Press, 1950), p. 3.

purposes have important implications for program development, curriculum design, and instructional planning. The middle school does the following:

1. Serves young people in the age ranges of ten or eleven to fourteen or fifteen.
2. Provides for general education, including opportunities for the development of a sense of inquiry, curiosity, and commitment to learning.
3. Facilitates self-development and self-actualization.
4. Provides opportunities for exploration.
5. Provides for the individualization of instruction.
6. Improves articulation with elementary and high school programs.
7. Provides opportunities for racial integration.[6]

These purposes (with the possible exception of the last one, which is certainly open to serious question) point the direction for the middle school program and set the limits within which it functions. They serve as criteria for the specification of programmatic and curricular objectives. Let us examine the meaning of these purposes.

First, the middle school focuses upon a specific age group consisting of students who are moving from the concrete operations stage of intellectual development to the point where they will soon be ready for propositional thinking. At the same time they are undergoing major physical and psychological changes. All of this has important implications for the content of curriculum and the selection of instructional procedures.

Second, it is the responsibility of the middle school to provide for the general education of its students. General education may be construed as the subject matter all young people should study and the skills and attitudes they should develop, or it may be perceived as those needs, problems, and concerns that are common to all young people growing up in our society. Although in the first instance general education is conceived in terms of subject matter and in the second in terms of personal-societal problems, each view sees general education as meeting common needs, however such needs may be defined. Thus, the middle school program has some sort of common core of subjects or experiences.

Third, the middle school is charged with the task of facilitating self-development, that is, of helping students to develop positive images

6. Bernard M. Gross, "An Analysis of the Present and Perceived Purposes, Functions, and Characteristics of the Middle School," doctoral dissertation, Temple University, 1972.

of themselves and to become all that their talents and interests will permit them to become. A correlative task is the fourth one—that of providing opportunities for exploration. The implications here are two-fold: (1) the middle school program and its curricula must provide opportunities for older children, preadolescents, and early adolescents to deal with areas relevant to their lives; and (2) in addition to those experiences that are required of all, a broad spectrum of experiences must be available for young people to sample or to pursue in depth as their interests may dictate.

Rather closely related to the foregoing task, yet with an additional and most important implication, is the fifth one—individualization of instruction. In addition to providing new and relevant experiences, individualizing instruction means giving the student an opportunity to move along at his or her own pace, not at the pace of classmates who may be faster or slower. This may mean computer-assisted instruction or other types of programmed materials, or it may mean carefully selected experiences that permit the student to individualize for himself. Either way, the problems of curriculum design and implementation are exceedingly complex.

Sixth, the middle school must both build upon what has gone before and be articulated with the subsequent program for adolescents. The very title of the middle school says something important. It is no longer a *junior* high school; it is now a school in the middle. It is, according to Alexander, a "school providing a program planned for a range of older children, preadolescents, and early adolescents that builds upon the elementary school program for earlier childhood and in turn is built upon by the high school's program for adolescence." Further, it is "a phase and program of schooling bridging but differing from the childhood and adolescent phases and programs."[7] Quite obviously a program from kindergarten through twelfth grade is assumed. These statements should make it clear that the middle school has an integrity of its own and hence requires a program of its own.

Finally, the middle school is perceived as a means of providing opportunities for desegregation. There is still a great deal of controversy as to whether or not social integration—although it is an admirable goal and a necessary cause—is an appropriate function of any school. Integration as a purpose of the middle school is at least partially politically motivated. It receives its greatest emphasis in large urban areas, since large numbers of minority groups have congregated there.[8] Urban middle schools seek to achieve integration by increasing the geographical

7. William Alexander et al., *The Emergent Middle School* (New York: Holt, Rinehart and Winston, Inc., 1968), p. 5.

8. Gross, op. cit., p. 119.

spread of the service area of a particular school (taking grades five and six from nearby elementary schools and adding them to the middle school), by busing, and by the inclusion of ethnic studies among the school's offerings.[9]

OBJECTIVES Earlier in this chapter it was stated that the curriculum design is the basic plan from which instructional systems are generated and, further, that one of the essential elements of curriculum design is the clearly specified objective. Curricular objectives are broad, yet they are not stated as generally as the purposes of the school (previously considered), nor specified in as narrow and limited a manner as are instructional objectives. They lie somewhere between these two extremes in terms of specificity. In a somewhat different context, Hough and Duncan use the term *intermediate objectives*.[10] Curricular objectives must, of course, be consistent with the purposes of the school and its program, just as instructional objectives must be consistent with curricular objectives.

Considerable controversy exists concerning the manner in which objectives should be stated. However, since the majority of writers believe that objectives should be stated as behaviors and since there are certain advantages to so stating them, the present discussion will be limited to behavioral objectives.[11]

Curricular objectives expressed in behavioral terms specify the desired changes in the action patterns of students, that is, the ways the student should think, feel, or act after exposure to an educational experience. Statements of behavioral objectives at the curricular level are typically broad and include appropriate content limitations. Statements of curricular objectives do not specify teaching strategies, nor do they include criteria for success. Curricular objectives state in broad terms the kinds of ideas, skills, techniques of thinking, and feelings that planners desire the students to learn, utilize, and develop—such as thinking critically or writng and speaking clearly and coherently.

9. Thomas E. Gateswood, "What Research Says about the Middle School," *Educational Leadership*, Vol. 31, December, 1973, pp. 221–224.

10. John B. Hough and James K. Duncan, *Teaching: Description and Analysis* (Reading, Mass.: Addison-Wesley Publishing Co., Inc., 1970), p. 47.

11. For a contrary viewpoint, see Elliot W. Eisner, "Instructional and Expressive Objectives: Their Formulation and Use in Curriculum," in *Instructional Objectives*, AERA Monograph Series on Curriculum Evaluation, No. 3 (Chicago: Rand McNally & Co., 1969), pp. 1–31.

The problem of determining the degree of specificity required in stating an objective is a knotty one for many curriculum writers. The difficulty arises from two sources. First, confusion often comes from a failure to understand that there is a difference between curricular and instructional objectives. Second, curriculum writers tend to mistake specificity for clarity. The curriculum writer must state objectives clearly in terms of the generality of the behavior expected.

Curricular objectives must be consistent with the purposes of the school. The objectives that follow meet this criterion, for they fall very clearly under the broad middle school purpose of self-development. They are from one source unit of a series dealing with the personal-social problems of preadolescents and early adolescents. The unit was designed as a base from which teachers could plan instruction for and with particular groups of young people. These objectives are stated broadly in terms of student behavior. Although the example is problem-oriented, the same principles for stating behavioral objectives apply to the disciplines. Each statement should be limited to a single idea, should be worded in action terms (verbs are a must), should specify content limitations, and should avoid references to teaching methodology and achievement criteria.

Getting Along with My Family

A. Gaining independence at home.
B. Getting along with my brothers and sisters.
C. Sharing family possessions.
D. Earning and spending money.
E. Getting my family to accept my friends and dates.
F. Getting help from my family with my personal problems.[12]

Since this chapter is concerned with curriculum design, space will not be devoted to a discussion of the specification of instructional objectives. For those interested in pursuing the subject further, many useful texts are available.[13]

In summation, statements of curricular objectives define intent, provide criteria for the selection of content and the determination of basic instructional strategies, and delimit that which is to be evaluated.

---

12. John M. Mickelson, ed., *Getting Along with My Family* (Philadelphia: Curriculum Laboratory, Temple University, undated, out of print), pp. 2–4.

13. See Robert F. Mager, *Preparing Instructional Objectives*, 2nd ed. (Belmont, Calif.: Fearon Pubs. Inc., 1975); and Paul D. Plowman, *Behavioral Objectives* (Chicago: Science Research Associates, 1971).

READINGS FOR TEACHERS

Gronlund, Norman E., *Stating Objectives for Classroom Instruction.* New York: Macmillan Publishing Co., Inc., 1978 (paperback). This is a practical guide for preparing instructional objectives in terms of student performance.

Krathwohl, David R., "The Taxonomy of Educational Objectives—Its Uses in Curriculum Building," in *Curriculum: An Introduction to the Field,* James R. Gress with David E. Purpel, eds. Berkeley, Calif.: McCutchan Publishing Corporation, 1978, pp. 341–357. Deals with the classification of objectives in both the cognitive and affective domains.

Ragan, William B., and Gene D. Shepherd, "Educational Objectives," in *Curriculum: An Introduction to the Field,* James R. Gress with David E. Purpel, eds. Berkeley, Calif.: McCutchan Publishing Corporation, 1978, pp. 326–340. Article focuses on identifying, stating and categorizing objectives. Examples of statements of objectives are given.

CONTENT

Once agreement has been reached concerning school purposes and curricular objectives, it is possible to determine curricular content. Even though the objectives of the curriculum may be stated in behavioral terms and with a high degree of precision, they are still broad. This is both an advantage and a disadvantage. Broad objectives ultimately make possible a greater degree of individualization, but differences of opinion may arise concerning the exact content to be included in a particular instructional system to meet a particular set of objectives.

SCOPE Scope refers to breadth or the actual coverage of the curriculum. It should be readily apparent that any set of curricular objectives determined without some sort of organizing principles or rationale can only result in disorder. One part of the curriculum may be contravening another, and each may be contrary to the stated purposes of the school. In the case of the middle school, the purposes enunciated at the beginning of the present chapter provide a rationale and delimit the broad scope of the curriculum.

Subjects such as arithmetic, the language arts, and Spanish define the scope of the curriculum somewhat more precisely than do broad statements of purpose. Similarly, topics drawn from areas such as personal-social problems, or based upon unifying themes such as the community, the school, or conservation, also serve to delimit.

The specification of the scope of the curriculum depends upon the rationale, as does the selection of particular objectives. Tyler has stated that consistency and discrimination in the selection of objectives are provided through the use of twin filters—a philosophy of education and a psychology of learning.[14] Certainly the rationale for the design of the middle school curriculum will depend upon what is conceived to be educationally "good" and what is believed concerning the ways in which young people grow and learn. Rationale plus objectives equals scope. Scope is narrowed as objectives are refined.

SEQUENCE Sequence, which is related to scope much as curriculum is related to instruction, refers to the ordering of the content of the curriculum. Every curriculum must provide for some form of orderly, progressive arrangement of subject matter; this is sequence.

Determination of sequence is dependent upon three factors: objectives, content, and the learners. Obviously there can be no sequence without objectives, things to be learned, and persons to learn those things. This seemingly simple problem is often more difficult to solve than the question of scope.

In the past, sequence was usually determined by chronology and difficulty. For most of us, American history began with the period of discovery and exploration, moved through colonization, then the Revolution, and so on. Arithmetic began with simple number combinations of addition and subtraction, then continued with the introduction of multiplication and division. Teachers assumed they were moving from the least difficult to the more difficult. Today curricular sequence is still based on chronology and difficulty, but with certain modifications. There are different views as to what constitutes difficulty and as to what children should learn at a given age, particularly in light of the writings of Bruner and Piaget. The work of Piaget in particular has much to offer the middle school curriculum designer (see Chapter 3) for planning sequence as well as selecting content.

---

14. Tyler, op. cit., pp. 22–28.

The knowledge explosion has resulted in a necessarily greater selectivity by school planners as to the content of the curriculum. At one time every United States history course, whether elementary, junior high school, or high school, included the period of discovery and exploration and the period of colonization. Because of the vast outpouring of knowledge, these historical periods are increasingly being left to the middle school; the high school course begins with the Revolutionary War.

Other shifts in sequence will undoubtedly occur. For example, some experimentation is being conducted with the introduction of computer-assisted instruction in algebra at the middle school level rather than at the high school level. Science, which formerly began in grade eight or nine, is now included at all the levels of the middle school.

Among the modifications of the chronology-difficulty sequence is an approach known as *spiraling*. Spiraling is not a new concept, but was given new life by Bruner at the time he began his advocacy of basing curriculum content on the structure of subject matter. As Bruner perceives it, spiraling is a curriculum design in which basic concepts, principles, and generalizations are first presented, ignored for a time, and then returned to; in this way the curricular plan progresses continuously toward a more sophisticated and deeper presentation of the subject matter.[15] The concept of spiraling may be applied just as readily to a needs- or problems-based curriculum.

The danger inherent in the spiral curriculum is that it can very easily become the repetitive curriculum.

> Essential to the success of a spiral curriculum is the clearcut understanding . . . that spiraling is organized in terms of the structure of the subject matter . . . not in terms of the traditional view that subject matter is the continued incrementation of bits and pieces of information organized in some logical fashion to facilitate their mastery.[16]

Curricula that were designed to spiral have not achieved notable success in doing so. This is caused chiefly by the failure of those who design and implement the curriculum to understand that spiraling must be based on constantly expanding and deepening presentations of concepts, principles, and generalizations, and not on increasing the quota of incremental bits and pieces of information to be covered.

---

15. Jerome S. Bruner, *The Process of Education* (Cambridge, Mass.: Harvard University Press, 1960), pp.12–13.

16. John M. Mickelson, "Curriculum Designs," in *The Intermediate Schools*, Leslie W. Kindred, ed. (New York: Prentice-Hall, Inc., 1968), p. 113.

An excellent example of an effective spiraling needs-based curriculum is to be found in *Developing a Curriculum for Modern Living.* The authors present "persistent life situations," which they define as "those situations that recur in the life of the individual in many different ways as he grows from infancy to maturity."[17] These life situations are classified with reference to four main states in life: early childhood, later childhood, youth, and adulthood. The various categories of life situations include such things as maintaining both physical and mental health, meeting social needs, developing the intellect, making moral choices, developing aesthetic appreciation, and maintaining good group relations.

It is obvious that whether spiraling is by subject matter or by needs, any long-range curriculum plan involving spiraling must be on a kindergarten-through-twelfth-grade basis; otherwise there can be no spiral. All long-range curriculum plans should be kindergarten-through-twelfth-grade in scope—no respectable middle school curriculum can be designed and planned without attention to what has gone before at the elementary level and what is to come after in the high school.

SUBJECT MATTER Although the middle school represents a new approach to education for the "middle years," Gross determined that approximately 55 percent of the middle schools queried in a study had apparently based their curricula on subject matter.[18] In any case, they did not utilize a block-of-time program, which the remaining 45 percent acknowledged. Of additional interest is the fact that 67 (almost 42 percent) of the 160 schools reporting block-of-time programs stated that the subjects maintained their identity within the blocks. (The self-contained classroom seems a likely explanation.) Thus, it appears that conventional subject matter areas not only provide the content for most middle school curricula, but also help to define scope. A more recent study by Brooks and Edwards, although not directly comparable, reveals that Gross's findings are still valid.[19] This tendency to cling to

---

17. Florence B. Stratemeyer et al., *Developing a Curriculum for Modern Living,* 2nd ed. (New York: Teachers College Press, 1957), p. 115.

18. Gross, op. cit., pp. 132–146. See also Gateswood, op. cit., p. 222.

19. Kenneth Brooks and Francine Edwards, *The Middle School in Transition* (Lexington, Ky.: Center for Professional Development, College of Education, University of Kentucky, 1978), p. 14.

the old and to disregard the opportunities for experimentation and innovation is unfortunate. It appears that in the majority of instances the middle school is simply perpetuating some of the less desirable practices of the junior high school.

Definitive data are unavailable, but it does seem likely that many of the 75 percent of the above schools designing curricula based on conventional subject matter areas may have utilized recent approaches to curriculum design within subject matter areas. For a number of years much emphasis had been placed on designing the curriculum in terms of the structure of subject matter. Jerome Bruner, who is generally credited with bringing this approach to national prominence, uses the term structure to mean the basic concepts, principles, generalizations, and the like that are peculiar to a specific discipline.[20] For example, the emphasis in mathematics shifted from computational skills to sets, and people who had attended school some years ago found themselves in classes in modern mathematics for parents! Computational skills were not ignored by the curriculum planners; mathematics curricula were simply cast in a different context. Today there is a movement back to the "traditional" mathematics. Similar emphasis on the structure of subject matter may be found in programs developed or proposed in English, science, and social studies. The emphasis in these cases is on the cognitive.

STUDENT NEEDS Bruner has shifted his earlier position, noting that the "rational is not enough," and has publicly called for greater emphasis on the affective in curriculum building.[21] Interesting, in connection with this change of emphasis advocated by Bruner, is the fact that about 25 percent of the middle school programs surveyed by Gross are based on some sort of personal-social needs or problems approach.[22] (Needs are usually assumed to be common to the students for whom the curriculum is planned.) Thus, although the notion may have struck Bruner late, the desirability of somehow emphasizing the affective has permeated the thinking of curriculum specialists for many years. This has been particularly true of those concerned with the middle years of schooling.

20. Bruner, op. cit., pp. 6–8.

21. Jerome S. Bruner, "The Process of Education Revisited," Address given at the Annual Conference of the Association for Supervision and Curriculum Development, St. Louis, Mo., March 9, 1971.

22. Gross, op. cit., pp. 132–146.

The necessity for the middle school to meet the needs of the students it serves is clearly stated in the list of purposes at the beginning of this chapter. The notion of needs implies a concommitant lack or weakness in the student or society.

Unfortunately, the concept of needs is extremely ambiguous, a characteristic that led Havighurst to develop his well-known list of developmental tasks,[23] and that also led Stratemeyer, Forkner, McKim, and Passow to develop their list of persistent life problems.[24]

Needs can be roughly divided into two categories: personal-social and societal. The personal-social needs of middle school youth are those any boy or girl must face while growing up. The complexity, difficulty, and impact of the problem of meeting these needs will vary with the individual. Havighurst called these needs developmental tasks; for him a developmental task is one "which arises at or about a certain period in the life of an individual, successful achievement of which leads to his happiness and to success with the later tasks, while failure leads to unhappiness in the individual, disapproval by society, and difficulty with later tasks."[25] Examples of developmental tasks at the middle school level would include getting along with peers, achieving a satisfactory sexual adjustment, laying the basis for a career choice, and becoming less dependent upon one's parents.

At the opposite pole of the needs concept lie the needs perceived as the needs of society. Any society makes certain demands upon its citizens; these are perceived by the curriculum designer as student needs even though the student may not share the percept. Society-based needs can be construed in many ways, such as the "need" to be a good citizen, the "need" to understand the American heritage, the "need" to support the "American way of life," and so on.[26]

Designing a curriculum plan based solely upon either of the categories of needs is not really satisfactory for middle school students. As a result, curricula that are designed to "meet needs" generally reflect some sort of compromise between personal–social and societal needs. The determination of which needs to select at a particular time, which to reject, and which merely to postpone to a later date depends upon the children and the community to be served.

---

23. Robert J. Havighurst, *Human Development and Education* (New York: Longman, Inc., 1953).

24. Stratemeyer et al., op. cit.

25. Havighurst, op. cit., p. 2.

26. John M. Mickelson, "Curriculum Designs," in *The Intermediate Schools*, Leslie W. Kindred, ed. (New York: Prentice-Hall, Inc., 1968), p. 112.

READINGS FOR TEACHERS

Appel, Marilyn H., "The Application of Piagetian Learning Theory to a Science Curriculum Project," in *Topics in Cognitive Development*, Vol. I, Jean Piaget Society, Marilyn H. Appel and Lois S. Goldberg, eds. New York: Plenum Press, 1977, pp. 183–197. Although the rationale is aimed at the elementary school level, it is equally applicable to the middle school.

Presseisen, Barbara Z., "Piaget's Theory Applied to a Social Studies Curriculum," in *Topics in Cognitive Development*, Vol. I, Jean Piaget Society, Marilyn H. Appel and Lois S. Goldberg, eds. New York: Plenum Press, 1977, pp. 165–181. A most interesting application of Piaget to social studies curriculum development. Rationale can be applied to the middle school level.

Rubin, Louis, ed., *Curriculum Handbook*, abridged ed. Boston: Allyn and Bacon, Inc., 1977. See Section 1 for a selection of readings on schooling and subject matter.

STRATEGIES

In the lower right-hand corner of Figure 4–1 appears the word *strategies.* Strategy refers to planning for instruction at the curricular level. It is used in the broad military sense—that is, the planning and directing of projects involving the movement of forces (for our purpose we substitute the broad planning of programs of instruction). This is in contrast to *tactics,* which refers to the actual processes or procedures for moving or handling forces (for present purposes we substitute classroom methodology for tactics). This phase of the discussion of curriculum design will be concerned with instructional strategy at the broad planning level.

We have noted several times that objectives, content, and strategy are interrelated and that no one part can be emphasized at the expense of the others if a complete design is to be the outcome. Like content, strategies are determined by the objectives to be reached.

METHOD OF INQUIRY New strategies commonly used include critical thinking, discovery, the method of inquiry, and problem-solving. In practice there is not a great deal of difference between them, and it seems likely that the basic cognitive abilities required in their performance are not substantially different, no matter what the strategy is called.[27] Consequently, only one of the strategies will be described here.

The great majority of middle school curricula include science; unquestionably all should contain it. One of the broad objectives commonly assigned to science courses is that "the student shall act in the manner of a scientist," even though it is clearly understood that the degree of scientific expertise expected of or achieved by the student is far below that expected of a professional. This curricular objective has meant not only new subject matter and new ways of organizing subject matter, but also new ways of organizing for instruction. The instructional strategy most often selected to achieve this objective is the method of inquiry.

Inquiry is a fundamental process in basic science, for the scientist is engaged in an unending quest for knowledge. "The method of inquiry" provides a handy label for describing what the scientist does to discover what he or she wants to know. Although it is true that the method of inquiry is usually associated with new science programs, "it has application wherever there is a need for the development of understanding, for generalizations, or for new knowledge."[28] Inquiry procedures are essential to critical thinking, to problem-solving, and to the discovery method. It is therefore, a useful example for present purposes.

The method of inquiry is not something that proceeds by numbers or any set procedure. However, it does possess identifiable elements which it will be helpful to examine. One of the ways in which the method of inquiry can be represented is shown in Figure 4–2.

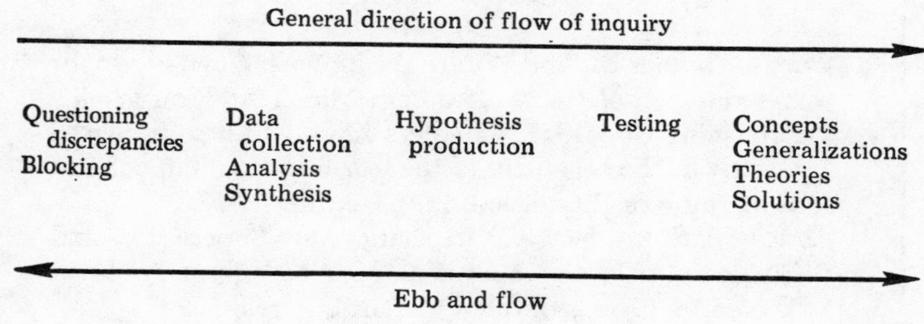

Figure 4–2. The Inquiry Process

27. J. P. Guilford, "Intellectual Factors in Productive Thinking," in *Productive Thinking in Education*, rev. ed., M. J. Ashner and C. E. Bish, eds. (Washington, D.C.: National Education Association, 1968).

28. John M. Mickelson, "Instructional Processes," in *The Intermediate Schools*, Leslie W. Kindred, ed. (Englewood Cliffs, N.J.: Prentice-Hall, Inc., 1968).

It cannot be emphasized enough that if curricular objectives require that the method of inquiry be the instructional strategy, then a major shift in the usual instructional practice will have to take place. Over the years the emphasis has been on learner intake, storage, and retrieval of information, accompanied by instructional strategies appropriate to these demands. The inquiry method as represented in Figure 4–2 requires first some kind of blocking. The inquirer then needs opportunities to secure the essential raw data, the freedom to hypothesize, the chance to test these hypotheses, and, ultimately, the ability to develop concepts and generalizations. This is a slow process, and there is much ebb and flow among data analysis, hypothesis production, and testing. The implications for content selection and organization of curricula are enormous. The importance of the choice of the method of inquiry (or a similar approach) as the broad instructional strategy to be used in planning a curriculum for middle schoolers who are just moving into the formal operations stage of intellectual development should be readily apparent.

With this brief account of instruction as it relates to curriculum design (brief because the major focus in curriculum design is on content) our discussion has come full circle.

READINGS FOR TEACHERS

Curtis, Thomas E., and Wilma W. Bidwell, *Curriculum for Emerging Adolescents.* Reading, Mass.: Addison-Wesley Publishing Co., 1977. Chapters 12 and 13 describing the teacher as the organizer of the learning environment and as learning facilitator are quite helpful.

Educational Leadership, Association for Supervision and Curriculum Development, Vol. 36, No. 4, January, 1979. The entire issue is devoted to learning styles.

Joyce, Bruce R., *Selecting Learning Experiences; Linking Theory and Practice.* Washington, D.C.: Association for Supervision and Curriculum Development, 1978 (paperback). Describes role of teacher in selecting learning experiences by matching teaching models and the learner's style of learning.

PUTTING IT ALL TOGETHER

Curriculum design must be concerned with objectives, content, and strategy. Along with these basic elements go related problems of determining scope and sequence.

The Social Science Studies Curriculum Project has developed a curriculum called *Man and Politics,* designed for use at the upper middle school level.[29] One of its units is "From Subject to Citizen." A major objective of this unit is to have the student function as a historian functions; content selection is based on the structures-of-knowledge notion, and the broad instuctional strategy is the discovery approach. The case study provides the format. In the following quotation, Patterson describes the implementation of the curriculum in the classroom. "Sudbury: A Case Study in New England Land Settlement" follows a young Englishman, Peter Noyes, who left his home in Weyhill, England, in 1637, to go first to Watertown, Massachusetts, and finally to Sudbury, Massachusetts. There he remained, as do his descendants today.

> [As Peter Noyes] moves from Weyhill to Watertown to Sudbury— and as others move farther to Marlborough—relevant records of the time are used. These include land distribution lists, maps, town records, and the like. Students work through these materials, formulating hypotheses step by step as they go. In the process, they encounter an evident breakdown of medieval concepts of social status and land rights. Common land ownership in a ranked society gives way to individually owned land in a much more equalitarian and mobile society. "Sudbury" involves students in speculating about factors that conditioned the distribution of land, and has them try their own hands at dividing up land and comparing their own decisions with decisions that were actually made by colonial settlers. They generalize about the causes of change and the democratization of land ownership; in addition they hypothesize about the relationship between increasing equality of land ownership and political attitudes and behavior.[30]

This quick summary by Patterson reveals the careful curricular planning underlying the implementation of the unit. The broad objective is clear, and it is accurately reflected in the choice of curriculum

---

29. Educational Development Center, Newton, Mass.

30. F. K. Patterson, *Man and Politics,* Occasional Paper No. 4, The Social Sciences Curriculum Study Program (Cambridge, Mass.: Educational Development Laboratory, 1965).

content and basic instructional strategy. There are no dry-as-dust facts to be memorized; there are only primary materials of the type with which historians themselves work. There is the challenge to develop hypotheses, to test them, and, ultimately, to develop generalizations with implications far beyond seventeenth-century Sudbury.

EVALUATION

At the start of the present chapter we noted that a factor *related* to the design of curricula is evaluation. The Eight Year Study presents a contrary point of view in which evaluation is perceived as an integral part of the basic curriculum design.[31] There is no question of the importance of evaluation—the question concerns the function of evaluation. The function appears to have several components:

1. Diagnosis of student strengths and weaknesses.
2. Assessment of student achievement.
3. Assessment of teacher effectiveness.
4. Assessment of the curriculum.

None of these are really part of the curriculum. The first two represent something carried out upon the student, the third something done to the teacher, and the fourth judgments concerning the curriculum itself. The confusion arises from an inability to distinguish between curriculum and instruction. Item one is unquestionably a part of instructional tactics; item two could be either an effort to assess a student's level of achievement for guidance purposes or an attempt to assess the effectiveness of instruction. Item two might also provide data for item three. Item four represents a very complex problem that certainly cannot be a part of a curriculum design without disarranging the basic design itself. The design for a bridge does not include within the design provisions for evaluating the bridge. The design is first conceived and then ways of testing the design are conceived.

Thus, evaluation of curriculum design may be part of instruction on the tactical level, it may be used to assess the teacher, or, more broadly, it may be used to assess the curriculum itself. *In any event,*

---

31. See Hilda Taba, *Curriculum Development: Theory and Practice* (New York: Harcourt Brace Jovanovich, Inc., 1962), pp. 424–425; or Virgil E. Herrick, in *Strategies of Curriculum Development*, James B. MacDonald, Dan W. Anderson, and Frank B. May, eds. (Columbus, Ohio: Charles E. Merrill Books, Inc., 1965), p. 24.

evaluation requires its own designs and models, which must be consistent with its own purposes. It is not and cannot be a part of the basic design of the curriculum. (For a discussion of evaluation see Chapter 10.)

READINGS FOR TEACHERS

Bondi, Joseph, *Developing Middle Schools: A Guidebook.* Wheeling, Ill.: Whitehall Publishers, 1977 (paperback). Designed for schools seeking to make the transition from an existing plan of organization to a middle school plan.

Combs, Arthur, et al., *Humanistic Education: Objectives and Assessment.* Washington, D.C.: Association for Supervision and Curriculum Development, 1978 (paperback). Helpful for those seeking to organize schools that are "humanistic."

Leeper, Robert R., *Middle School in the Making.* Washington, D.C.: Association for Supervision and Curriculum Development, 1974 (paperback). Series of articles on the middle school; Parts 4 and 5 are particularly useful.

Pumerantz, Philip, and Ralph W. Galano, *Establishing Interdisciplinary Programs in the Middle School.* West Nyack, N.Y.: Parker Publishing Co., Inc., 1972. A how-to book.

Chapter 5

Middle School Organization and Programs

As important as it is to examine the basic elements of curriculum, it is equally important to examine actual curricular practice. This task will be accomplished in two ways in this chapter—first by looking at the curricular practices of middle schools in general, and then by examining several selected programs in particular.

ASPECTS OF THE MIDDLE SCHOOL CURRICULUM

The mere fact that "everybody's doing it" does not of necessity mean that a particular curriculum or curriculum-related practice is either right or desirable. Data concerning the trends in middle school curriculum design and development do make possible the comparison of specific programs with general practice; data also provide a reservoir of ideas and experience upon which persons contemplating the organization of a middle school program may draw, and constitute a basis for ascertaining whether or not middle school programs are fulfilling the purposes for which they were developed.

Four aspects of general middle school practices have been selected as having particular relevance to present purposes: grade-level organization, school size, curricular provisions, and program implementation. The data cited in this section of Chapter 5 are drawn primarily from two sources: a study by Gross, "An Analysis of the Present and Perceived

Purposes, Functions, and Characteristics of the Middle School,"[1] and a study by Brooks and Edwards, "The Middle School in Transition."[2]

GRADE-LEVEL ORGANIZATION Differences of opinion have continuously existed concerning the grade levels that ought to be included in the middle school, and a variety of practices have evolved. However, it is now possible to describe firm trends. The findings of the studies of Gross, and of Brooks and Edwards, viewed in the light of baselines established by Alexander[3] in 1967, reveal several clear patterns of practice.

Of the 4,060 schools responding to the questionnaire distributed by Brooks and Edwards, almost two-thirds included grades six through eight, whereas less than one-third encompassed some arrangement of grades five through eight. These findings represented substantially the same proportions as those discovered by Gross in 1970 and by Alexander three years earlier.

Thus, nearly two out of three schools have resolved the question of placing the point between the lower and middle schools in favor of beginning with grade six. The majority of those middle schools that begin with grade five are located in very large urban areas. This suggests that attempts to resolve the problems of housing and de facto segregation may have exercised the greatest influence on the decision to begin schools at grade five.

In the minds of some middle school advocates, the ninth grader is not yet ready to enter the specialized academic situation found in the senior high school. Placement of the ninth grade is being debated by an increasing number of educators. Should it be in a separate unit such as the junior high school, or does it really belong in the senior high school, where a continuous, integrated four-year sequence would be the result?

An increasing emphasis on post–high school education, of which the growing numbers of community colleges are evidence, is causing

1. Bernard M. Gross, "An Analysis of the Present and Perceived Purposes, Functions, and Characteristics of the Middle School," doctoral dissertation, Temple University, 1972.

2. Kenneth Brooks and Francine Edwards, "The Middle Schools in Transition: A Research Report on the Status of the Middle School Movement," Center for Professional Development, College of Education, University of Kentucky, Lexington, Ky., 1978.

3. William M. Alexander, *A Survey of Organizational Patterns of Reorganized Middle Schools* (Washington, D.C.: U.S. Dept. of Health, Education, and Welfare, 1968). See also Ronald D. Kealy, "The Middle Schools Movement, 1969–1970," *The National Elementary School Principal*, Vol. 51, November, 1971, pp. 20–25; and Joe T. Raymer, "A Study to Identify Middle Schools and to Determine the Current Level of Implementation of Eighteen Basic Middle School Characteristics in Selected United States and Michigan Schools," doctoral dissertation, Michigan State University, 1974.

school people to look again at the desirability of a unified four-year college preparatory sequence. With this sequence, basic subjects can be pursued with improved articulation. The feeling is reviving (it never completely disappeared) that the ninth grade is more closely related to the grades above than to those immediately below. The findings of the studies cited suggest that the question is being resolved by adding grade nine to the senior high school.

It cannot be stated definitively that one particular organizational pattern is better than the others. Each school district must determine for itself the pattern best suited to helping its student population meet the specific educational objectives established for the projected unit. Certainly the overwhelming employment of the five-three-four and four-four-four patterns of grade organization means that the majority of public middle schools are serving the children who are in the developmental stages for which the schools were designed.

SCHOOL SIZE In addition to grade-level patterns, another important factor influencing the organization of middle schools is the number of students a school accommodates. Extremely large schools may defeat the purposes of the middle school simply because of sheer numbers; on the other hand, schools with small enrollments may be uneconomical. Obviously, neither extreme is desirable.

Brooks and Edwards reported that almost 65 percent of the schools surveyed enrolled 800 or fewer students, while in 1970, Gross reported the same percentage enrolled 700 or fewer students. Brooks and Edwards concluded that the majority of middle schools enrolled between 400 and 800 students. While average school size has increased, slightly less than 13 percent enrolled 1,000 or more students, and three-fourths of those fell in the range from 1,001 to 1,300 students.

Although the history of the middle school concept is still quite brief and schools have a way of changing unexpectedly, it seems reasonable to infer that a serious effort is being made to keep the size of the middle school in line with its purposes. The "typical" middle school probably enrolls about 650 students.[4]

What determines the optimum size for a middle school? The school must be large enough to provide economically for the services and curricular alternatives needed by middle school children, but it must not be so large that regimentation and depersonalization become the order of

4. Brooks and Edwards, op. cit., p. 14.

the day. These criteria suggest a school with an enrollment of 650–1,000, with the lower figure preferable. More than 1,200 students is undesirable.

CURRICULAR PROVISIONS The middle school may very well be enrolling the older children, preadolescents, and early adolescents for whom it is intended, but if the program provided is irrelevant to their needs, then the whole is wasted effort. Caught in the midst of such a program, any teacher, no matter how competent, will find it extremely difficult to meet the needs of the students in his or her charge. In short, a school may put itself in the paradoxical position of actually creating a great many of the problems with which it then must contend.

This overview of curricular provisions is divided into three segments for convenient analysis: that part of the curriculum required of all, electives, and cocurricular activities. We will also take a brief look at the concept of mini-courses.

Required Areas. What curricular experiences are required of all students? It is not surprising to discover, upon examining Table 5–1, that such basic subjects as mathematics, science, social studies, English, reading, and spelling are required of nearly all students. Nine out of ten students are required to take physical education, and nearly as many take health. It is clear that the middle school need make no special effort to return to the basics; it has never abandoned them.

The findings reported in Table 5–1 are similar to those of Gross and others who have studied the middle school over the last decade.

Unfortunately, the Brooks and Edwards study did not probe very deeply into the status of interdisciplinary programs. Suffice it to say that: (1) such programs do exist, (2) they are more often found in grades five and six, in descending order, and (3) they are most likely to be self-contained classrooms or a modification thereof. Most middle schools are organized to teach separate subjects, even those which claim to have an interdisciplinary format.[5]

Other subjects long associated with the middle years—general music, art, industrial arts, home economics, foreign languages—are regularly required in the middle school. None are required every year or of all students in all schools. With the exception of foreign languages, each is required in more than half the schools. In an apparent turnaround of what was a downward trend, foreign language offerings—both required and elective—have increased since Gross's study of 1970.

5. Brooks and Edwards, op. cit., p. 12.

Table 5–1 Content Areas in the Middle School

CONTENT AREA	*PERCENT REQUIRED*	*PERCENT ELECTIVE*	*CONTENT AREA*	*PERCENT REQUIRED*	*PERCENT ELECTIVE*
Math	98.3	0.7	Photography	6.0	17.8
Science	98.0	0.7	General Music	63.4	14.4
Social Studies	98.3	0.3	Vocal Music	34.6	27.2
English	98.3	0.7	Chorus	31.5	46.0
Reading	96.6	3.0	Band	40.9	61.4
Spelling	95.0	1.0	Orchestra	9.1	22.5
Health	85.2	1.7	Physical Education	90.9	4.4
Foreign languages	17.8	24.5	Intramural Athletics (boys)	28.9	41.9
Typing	10.7	13.8	Intramural Athletics (girls)	28.5	41.9
Art	69.5	23.8	Interschool Athletics (boys)	29.2	45.6
Arts & Crafts	26.8	21.5	Interschool Athletics (girls)	26.8	40.3
Home Economics	56.4	24.5	Student Government	22.8	41.9
Industrial Arts	56.0	21.8	Student Publication	17.1	41.3
Speech	14.8	15.4	Student Clubs	20.1	39.3
Dramatics	15.4	29.9	Honor Societies	8.7	14.4
			Other	6.0	5.4

Source: Kenneth Brooks and Francine Edwards, "The Middle Schools in Transition: A Research Report on the Status of the Middle School Movement," Center for Professional Development, College of Education, University of Kentucky, Lexington, Ky., 1978.

Two conclusions may be drawn from the preceding data; one is positive, the other may be negative. The first conclusion is that the middle school takes quite seriously its responsibility to provide for the general education of its students. The second conclusion, which requires a familiarity with the curricular offerings of the earlier junior high schools, is that the majority of middle schools do not differ significantly from their predecessors.

Electives. In addition to the basic education of its clientele, another commonly accepted purpose of the middle school is to provide opportunities for exploration, both to enhance the richness of the student's experiential background and to provide the student with a broader base of knowledge from which to make academic and career decisions. If this is indeed an accepted purpose, and there seems to be little disagreement, then it follows that a wide range of course alternatives should be available to the student.

The subjects most often offered as electives are music, art (including crafts), home economics and industrial arts, and foreign languages. Other electives available include speech, typing, dramatics, and photography. There exist, of course, even more electives, but they are offered so infrequently as not to merit separate listings. There is little to suggest that Alexander and his colleagues were correct in applying the term "emergent" to the middle school, at least so far as program is concerned.[6]

The findings concerning elective offerings, especially when compared with the required courses described earlier, lead to a telling conclusion. Unless a great deal is hidden behind the titles of the various categories, there is little to suggest that the formal elements of the curriculum are contributing much to the exploratory function of the middle school.

Cocurricular Activities. If it exists at all, the middle school without a cocurricular program would be considered a rarity. All of the middle schools surveyed by Gross in 1970 reported cocurricular programs, although the nature of the programs varied from school to school.[7] Brooks and Edwards, in their 1977 study, do not clearly distinguish between electives and cocurricular activities (see Table 5–1).[8] However, the judicious application of "extra-sensory extrapolation" permits the conclusion that the major changes in the intervening years between the Brooks and Edwards study and the one by Gross have been limited to an increase in interschool athletics for girls, and a decrease in club programs. In descending order, then, cocurricular programs are as follows: band, chorus, athletics for boys and girls, student government, student publications, and clubs. It should be noted that musical activities are the most widely offered, followed by intramural and interschool athletics.

Diversified musical activities and well-run athletic programs are important, but the various studies of middle school programs suggest an imbalance, especially since participation may be limited in many schools. Club programs, available today in less than half the schools and often of questionable value, are being required to shoulder a disproportionate share of the burden of providing a variety of options for broadening the experiences of boys and girls.

Once again the question must be raised: Are most middle schools really providing for self-development, for exploration, and for individualization? These should be the real goals of the designers of middle school programs. (See Chapter 8 for a detailed discussion of the activity program.)

Mini-courses. Increasingly, middle school principals have recognized that the pre- and early-adolescent have the capacity to assume greater

6. William Alexander et al., *The Emergent Middle School* (New York: Holt, Rinehart and Winston, Inc., 1968).

7. Gross, op. cit., p. 147.

8. Brooks and Edwards, op. cit., p. 14.

responsibility for their own learning. Exploiting this capability, innovative middle schools have encouraged students to enroll in short-term courses geared to their own interests. These mini-courses are often planned cooperatively by teachers and students.

The number, variety, and length of mini-courses depend upon such factors as availability of staff, student interest, and the particular topic. Courses may be credit or non-credit, and may vary in length from two, three, or four weeks to six weeks. Some mini-courses last as long as nine weeks.

The following titles are drawn from the many that have been offered in middle schools:

Fine and Practical Arts

African music and dance
Creative stitching
Dancing—folk
Dancing—ballet
Glass blowing
Basic electricity, including repairs
Projects in jewelry-making
Puppetry
Flower arranging
Photography
Painting
Sculpture
Industrial arts projects (selected)

Humanities

Archaeology
Great events (selected)
Ethnic studies (selected)
Black cowboys
Easter Island
Major religions
Great men (selected)
Who discovered America?
Forms of government
Current events
Cartography
Stock market
Anthropology—cultural
Animal communication
The not-so-simple simian (psychology)
Map reading

Mathematics

Number systems
Probability
Chess
Compass, straight-edge and pencil
Logic
Geometry in design
History of numbers
The uses of mathematics
Statistics

Science

Butterflies	Space biology
Basic rocketry	Nuclear energy
Anthropology—physical	A tree is a tree
Oceanography	Fossils
Marine biology	Rock collecting
Laser beam	
Suburban (or city) conservation	

A comparison of the mini-course idea with the old club program of the junior high school clearly demonstrates the improvement. The topics, rotated frequently, are geared to current interests rather than being static year-long choices. These short-term programs accord better with the unpredictability of ten- to fourteen-year-old students.

IMPLEMENTATION The manner of implementation of any curriculum is of critical importance. The way in which the curriculum is organized and staffed has much to do with whether or not the school's mission is achieved. Consequently, a brief examination of selected aspects of implementation may yield additional valuable insights into the degree to which the middle school is achieving its purpose.

Block-of-time Classes. Classes utilizing two or more consecutive periods and classes operating as self-contained units are not new. Both types were reported by approximately one-half of the respondents to Gross's questionnaire.[9] The findings of Brooks and Edwards, although difficult to compare with Gross's because of differences in the survey instruments used, suggest that the same proportion of self-contained and block-of-time classes persists.[10] Of the two types, the two-or-more-consecutive-periods type is probably the nearest thing to a minor crack in the shell of conventional curriculum design in most middle schools. Self-contained classes, generally operative at the fifth- and sixth-grade levels, are mainly holdovers from former elementary programs. The purposes of the self-contained classroom, in this instance, are to facilitate the articulation of programs and to ameliorate student adjustment problems in a new situation.

More than 90 percent of the block-of-time classes identified by Gross included English or social studies in combination with some other

9. Gross, op. cit., p. 144.

10. Brooks and Edwards, op. cit., p. 13.

subject(s) or with each other. Further, in actual practice, even the block-of-time arrangement represented a minimal change from the conventional system, since each subject tended to retain its identity within the block, or, if the subjects remained separate, there was a planned effort at correlation within the block. Evidence indicates that perhaps only one-fourth of the schools are developing programs that go beyond the conventional programs—which have been so often tried and so often found wanting.

This does not mean that the middle school program does not reflect a serious effort to provide for the general education of its students. What is questionable is whether the middle school is in reality meeting the closely related purposes of individual self-development and self-actualization when the bulk of the students' school day is occupied by a mandated curriculum that appears to be little different from that which it is supposed to supplant. The only redeeming hope is that this regrettable situation is merely transitional.

Modular Scheduling. Reams of paper have been used in advocating modular scheduling, but apparently the designers of middle school programs have as yet been little influenced by this movement. The modal school day in the schools surveyed by Gross consisted of seven periods of forty to forty-five minutes in a six-hour school day, exclusive of lunch.[11] Although a number of the schools scheduled fewer periods and larger blocks of time, only 5 of the 327 stated that they used a modular schedule. The time range of the school day for most schools was five and one-half to six and one-half hours, and the number of periods was six to eight. It is apparent that middle schools in the early seventies were approaching cautiously the notion of dividing the school day into many short time blocks, or modules, which can be combined according to need.

Another factor accounting for the apparent reluctance to employ modules is that many middle schools use the self-contained classroom in grades five and six. It is also possible that a sort of modular scheduling takes place within the longer blocks of time, especially if a teaching team is involved. In any event, data presently available do not suggest any major change in the patterning of the middle school day.

ORGANIZATION FOR INSTRUCTION Previously we noted that the middle school curriculum is generally conventional in its organization, although the block-of-time approach appears as an innovation in a

11. Gross, op. cit., p. 135.

number of schools. There is more to organizing for instruction, however, than simply setting the limits within which learning is to occur. Careful attention must be given to what will happen within those limits.

Team Teaching. The most frequently reported innovative pattern of organization for instruction is team teaching, although the number of middle schools employing team teaching appears to be decreasing. Perhaps the problem is that relatively few teachers at either the preservice or inservice level are prepared to function as team members. If this is true, then it poses a very real problem in staff development.

Large-group instruction is usually thought of in connection with team teaching, possibly because of the Trump recommendations.[12] Therefore, it is surprising to find that relatively few of the schools report the use of large-group instruction. Possibly large-group instruction is perceived as a part of team teaching and hence not reported separately. This quite possibly accounts for rather large variations among the reports of middle schools.

Independent Study. Along with various other approaches to grouping, some middle schools have experimented with independent study as a means of individualization (as opposed to individualizing by means of specially prepared learning materials). Independent study may range all the way from a project carried on within the confines of a conventional class to a student's working alone under the supervision of a teacher. As in the case of team teaching, present performance leaves something to be desired, for only a few schools make provision for independent study, even though it offers great potential in meeting individual needs.

Class Size. Consistent with the goal of individualization are efforts to place limitations on class size. Even though it is a crude and insufficient measure of individualization, class size is one of the few gauges available. Although data from recent national studies are lacking, there is reason to believe that findings from earlier studies still apply. Thus, it is possible to say that seven out of ten classes in the middle school fall in the range of twenty-five to twenty-nine students, with slightly over two out of ten containing thirty to thirty-four students.

Obviously, in schools where the average class size was in the range of twenty-five to twenty-nine, some classes enrolled more than thirty

---

12. See J. Lloyd Trump and Dorsey Baynham, *Focus on Change: Guide to Better Schools* (Chicago: Rand McNally and Co., 1961).

students. However, in view of the pressures on the schools to increase class size, it would appear that a definite attempt is being made to keep the student-to-teacher ratio at a reasonable level. This is, of course, helpful in increasing opportunities for individualization in the conventional classroom setting. Perhaps what is most needed is for the middle school to develop new strategies for instruction and new patterns for staffing in the face of the economic and other pressures operating on today's schools. (See Chapter 6 on individualizing instruction for a discussion of strategies.)

TRENDS In summarizing the chapter this far, several trends may be discerned in the middle school.

1. Nearly two out of every three middle schools include grades six, seven, and eight, and most of the remainder use the five-six-seven-eight combination.
2. All schools require English (including reading), mathematics, science, social studies, health, and physical education at all grade levels. Other required subjects include industrial arts, vocal music, a foreign language, arts and crafts, and home economics.
3. Only about 25 percent of the schools appear to have block-of-time programs, most of which are not innovative.
4. The most commonly offered electives are instrumental music, vocal music, art and crafts, home economics and industrial arts, and foreign languages, in that order.
5. The majority of cocurricular activities are centered around music and athletics for both boys and girls. Other major activities include student government, publications, and clubs.
6. Team teaching (although it appears to be decreasing) and independent study are the instructional innovations most frequently reported.
7. Average class size is from twenty-five to twenty-nine students.
8. The modal school day is six hours long and includes seven periods of forty to forty-five minutes plus lunch.
9. Very few schools report modular scheduling.

It is possible to draw a number of conclusions about the middle school. Since these have already been discussed, they will only be summarized here.

1. The middle school is enrolling the population for which it was designed.

2. An attempt is being made to achieve individualization through the use of appropriate instructional materials and through organizational means.
3. The middle school is attempting to provide for the general education of its clientele, although questions must be raised concerning its relevancy.
4. A serious question must be raised as to whether or not the middle school is meeting its obligations in terms of exploration, self-development, and self-actualization.
5. It is questionable whether the instructional strategies vary greatly from the conventional procedures they were supposed to replace.

SELECTED MIDDLE SCHOOL PROGRAMS

The preceding survey of general practices provides a useful overview of the curriculum and its implementation at the middle school level. It is also worthwhile to engage in some "post-holing," digging somewhat deeper than a survey permits.

In the pages that follow, several actual middle school programs are described, although the real names of the schools are not given. Although there are available many other fine programs worthy of scrutiny, the examples that follow reflect both imaginative and practical approaches to the development of the middle school program.

SMALL TOWN MIDDLE SCHOOL Small Town Middle School is located in a town in a fertile farming area, although the chief businesses of the community are education and manufacturing. A few of the residents commute a considerable distance each day to jobs in nearby cities. The parent group consists of blue-collar workers, white-collar workers, and well-educated professionals. As might be expected, parents demonstrate an active concern in their children's schools.

The Rationale. The staff and administration of Small Town Middle School agree, along with their counterparts at many other middle schools, that the approach to the education of pre- and early-adolescent boys and girls should be a unified one. The staff perceives the major goals of the middle school as responding to the students' needs to refine basic skills, to cope with the problems of their changing physical and psychological structures, to develop their interests, and to be satisfied with their personal relationships.

Purposes. The purposes of Small Town Middle School may be summarized quite briefly. Small Town firmly believes that the middle school should do the following:

1. Provide for the intellectual development of each student.
2. Aid the student to develop his or her independence as a learner.
3. Help the student to strengthen or develop positive self-concepts.
4. Assist the student to learn to cope with change through intelligent choices from responsible courses of action.

Organization and Program. The organization of the program of studies at Small Town Middle School is conventional. (See Figure 5-1.) However, to assist in providing for a more individualized program, stu-

GRADE 6	*GRADE 7*	*GRADE 8*
Language Arts	Language Arts	Language Arts
Reading	Reading	Reading
Mathematics	Mathematics	Mathematics
Science	Science	Science
Social Studies	Social Studies	Social Studies
Physical Education	Physical Education	Physical Education
Music	Music	Music
Art	Art	Art
Industrial Arts	Industrial Arts	Industrial Arts
Home Economics	Home Economics	Home Economics
Health	Health	Health
Conversational French	French—Depth and Conversational	French—Depth and Conversational
Conversational Spanish	Spanish—Depth and Conversational	Spanish—Depth and Conversational

The Library Resource Center is a program in which all students are welcome to participate at all times.

DAILY TIME SCHEDULE

7:55 a.m. Homeroom period begins
8:00 a.m. Student tardy bell
8:10 a.m. Period 1 begins
2:35 p.m. Students return to homeroom
2:40 p.m. Students dismissed

Figure 5-1. Program of Studies at Small Town Middle School

dents are organized into groups of approximately twenty-five; each group is under the supervision of four teachers covering language arts, mathematics, science, and social studies. In addition, a specialist provides help for the regular classroom teachers in developmental reading. (Remedial reading is also available.) The teacher teams change personnel annually, while the groups of children remain together throughout the three-year period, except, of course, for the expected normal turnover in any group of students. To provide for continuity of staff, a guidance counselor is assigned to each group of students for the duration.

The Small Town program includes—in addition to the basic four subjects (plus reading)—physical education, music, art, industrial arts, home economics, health, and foreign languages. Both the languages taught—French and Spanish—are offered with two emphases, conversational and in-depth. In the sixth grade, *all* students select one language for a seven-week introductory conversation course. In grades seven and eight, students select either language in seven-week cycles to further conversational proficiency. Students may begin in-depth French or Spanish in grade eight. However, only those students who show promise of success are admitted to the in-depth classes, since the school is unable to provide for all students. The two-year sequence is the equivalent of high school French I or Spanish I. Upon reaching high school, students are placed in second year French or Spanish.

It is believed that the arrangement whereby four teachers, supplemented by a counselor and a reading specialist, are responsible for a single group of boys and girls increases the possibilities for individualizing instruction and improving guidance. It should be noted that the program at Small Town is very definitely teacher-directed. Opportunities for students to participate in planning are limited or nonexistent. Content, judging by course outlines, is centered on intellectual development.

Career Education. Small Town Middle School is proud of its "Career Education Program." It is an exploratory type of program in which students are encouraged to learn about a wide range of opportunities both for jobs and for lifetime interests. The program involves about twenty staff members and is an integrated, carefully planned part of health, physical education, social studies, mathematics, guidance, science, language arts (in grade seven), industrial arts, and home economics.

Library Resource Center. The "Library Resource Center" is an important part of the total program at Small Town Middle School. It has received national attention for its success as an instructional resource for all subjects. In addition to its services in supplying references, books, and media materials, it also maintains a very carefully planned instructional program designed to teach the student how to make independent use of the resources available in any modern library.

SUBURBAN MIDDLE SCHOOL Suburban Middle School is located in a town of more than 20,000 residents, many of whom are employed in the nearby large city. Others work in local industry, which is mostly of the "smokeless" variety. The school district has two middle schools serving not only the town but also surrounding semirural areas.

Rationale. Suburban Middle School recognizes and attempts to provide for the uniqueness of the middle school youngster; it is deemed important to provide each student with opportunities for maximum growth in self-knowledge, in personal discipline, in citizenship, and in intellectual development. These opportunities, it is hoped, will lead the student not only to discover his or her own self-worth and potential, but also to develop a sensitivity in human relationships and respect for the abilities, values, and attitudes of others. Suburban Middle School wants to be a "humane" school.

Purposes. The expressed purposes of Suburban Middle School are consistent with the rationale. Briefly, the goals of Suburban can be stated as follows:

1. To help students develop and refine intellectual skills.
2. To help students understand the principles of democracy and their responsibilities in a democracy.
3. To help students identify and clarify their values.
4. To help students understand and cope with the mental, physical, social, and emotional changes they are undergoing.
5. To help students develop and refine the basic skills.
6. To help students to explore a wide range of experiences.
7. To help each student to discover his or her own uniqueness.

Program and Organization. Suburban Middle School serves boys and girls in grades five, six, seven, and eight. The school is contained within a single building, formerly the high school, which has been divided into two smaller schools, known as "houses." One house contains all the fifth and sixth graders, while the other shelters grades seven and eight. Each is composed of approximately 600 students, who are further divided into learning teams of varying sizes to reduce the impersonality likely to be associated with a 1,200-pupil school.

The house-team plan of organization is designed to help students retain their individual identities and to enable Suburban to maintain its child-centered philosophy. Teams are interdisciplinary, with two to four teachers from different subject areas assigned to each. Presumably, the team arrangement promotes communication, coordination, and cooperation among subject-matter specialists. It is intended that students will benefit from instruction that is planned and presented by specialists. Also, the teams are seen as a means to avoid the fragmentation characteristic of most departmental plans of organization. Suburban does not want to be a subject-centered school.

The team form of staff organization as practiced at Suburban requires teachers to assume an active role in planning, scheduling, grouping, and guiding. Each team has time during *every* school day for planning the team's program. Since the learning teams in each house are grouped heterogeneously, it becomes the responsibility of each teaching team to determine the manner of grouping for its students. In addition to time for program planning, teams are allotted time to discuss individual students, and to meet with parents, counselors, and various specialists so that the needs of individual boys and girls can be met.

Program offerings include such usual subjects as English, reading, science, social studies, mathematics, foreign languages (French and Spanish), music, fine and practical arts, physical education, and health education. In addition, a wide variety of teacher-developed short courses and other activities are provided in the activity blocks. (For a sample student program see Figure 5–2.) It is interesting to note that the practical arts are introduced in grade six and health in grade five, and that the physical education classes are coeducational. Reading is not only taught in grades five and six, but is also required of all students in grades seven and eight.

It is not considered necessary to allocate the same number of minutes for each subject each day. In fact, the school day is divided into twelve-minute modules. Thus the team is able to vary the time devoted to various activities according to need. (See Figure 5–2.) This flexibility would not be possible without the generous provisions of time for team planning.

Media Center. Every outstanding middle school appears to have established a first-class media or instructional materials center; Suburban is no exception. Its center, a spacious arrangement composed of the former high school library and an adjoining room, is divided into two sections—"Print" (library) and "Non-Print" (audiovisual). The center contains an extensive collection of standard references, other books, and audiovisual materials and equipment. In addition to circulating books,

NAME ________ LOCKER NO. ________ HOUSE ________ GRADE ________ HOMEROOM ________

	Monday	Tuesday	Wednesday	Thursday	Friday
*8:05					
8:15	Homeroom Period	Homeroom Period	Homeroom Period	Homeroom Period	Homeroom Period
8:27	Reading	English	Math	Social Studies	Science
8:39					
8:51					
9:03		Science	Science		
9:15	Social Studies			French	
9:27					Math
9:39					
9:51	Practical Arts	Art	Reading		
10:03				English	
10:15					
10:27			Physical Education		Physical Education
10:39		Music			
10:51				Math	
11:03					
11:15	English	Math			
11:27			Social Studies	Reading	French
11:39					
11:51					
12:03					
12:15	Lunch	Lunch	Lunch	Lunch	Lunch
12:27					
12:39	French	Social Studies	Art	Science	Music
12:51					
1:03					
1:15					English
1:27	Science		Homeroom		
1:39		Activity	Tutorial	Activity	
1:51		Block	-or-	Block	
2:03	Math		Early		Social Studies
2:15			Dismissal		
2:25					

Figure 5–2. Sample Student Schedule from Suburban Middle School (shaded areas are team-taught classes)

materials, and machines, the center prepares bibliographies, produces audiovisual items, and offers small-group instruction in the use of its facilities.

HILL MIDDLE SCHOOL The third and last example is a school within easy commuting distance of a major eastern city. A high proportion of local residents are either professional or self-employed. As a result, their educational achievement is generally high, and they have been generous in their support of education. Hill is one of three middle schools serving its district; each school includes grades seven and eight.

Rationale. The staff believes that Hill Middle School should be free to differ from existing elementary and high schools, and free to provide the unique educational experience required by students of the middle school age-group.

Purpose. The Hill Middle School is similar to other middle schools in the purposes it espouses. Briefly, the faculty believes the environment of the middle school should provide opportunities for each child to progress and success at a rate and to a depth commensurate with his or her readiness, abilities, needs, and interests. Developing this environment requires a keen understanding of the middle school child. Course offerings of the Hill Middle School reveal that the faculty takes seriously the responsibility of providing for the basic and general education of the students.

Program and Organization. The teachers at Hill Middle School are organized into seven teams, under the direction of two full-time "instructional consultants." The teams are interdisciplinary, including for the eighth grade, teachers of language arts, social studies, math, and science, and for the seventh grade, teachers of mathematics, science, social studies, language arts, and reading. Learning experiences are provided for students through both subject-centered and interdisciplinary approaches.

Subject-centered Approach. Mathematics is provided by means of a continuous, sequential two-year program through which students proceed at their own rates. The student must achieve clearly stated, sequential objectives in order to progress from one level to the next. Students who require added reinforcement are referred to the "Mathematics Center" for additional work. Those students who demonstrate high achievement in mathematics are referred to the "Algebra Center."

The science program utilizes the discovery method. Students are exposed to the scientific method, laboratory procedures, experiments, and working in group situations.

The language arts program, which is characterized by depth, encompasses: (1) language and communications, (2) literature, (3) listening and speaking, (4) reading, (5) writing, and (6) study skills. A wide variety of learning materials and approaches are employed to meet the varied interests and ability levels of the students.

Social studies covers world cultures in grade seven, and United States culture and history the following year. During both years emphasis is placed on using the library, locating and organizing material, map-reading, and analyzing information.

A developmental reading and literature program is run for eighteen weeks in grade seven. Its purposes are to improve comprehension and vocabulary, to improve reading in the content area, to improve listening and oral reading skills, and to increase recreational reading.

Interdisciplinary Approach. In addition to the subject areas just described, interdisciplinary units are studied. These units are designed to foster skill and concept development; they combine the skills and content from two or more subject areas to demonstrate to students the interrelationships among areas of knowledge in life outside of academic centers. One unit might combine language arts, social studies, and developmental reading and literature; another might blend mathematics and science (metrics).

Expressive Arts. The subjects included in this category are home arts, industrial arts, art, and music. The expressive arts program of instruction is designed to relate directly to the needs of the middle school student to explore, to stretch, and to exercise his or her intelligence, initiative, and growing maturity.

Independent Study. Of particular interest is the "Independent Study Program" which is used to provide opportunities for *all* students to plan and organize their own learning. Independent study may or may not be apart from regular class or group activities. School personnel, other students, and people from the community are utilized as technical consultants by the student. Students choose, plan, pursue, and evaluate projects with the guidance of an "Independent Study Staff."

Other Areas. In addition to the subjects already noted, Hill Middle School students take foreign languages (French or Spanish), physical education, health education, and a daily activities period. The activity period program includes, among other options, mini-courses, intramural athletics, quiet study, and group guidance.

Special Interest. Of particular interest is the school environmental camping program, which makes use of a nearby state park. Students, under the supervision of school personnel, spend three days in the open. While at the camp the students investigate, in groups and individually, a variety of topics pertinent to environmental science.

Chapter 6
Individualizing Instruction

The adaptation of instructional practices to meet the diverse intellectual, physical, emotional, and social needs of students should be the major concern of a teaching staff. After all, it is through the vehicle of instruction that the program of studies is applied to serve these needs. The material in this chapter will be helpful in adapting instruction in a way that reflects a faculty's understanding of human individuality and the diverse needs of middle school students.

DEVELOPING STRATEGIES

Given a goal, the plan by which the goal is to be achieved is the strategy. In education, the achievement of goals and objectives is a complex task involving the consideration of many variables; therefore, the development of a teaching strategy is a complicated matter. Before we can proceed to consider strategies for individualization, we must first agree upon what individualizing instruction means. Is it setting students off on their own and making them responsible for what they learn? Is it plugging them into computers which then manage programs, instruct, evaluate, and reward with advancement to the next learning stage? Is it a teacher in a classroom with thirty students trying to go in thirty different directions in five or six subject areas all at the same time? It is none of these; a much broader definition is needed. Individualizing instruction is the tailoring of instructional arrangements to individual needs and abilities. While the authors recognize that it is impossible for any teacher to meet all of the needs of all students at all times, each teacher does have the responsibility for "providing the most nearly appropriate task possible for each learner, given a specific teacher and the resources available to him/her at a specific point in time."[1]

In developing strategies for individualized learning, our first concern must be the students. Since strategy is a planned design for achieving particular goals, we must look at learning objectives. Program is the vehicle through which we work, so it must also be considered. Since we are concerned with instruction, we must look at the teacher and what he or she does to make learning appropriate for each student. We must assess each student's progress toward the objectives to determine how much learning is taking place. Our strategy, then, develops on the basis of answers to the following questions: Who are my students? What are the learning goals? What is the program with which we will work? What will I, the teacher, do? How will each student's progress be evaluated? Following is an outline of illustrative questions that could be considered in each of these areas.

A. Who are my students? (Looking at them individually)
   1. Where is he or she developmentally?
   2. What are each one's unique attributes as a person?
   3. Where is each one in the group?
B. What are the learning goals?
   1. What are the specific behaviors that are to be developed? Are they cognitive, affective, or psychomotor?
   2. How are they best ordered?
   3. How can these goals be differentiated?
   4. How will achievement of these goals manifest itself?
C. What is the program with which we will work?
   1. What are the concepts that are involved in this program?
   2. How can the material be sequenced?
   3. At what points can the material be approached?
   4. What kinds of learning resources are pertinent to this material?
   5. To what activities does the material lend itself?
D. What will I, the teacher, do?
   1. How will I organize students for this learning?
   2. How can I adapt the learning tasks?
   3. What must I do to make each student's learning more efficient and successful? (Considering the students individually)

1. L. Leon Webb and Theresa E. Howard, "Individualized Learning: An Achievable Goal for All!" *Educational Leadership*, Vol. 34, February, 1977, p. 360.

E. How will I evaluate each student's progress?
1. What methods and instruments should be used?
2. How can I best help each student move toward an effective self-evaluation process?
3. How should evaluation results be interpreted and used?

By raising such questions, developing the most accurate answers possible, and utilizing the professional talents of the teacher, a strategy for achieving specific goals and objectives with particular learners is formulated. Strategy is the day-by-day plan of operation by which the teacher attempts to help learning take place, and it grows out of attention to concerns like those above. Each teacher's strategy is unique; it is based on individual professional talents and understandings, the students involved, and the particular teaching situation.

Lesson planning is daily application of the above process of strategy building. Each daily session builds toward the overall objective of actualizing more fully the potential of each student. How can the teacher determine if the instructional strategies being planned and implemented are indeed promoting individualized educational experiences? What are the characteristics of individualized learning situations? The examples in Table 6–1 help answer such questions.

Table 6-1

Opportunities for individualized learning are being afforded	Opportunities for individualized learning are not being afforded
If subgroups formed include only those children ready for the specific learning task to be undertaken.	If subgroups formed include children for whom the specific learning task will be too easy or too difficult.
If learning tasks provide for the expression of individual interests, for obtaining information particular students require, or for activities that individual students need for specific reasons.	If learning tasks require that all students do the same things in the same way.
If learning expectations are varied according to the student's ability and previous acquaintance with the learning task.	If learning expectations are the same for all students.
If time schedules vary according to the needs of each student.	If all students are expected to complete tasks in the same amount of time.
If provision is made for the expression of each student's ideas and creative contributions.	If all students are expected to emerge with the same ideas and conclusions.

TEACHER-PUPIL PLANNING Middle school students need opportunities to begin assuming responsibility for their own learning. They need to find the kind of learning system that will "turn them on." This is particularly important when they are involved in areas beyond the boundaries of the basics. Realistic individualized performance standards need to be established and achieved. Students need experience in making decisions and opportunities to "move forward in areas of their own choosing at their own speed according to their own unique purposes, desired, and needs."[2] Through this process, students will gain a better understanding of their own capabilities.

While they need opportunities for developing decision-making skills and for assuming responsibility for their own learning, middle school students are far from ready to assume all this on their own. Teacher-pupil planning on a one-to-one basis is needed to provide students with assistance in clarifying their goals and objectives, structuring their procedures, and developing appropriate processes for evaluating their achievement. Teacher-pupil planning provides opportunities for discussing problems, examining alternatives, and projecting solutions. However, teachers must be ready to accept student goals, and approaches for achieving them, even if they differ from those the teacher would have planned.

MASTERY LEARNING In order to implement the concept of mastery learning, a variety of strategies are needed as well as a systems approach. That which is to be learned must be broken up into units that are manageable and easy to analyze. The criterion for what constitutes mastery must be established. As each unit or module is mastered, the individual student moves on to the next in sequence. (A number of individualized learning systems as described in Chapter 7 may be utilized for this purpose.)

Bloom emphasizes the need for favorable learning conditions that are appropriate to the characteristics and needs of each learner.[3] This implies providing students with a variety of ways to learn. Caution must be exercised so that variety is not introduced merely for the sake of variety, but because there are a variety of effective ways for achieving the established goals and objectives.

The concepts of individualized instruction and mastery learning do not negate group methods. Following group instruction that has been

---

2. Thomas E. Curtis and Wilma W. Bidwell, *Curriculum and Instruction for Emerging Adolescents* (Reading, Mass.: Addison-Wesley Publishing Co., 1977), p. 274.

3. Benjamin S. Bloom, *Human Characteristics and School Learning* (New York: McGraw-Hill Book Co., 1976).

teacher-paced, evaluative feedback may provide information regarding those whose progress toward mastery is unsatisfactory at that point. A variety of alternative and supplemental procedures may then be prescribed. Block refers to these as "correctives" whereby students may attempt to overcome particular learning difficulties.[4] Some correctives are for use primarily by a group of students, while others are for use by individuals. In addition, correctives may focus on re-presenting the problematic material or on reinvolving students in learning.

READINGS FOR TEACHERS

Block, J. H., ed., *Schools, Society and Mastery Learning.* New York: Holt, Rinehart and Winston, Inc., 1974.

Block, J. H., and L. W. Anderson, *Mastery Learning in Classroom Instruction.* New York: Macmillan Publishing Co., Inc., 1975.

Bloom, Benjamin S., *Human Characteristics and School Learning.* New York: McGraw-Hill Book Co., 1976.

THE LEARNING ENVIRONMENT

Schools should be happy places where people are comfortable, where success abounds, and where failures are viewed only in relation to potential for further understanding. Schools should be places where students and teachers come together in an effort to seek truth, develop potential, and extend human abilities. Schools should be places where the most important considerations concern people and where students feel wanted, respected, and competent as human beings. Only if schools are such places can they contribute to the development of positive, healthy self-images. Only then can they capitalize on the individual's natural desire to grow, to become, and to direct motivation into desirable avenues. Only if such an environment exists can each young person continue to develop the faith and belief in self that is necessary to tackle the tasks of intellectual, social, and psychological development that are a part of growing up.

4. James H. Block, "Individualized Instruction: A Mastery Learning Perspective," *Educational Leadership*, Vol. 34, February, 1977, p. 339.

PHYSICAL ENVIRONMENT AND MATERIAL RESOURCES

Because students use different modes and strategies in learning, the physical environment of a middle school must be flexible. Rooms with desks that are permanently affixed to the floor have become relatively rare. Nevertheless, many teachers still cling to the security of neat rigid rows of desks and chairs despite the introduction of movable furniture. If varying instructional strategies are to be utilized, the teacher must be willing to have students shift furniture in order to accommodate varying grouping patterns. Space must be allocated for "Learning Centers." Above all, the room should be attractive. The following is a description of how an ideal middle school classroom might look.

> *The Classroom*—pleasant, carpeted, colorful. Student-made mobiles suspended from the ceiling. Tables, chairs, clusters of desks. Learning Centers located around the periphery of the room with multi-level materials geared to a concept . . . books, filmstrips, listening centers, tapes. Definitions and directions printed on large, laminated posters. One corner filled with construction paper, posterboard, crayons, magic markers, glue, scissors, stapler, magazines. Another corner a mini-media production center with a drymount press, typewriter, laminating film, chartex. A well organized classroom layout.[5]

Classroom space should be adapted to the specific kind of learning situation required at a particular time—meaning that classroom areas might even be organized differently several times in a single day or from one day to the next. Open and closed storage facilities should be available for the teacher, as well as sufficient file cabinet space for student records and sufficient storage for student work, projects, and individual materials. Clutter indicates that space is being misused and can only lead to disorder and disorganization.

In addition to flexible physical arrangements, individualization for optimum learning requires a variety of methods and a variety of resources. Many kinds of materials should be available to all students, in activity and interest centers. Books of different levels should be used in the various subject areas. There should be a balance between teacher-made materials and commercially prepared posters, charts, and other learning aids and devices.

A comprehensive media center can help provide needed resources. Some instructional materials may be stored in the media center for immediate retrieval. The center may also make available services, additional materials, and some resources for preparing instructional aids,

---

5. Joseph A. Young, Billie Bittinger, and Edward Mahoney, "Students Talk . . . Teacher Changes," *Middle School Journal*, Vol. 9, August, 1978, p. 5.

including overhead visuals, audio and video recordings, and laminated materials. However, although the media center may be an important resource, it must not replace the classroom as the primary resource.

INTELLECTUAL ENVIRONMENT The intellectual environment in a middle school classroom should facilitate student learning. A teacher who understands the intellectual nature of the middle school youth will provide a classroom with the physical characteristics described above as well as a nonmaterial environment that is challenging and motivating. To achieve this, the teacher must promote student self-direction, initiative, and responsibility. Learning activities that promote student interest and involvement will be selected by the teacher. A problem-solving framework that involves students in relevant inquiry processes will be the starting point from which the teacher goes on to utilize a variety of group sizes and other instructional devices. Finally, for a truly intellectual environment, the teacher will use methods that encourage students to raise the level of their thinking beyond the level of recall.

HUMAN RELATIONSHIPS Students must be able to pursue learning in a way that will make them feel secure as well as successful. Despite the challenges from "back-to-the-basics" and accountability movements, a humanistic approach need not be discarded. Giving each student individual attention, encouragement, and praise is one way in which teachers can establish a learning climate that provides students with the emotional security they need, as well as contributing to the development of adequate self-concepts and personal stability. To accomplish this, the teacher must personally be emotionally secure as well as sensitive to the learners' needs.

Education can only take place in an environment where teachers and students are free to share their own humanity with one another, where a mutual feeling of respect exists, and where there is a deep bond of understanding. The first step in individualizing instruction should be the development of a relationship between the teacher and each student that as far as possible satisfies Carl Rogers's description of the ideal situation:

> If I can create a relationship characterized on my part: (a) by a genuineness of transparency in which I am my own real feelings; (b) by a warm acceptance of and a genuine liking for the other person as a completely separate individual; and (c) by a sensitive ability to see his world and himself as he sees them; then the other individual in the

relationship: (a) will experience and understand aspects of himself which previously he repressed; (b) will find himself becoming better integrated, more able to function effectively; (c) will become more unique, more self-expressive; and (d) will be able to deal with the problems of life more adequately and more comfortably.[6]

READINGS FOR TEACHERS

Association for Supervision and Curriculum Development, *Feeling, Valuing, and the Art of Growing: Insights into the Affective*, 1977 Yearbook. Washington, D.C.: ASCD, 1977. Pages 292 to 295 are particularly useful because numerous references have been classified according to their emphases which range from the theoretical to practical suggestions for teachers.

Association for Supervision and Curriculum Development, *Perceiving, Behaving, Becoming*, 1962 Yearbook. Washington, D.C.: ASCD, 1962.

There are very real and significant implications for educational success or failure in the relationship between teachers' attitudes and significant learning. Favorable teacher attitudes have a favorable effect upon intellectual and psychomotor development as well as upon student behavior. More content can be absorbed and faster learning paces can be established when the teacher has favorable expectations regarding the potential of students. Learning is thus improved; and there should be an accompanying positive effect upon self-concept and the attendant motivational aspects of self-feelings.

The attitudes and policies of administration are also important affectors of the school environment. These attitudes and policies affect staff and students alike; they either promote an openness to experience and a resulting growth potential, or they cause people to become closed to their experiences. Thus administrators, without even entering a classroom, may increase or diminish the possibilities for educational growth by the effects on the school environment of their policies and their attitudes.

There has been some concern recently that middle schools are not meeting the original expectations in program improvement. Research

6. Paul E. McClendon, "Teacher Perception and Working Climate," *Educational Leadership*, Vol. 20, November, 1962, p. 105.

on the practice of supervision in Tennessee suggests that one reason may be the lack of instructional support provided for the teachers. McGee and Eaker summarize this particular aspect of the study with the following conclusions:

> When Jr. High/Middle School teachers were asked if the service (supervisory) is provided when needed, they reported the following:
>
> A. Classroom demonstrations were usually not provided. 84.4% also perceived this service was needed.
> B. Serving as a link with the central office was usually perceived as not occurring. 77.8% of the teachers also perceived this was an important service.
> C. 82.2% of the teachers indicated that help was usually not available as a change agent. An equal number judged this was an important service. The data showed both the elementary and high school teachers had significantly more help in this area.
> D. 77.8% of the teachers reported that psychological support to try new ideas was usually not there. 86.7% of the Jr. High/Middle School teachers reported they needed this support.
> It was also noted that elementary and high school teachers perceived they had significantly more psychological support than Jr. High/Middle School teachers.[7]

It is obvious that the support of administrators and supervisors is needed by the classroom teacher. While the study is limited by its restriction to one state, its implications are important enough to mandate that schools and school districts in general examine the effectiveness of the relationships among teachers, supervisors, and administrators.

The role of the supervisor has changed in recent years. Teacher behavior is no longer the sole focus for supervision; there is also an emphasis on student behavior. Students' movements in the classroom and the number of students at a particular task at a given time may be examined. Interaction of teachers and students becomes important. Verbal flow between teachers and students and between students may be charted. Student data in the form of attendance and health records, test results, anecdotal records, and participation in the activities program may be cooperatively examined and interpreted by teacher and supervisor. Working together on these kinds of activities, the supervisor and teacher may develop a feeling of mutual respect and understanding.

7. Jerry C. McGee and Robert E. Eaker, "The Practice of Supervision in Junior High and Middle Schools," *Middle School Journal,* Vol. 9, August, 1978, pp. 10–11.

GROUPING

Formal education in the United States was not originally organized by grade levels, but by 1860 such organization existed in nearly all city schools. The graded school with a ratio of about one teacher to thirty pupils housed in "egg-crate" fashion has persisted to the present decade with little change. However, the grade-level organization has not gone unchallenged. In the 1950s, there was a swelling tide of criticism, a growing interest in plans for nongraded instruction—especially in the elementary schools—and an increasing number of schools turned to ungraded organizational formats.

One of the greatest problems with schools organized along grade-level lines is the inconsistency with what we know about individuals and how they grow and develop. Contrary to the theory of this organizational plan, research has established beyond question that individuals of the same age vary widely in physical, mental, and emotional growth, and that they develop at different rates and according to different patterns. Every boy and girl of the same age will not be ready to have the same learning experiences or to pursue them at the same rate of development. Therefore, the traditional graded schools engender failure and frustration. Children who are not ready for learning accomplishments stipulated for their age or grade level must live with the stigma of being retained, then plod once more through the same set of experiences—some of which they have mastered and all of which are "old hat" even if they have not achieved them. Other students who might be ready to leap ahead in their learning programs must spend a full year waiting until promotion to be allowed to move on. The whole set of perennial problems concerning whether any student has mastered enough of the fifth-grade curriculum to go on to the sixth grade is created by an organizational structure based on a misconceived interpretation of human reality.

Grouping can help the teacher to cope with the arbitrariness of grade organization. Students may be grouped according to their growth in one or more areas, such as achievement, sexual maturity, interest, physical development, and social maturation.

GROUPING PHILOSOPHIES A learning group is an organizational device, a means to an end. Experience and research have shown that no single grouping philosophy can magically guarantee results. Just as no method of teaching reading can be applied with equal success to all learners, neither can a particular grouping arrangement serve equally well in all learning situations.

GROUPING PRACTICES Individualization of learning does not mean that each student must be working independently all of the time. Students need to interact with other students in order to develop communication and social skills.

Learning groups should be designed around specific purposes while allowing for as many options as possible. If flexibility in grouping students for learning can be maintained, group composition can be varied to fit instructional objectives. The more rigid the organizational structure, the less able the staff will be to utilize unique arrangements to promote specific outcomes. Flexibility implies the option to change when change is desirable, but also the ability to maintain a given structure when that is best.

Grouping practices may range from various forms of homogeneous and heterogeneous groups through procedures that allow students to work individually.

The old notion of an across-the-board homogeneous group has been discarded as invalid. In place of grouping based on generalized measures of ability and achievement, students may be placed together based on their similarity in specific traits. Mental growth and achievement may be considered, along with physical, social, and emotional maturity. In some academic learning areas, students may be assigned to groups according to their developmental level in each individual subject. In other areas, where the presence of learners with divergent backgrounds can enhance the learning situation, heterogeneous grouping is more appropriate. Whatever form grouping may take, the techniques applied must avoid gross generalizations about learning groups, must provide for flexibility in grouping according to instructional purposes, and must take into account current knowledge regarding individual differences among learners.

From the variety of possibilities existing, it is much easier to develop fluid, responsive arrangements if a school is divided into a number of smaller units. Based on their mental, physical, social, and emotional patterns of development, 120 to 150 students may be assigned to a specific unit. Learning situations that reflect the students' patterns are devised by the professionals working with a given unit. Such an arrangement provides for the flexible adaptation of learning groups to reflect the day-by-day developmental patterns of the learners.

Although a need for planned group flexibility has been stressed, one cannot overlook the fact that permanence is a desirable characteristic for some groups. The guidance-oriented group, typically referred to in the secondary schools as the homeroom, is formed with a concern for human relationships. In grouping and regrouping young people to assure them the best opportunities, the middle school staff must also be aware of their need for stability and security. Certain human relationships must be allowed to continue over extended periods. It takes time to form the bonds that lead to lasting friendships and to a mutual trust allowing individuals to share their deeper hopes, problems, and other intimate feelings. If homeroom groups simply serve administration functions, the most important needs will, of course, go unrealized. On the other hand, if students feel that they have a fixed place where educational and personal problems can be shared with an interested and helpful adult and where friendships can be established, the arrangement can reach its highest apex in serving human needs.

For some students, it is necessary to provide highly specialized settings for learning. These individuals have particular needs that cannot be met in regular classrooms, and provisions must be made for them to work in self-contained areas where the setting, the learning materials, and the instructional staff are especially geared to their requirements. Children who have been diagnosed as educationally retarded, socially or emotionally disturbed, brain-injured, or physically impaired need such learning situations. Classes for these students represent learning groups organized around highly specialized considerations.

In summary, individualizing instruction does not mean that each student is working independently and alone all of the time. There are instances when participation in appropriately formed groups is the most effective vehicle for enhancing learning.

Ability Grouping. Ability grouping has been most frequently associated with the provision of experiences that provide for acceleration and/or enrichment. If, for example, a staff is concerned with forming a group of students thirteen or fourteen years of age who are ready to study algebra, the students should be selected on the similarity in their mathematics background and their ability to think abstractly.

For those working with the concept of ability grouping, a word of caution is appropriate. Ability, or, alternately, achievement level, grouping is the least refined approach to individualization. While such an approach has its place, teachers involved with groups formed on the basis of ability or achievement tend to teach all members as though they were alike. Teachers should remember that even similar students are not exactly alike. Methods involving projects, independent study, programmed instruction, etc., provide greater attention to individuals than does ability grouping.

Heterogeneous Grouping. Areas exist within every subject in which instruction can be organized around group activities. Social studies offers the most obvious opportunities. Although there are definite skills to be developed, there is also a concern for involving all students in broad social concepts. Thus boys and girls of different abilities with a wide range of developmental levels can, if they have some common interests, pursue a learning task with each contributing in relation to his or her ability. The goal is to achieve, through the combined efforts of the group, more than any individual could realize if he or she worked alone. Such situations, however, must still meet individual needs and provide differentiated opportunities. To illustrate these points about learning groups, let us look at an example.

Suppose the middle school staff were concerned with helping thirteen- and fourteen-year-old students to understand some of the basic functions that societies provide for people. Some of the important concepts in such an instructional unit might be the following:

1. Societies are groups of individuals who unite for mutually beneficial reasons.
2. Societies provide protection for group members.
3. Societies provide companionship and define relationships.
4. Societies provide for the care and indoctrination of the young.
5. Societies provide for the resolution of conflict within the group.

To promote understanding of these concepts the faculty might concentrate on compatible skill-development outcomes such as the following:

1. Use library reference skills.
2. Analyze and develop generalizations about a society's government, legal system, and educational system.
3. Select appropriate information relevant to situations under investigation.
4. Compare and contrast elements in two different societies.
5. Work as productive members of a peer group.

The general concepts and skills above could be incorporated productively into several learning units, such as studies of the American Indians, the Eskimos, early colonial settlements in America, and African nomads. If several topics are available for students to choose from at this point in their school program, learning groups can be formed around common interests. Also, students who have completed a unit of study, but need more experience with the same skills and concepts, have a number of other topics readily available to them for further work. Students who have developed sufficiently after completing one unit can proceed to another set of topics, which takes them on to other concepts and skills.

Modern teachers recognize that all students do not develop exactly alike even when pursuing the same learning units together. Each student makes a unique contribution to the project. William is good with his hands, Mary has a keen intellect, Jeff can get the group moving together, Sue is an organizer, and Margaret and Charles write well. Each therefore emerges with a slighlty different set of experiences, valuable in its own right to his or her development. The individual facts, skills, and concepts, and the level of their development, are not as vital a concern as is the process through which the students have worked. They have interacted and become intellectually involved with a segment of the world's culture. As a result, they have emerged with new conceptual insights, improved skills, and, ideally, a thirst for more such opportunities.

Musgrave recommends the following ten types of lessons for "whole class discussion." They provide an almost endless number of possibilities for group activities.

1. Sharing current events and affairs
2. Discussing controversial issues
3. Interpreting and discussing stories, poems, books, and all other types of literature
4. Sharing information and discussing subject-matter topics
5. Discussing school and class disciplinary rules and procedures
6. Talking about merits and demerits of mass media such as television shows, movies, radio, and recordings
7. Discussing topics that are relevant to the group members: sex, life and death, interpersonal relations, drug abuse, and tobacco smoking
8. Sharing riddles, jokes, personal stories, or imaginary experiences
9. Listening to music and discussing all aspects of the rendition
10. Reviewing any subject matter unit or topic[8]

Group participation in activities like the above promotes outcomes like the following:

1. Students with deeper insights suggesting ideas that would not occur to the others in the group.
2. Students of various talents recognizing the differences among the group members and coming to respect each for his or her uniqueness.

8. G. Ray Musgrave, *Individualized Instruction: Teaching Strategies Focusing on the Learner* (Boston: Allyn and Bacon, Inc., 1975), pp. 6–7.

3. Individuals of different intellectual levels learning to work with one another.
4. Students experiencing the social problems that arise in diverse groups and learning the conditions that lead to movement toward or away from the group objectives.
5. Students developing communication skills.

SIZE OF GROUPS

Large Groups. Some classes should be much larger than those typically found in schools; it can be advantageous for a class to run from 100 to 150 students or more. The specific size should depend on the kind of activities proposed for the group. Experiences that involve a presentation by a teacher or visiting lecturer might be held for 100 to 150 pupils, whereas film presentations might be limited in number only by the capacity of the room. Experimental studies show that both teachers and students adjust quickly to large-group instructional situations. Some of the reasons for large-group instruction are the following:

1. To carry out certain instructional functions compatible with larger groups such as introducing study units, explaining terms or concepts, demonstrating, hearing visiting personalities or special lectures, viewing films, and administering certain tests.
2. To present certain material to all students in a more uniform manner.
3. To expose more students to the more skillful and experienced teachers in all subject fields.
4. To make expensive instructional equipment more economically feasible.[9]

The role of the teacher in the large group varies considerably with the specific purposes of a class session. Often large-group instruction is handled by a team of teachers and teaching assistants, and other instructional activities are shared among team members.

The setting is important for all instructional situations, but it is particularly so for large groups. Because of the size of the group, any operational faux pas can cause a major snag, erode instructional time, and adversely affect the learning environment. Therefore, all details re-

9. J. Lloyd Trump and Dorsey Baynham, *Focus on Change: Guide to Better Schools* (Chicago: Rand McNally and Company, 1961), pp. 30–31. Adapted and reprinted by permission of Rand McNally College Publishing Company.

garding the session must be carefully preconsidered and proper arrangements provided. Traffic flow, adequate seating, proper lighting, sound amplification, and viewing arrangements are some of the basic variables. If materials are to be distributed or collected, the method of doing so must be determined beforehand. If questions from the floor are to be entertained, can these be heard adequately? If special equipment is to be involved, how will it be stationed and can it be operated efficiently as required by the lesson? If attendance must be taken, how will this be accomplished efficiently? These may seem to be insignificant considerations compared to the content of the lesson, but they are an important part of the planning for successful large-group sessions. Many a well-conceived lesson has collapsed because seemingly trivial elements of the situation were ignored.

In planning the content for a large-group situation, the teacher must also prepare carefully. The type of group, the particular kinds of individuals who comprise the class, the instructional goals of the session, and integration with other learning experiences must all be considered. Material presented must be relevant and of sufficient interest to all members of the group—and there will be a range of interest levels in any group of this size. The method of presentation must be compatible with the material with which the lesson deals. Attention span of the audience is important; it will depend on age, maturity, and other considerations relative to the individuals in the group. Variety must be built into the presentation. The teacher must have projected and practiced every aspect of the lesson plan. The lesson must move, hold the attention of the audience, and reach its conclusions in the time allotted to it. Planning such a lesson is not an easy task, but if the preparations are thorough, the educational profits can be considerable.

Small Groups. Small groups should consist of fifteen or fewer individuals and should serve to foster human interaction. The four major purposes of such groups are as follows:

1. Provide opportunities for teachers to measure an individual student's growth and development and then to try a variety of teaching techniques that will be suited to a student's needs.
2. Offer the therapy of the group process, whereby students are induced to examine previously held concepts and ideas and to alter sometimes mistaken approaches to issues and people. Students will learn, in other words, how to become better group members.
3. Permit all of the students to discover the significance of the subject matter involved and to discuss its potential uses, rather than to just receive it passively and return it in tests.

4. Provide students with opportunities to know their teachers on a personal, individual basis.[10]

The requirements for the teacher's role in the small-group setting are taken from the fact that the particular advantage of the small group is in promoting opportunities for human interaction. Teachers must remember that they are one of the group, even though they are in a different position from the others. They must avoid taking undue advantage of their privileges as the designated leaders. Their role is to promote participation by all, draw out the reticent, and encourage the sharing of ideas, experiences, and points of view. They must act in a way to preserve an atmosphere in which each group member feels comfortable and free to share his or her individuality with the others. Only in such an environment is it possible for students to experience the satisfaction of human sharing and to honestly examine ideas, concepts, issues, and values in order to open opportunities for new insights and opinions.

In the small group, the teacher can appear to the student as just another person, a unique human being with strengths, weaknesses, biases, endearing qualities, hopes, hang-ups, and all the other characteristics of a real person. When the teacher interacts honestly within the group, a whole new dimension in student-teacher understanding is opened. If the teacher expects students to become open, sharing, and accepting of others, he or she must lead the way in openness and acceptance. In the small-group setting, the teacher has an opportunity to come down from the front of the class, enter the group, and know and be known by the students. However, as another aspect of this role, the teacher should often be a quiet observer within the small group. After helping to establish the necessary environment within which the group can function and helping to stimulate the proper group processes for sharing and exchanging, the teacher becomes a watcher. The teacher observes students in action: How do they handle themselves? What does this tell me about the needs of each? Who bullies? Who ignores facts and clings to old biases? Who leads? How does each handle the learning material at hand? Who is the quick intellect with the keen insight? Who is the plodder? Who seems to be making progress? Who is not growing? Whom does the group accept or reject and for what apparent reasons? These and many similar questions are flooding through the mind of the quiet teacher who is watching the human dynamics within a seminar group. From astute watching, the teacher can decide how to help each of those who need special help.

10. Ibid., pp. 24–25.

INDIVIDUAL INQUIRY

Individualization of learning means that diverse approaches or options must be available to teachers and students. At times group interaction is needed to work toward achieving particular objectives, while at others individual inquiry is most appropriate. Some instructional practices for individual inquiry are briefly described in the following material.

CONTINUOUS PROGRESS In a continuous progress plan, each student is placed in a preplanned sequential curriculum. Each is expected to achieve at an established minimum level, with the primary variable being the amount of time necessary to achieve the preset objectives. To accomplish this, provision must be made for:

1. Focusing instruction on individual learners and accommodating current knowledge concerning learning theory and human growth and development.
2. Flexible organizations providing variations whenever these are appropriate to accommodate the developmental needs of children.
3. Patterns of staff assignment that will provide for better utilization of professional skills both by promoting staff collaboration in working with children and by employing teachers in tasks where their individual strengths and interests can be exploited.
4. Organizing curricular programs that will allow students to work individually at their own pace. (Some will be organized around group activity, with appropriate variations to accommodate individual circumstances.)

Since program is the basic building block of school systems, all possible arrangements conformable to the needs of individual learners should be considered. As an example, a model for reading development is presented in Figure 6–1. It should be noted that reading (as well as mathematics) involves sequential, cumulative skill development that can be organized so that learners proceed through the learning experiences at their own pace.

In Figure 6–1, the eighteen levels indicated on the vertical axis are all skills incorporated into the school's formal reading programs. The eighteen levels are arbitrary for the purposes of the model, but they would represent a normal developmental rate of about two levels per ten-month term up through age fourteen or fifteen. Skill development beyond these levels would be independent of formal instruction—except for specialized elective courses, such as speed reading, which would be

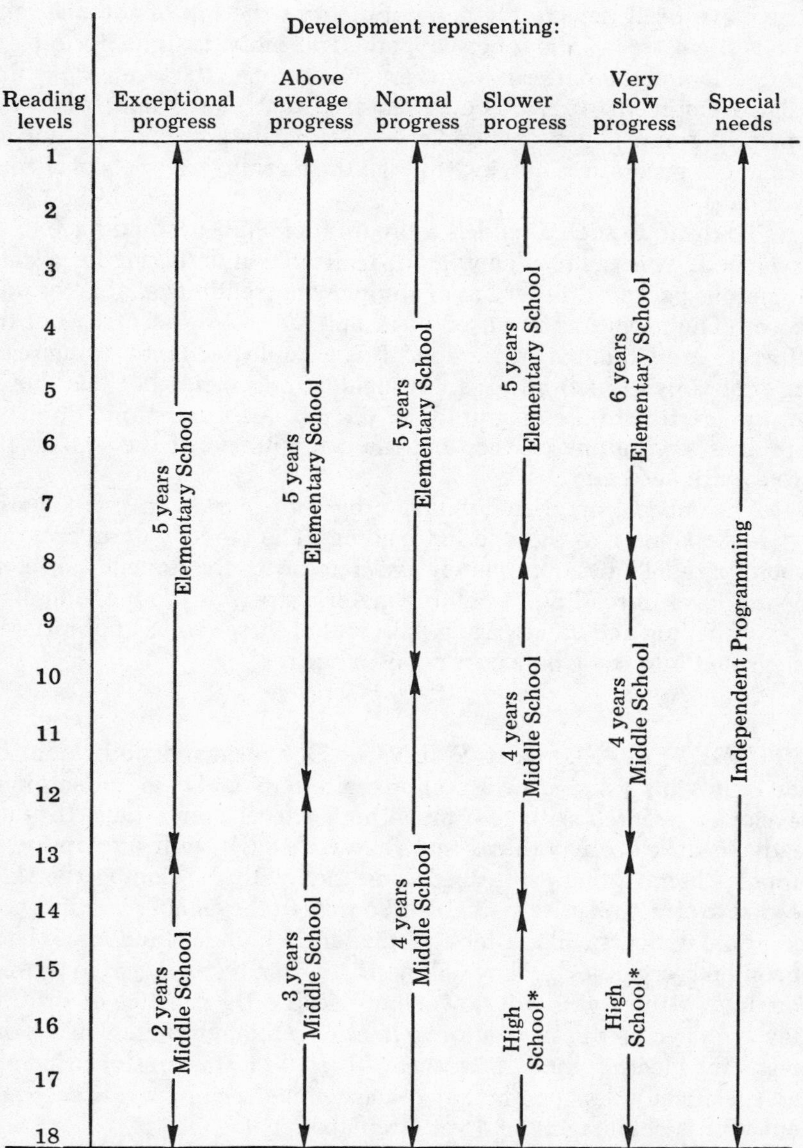

Figure 6–1. A Model of an Individual Progress Plan for Reading Development

available in the secondary school program. Various developmental patterns have been depicted horizontally across the top of the diagram. The vertical arrows show how hypothetical individuals conforming to the developmental patterns might progress through the levels of reading skill development. It must be emphasized that these examples do not represent groups, but rather depict representative patterns that individuals might generate in moving through the learning experiences at their own pace.

To institute such a model, a program of studies would have to be developed. This is a challenging but realizable undertaking for a staff. Numerous packaged programs of study are currently available for purchase. (The programs discussed in Chapter 7 are representative of the efforts to individualize instruction.) It is possible to adapt existing reading programs to such an organizational arrangement, but one should not underestimate the magnitude of the job. Adequate time, financial resources, consultant service, and the commitment of the staff to the project are necessary.

The model for an individual progress program in mathematics would be similar to the one for reading. The language arts program would parallel and be intimately associated with the student's developmental level in reading. Available materials permit the individualization of spelling and handwriting skills so that these can be appropriately integrated into the whole curricular pattern.

DIFFERENTIATED ASSIGNMENTS One means for individualization is providing students with tailored alternatives. Some students have developed research skills to a much higher level than others; they are ready to develop hypotheses and follow through with attempting to support them. Others still need assistance with developing the skills needed to effectively use available resources in the school's learning center. Some students will master a particular skill, understanding, or body of content very quickly; they will need additional challenges to prevent boredom. Others who are slower may need extra practice or drill, or may even need a different approach. Differentiated assignments is one means for meeting these differences—varied illustrations of principles and specifically designed homework assignments can provide each student with a challenging and yet attainable goal.

Interest centers provide a vehicle for differentiation. Formed to teach subject matter skills and concepts, they are stocked with materials covering a specific topic or subject. Students may select what they want to learn and how they will approach it, thus becoming involved in projects or other activities provided by the center. These activities must be designed to make possible real differentiation in interests and ability levels.

SELF-INSTRUCTIONAL MATERIALS Unfortunately, some educators believe that individualized learning can be achieved only through self-instructional materials. It is obvious from the preceding material that this is not true. However, self-instructional materials are an easily accessible means for achieving individualization. They make it possible for students to proceed at their own rate of development, since progress is based on mastery rather than on allotted units of study time. These materials also make provisions for the variances among students. Among the self-instructional materials, Individually Prescribed Instruction (IPI), Individually Guided Education (IGE), and Program for Learning in Accordance with Needs (PLAN) have contributed much to the effort. (The three systems are discussed in further detail in Chapter 7.)

CONTRACTING Contract plans are based on the premise that students can and will take responsibility for determining the extent to which their individual learning will take place. In its simplest form, a contract may stipulate that a specific assignment will be completed on a particular day. A more complex agreement will require student effort spread over many hours for a period of several weeks.

The first step in establishing a contract is an explanation of the system by the teacher. The student is then assisted by the teacher in determining the objectives to be met and the resources available. Agreement must be reached by the teacher and student upon both the extent of the assignment and the level of achievement to be reached. Upon completion of the contracted assignment, teacher and student jointly determine the degree to which the contract has been fulfilled.

An alternative to individually developed contracts is contracts that have been formulated beforehand by the teacher. These should indicate alternatives from which a student may select those that best meet his or her needs and interests. The teacher's role becomes one of arranging learning assignments developed in cooperation with each student.

In a contract it is not unusual to find a specification of the requirements that the student must meet to earn a particular grade. For example, completion of a specified amount might lead to the grade of "A," while completion of 90 percent of that which has been specified would result in assignment of a grade of "B," etc.

INDEPENDENT STUDY While contract learning may be applied to the subject areas in which students must achieve some level of competence, independent study projects make it possible for students to select and pursue areas free of most class restraints. This may be done either during school time or on the student's time. However, independent study must not be the same as those tasks that have been typically assigned as homework.

The term independent study has been interpreted in many ways. The following definition developed by Alexander and Hines is a valid one:

> *Independent study* is considered by us to be learning activity largely motivated by the learner's own aims to learn and largely regarded in terms of intrinsic values. Such activity as carried on under the auspices of secondary schools is somewhat independent of the class or other group organization dominant in past and present secondary school instructional practices, and it utilizes the services of teachers and other professional personnel primarily as resources for the learner.[11]

However, the definition indicates that independent study activity is generally carried on independent of the class and other group organizations. It need not be. Independent study projects provide a very appropriate means for individualizing learning within the framework of whatever group organization may exist at a particular point.

As can be seen from the list below, independent study may cover a large variety of interests and include projects that are oriented to library research or involve the investigation of various kinds of activities or processes.

Apollo Space Flights
Astrophotography
Child Care
Earthquakes
Famous Women in Sports
Fashion Designing
History of Aircraft
History of Singing
Microbes
Origin and Components of Pipe Organs
Profiles of Mathematics
Taxidermy
Tropical Fish
White-tail Deer
Writing Music

Not all students will be ready at a given stage to pursue special learning projects independently. The general aim of education is to develop individuals' ability to function independently and intelligently. However, this is a long-term goal, and teachers should begin in small ways to work toward it in the elementary school. Opportu-

11. W. M. Alexander and V. A. Hines, *Independent Study in Secondary Schools*, Cooperative Research Project no. 2969 (Gainesville, Fla.: University of Florida, 1966).

nities for small independent tasks can lay the groundwork for larger opportunities to come. Specific behaviors that independent study aims to develop are listed as:

1. The independent learner undertakes on his own initiative learning tasks that are important to him.
2. He uses sources of information efficiently.
3. He tests out reflectively possible answers, solutions, and ideas to see whether they are adequate.
4. He seeks to apply generalizations from former to new situations.
5. He is not easily discouraged by the difficulty of the learning task or by forces that would have him accept inadequate answers, solutions, and ideas.
6. He enjoys learning and seeks opportunities to learn.[12]

A middle school staff should encourage the participation of students in unique learning undertakings that promote their ability to function independently.

Before students are ready to move ahead on their own, some specific planning must be done. This planning can be accomplished by students and faculty sponsors through the formulating of independent study plans as shown in Figure 6–2. Each plan includes very concise, specific statements outlining the project objectives, procedures, final product, evaluative procedures, and a tentative time schedule. Such a plan establishes from the beginning a common perception by student and sponsor regarding the nature, limits, activities, and outcomes of the project.

Implementing the plan is, of course, primarily the responsibility of the students, since this is the essence of independent study. Teachers are not, however, divorced from the implementation stage; in fact, they have an important role to play. Although motivation can come only from the students themselves, teachers who are keenly interested in supporting it can have a positive effect. Teachers should express a sincere interest periodically without seeming to be primarily concerned with "checking up." Being available to counsel in time of difficulty, to act as a resource when progress seems to be stymied, to listen, to direct the student to new sources—all of these and many other supportive acts by the teacher are vital to the implementation of each student's plans. In guiding independent study, the teacher must do some delicate balancing between structure and freedom, between guiding and telling, and between monitoring progress and becoming overly supervisory.

---

12. W. M. Alexander and V. A. Hines, *Independent Study in Secondary Schools* (New York: Holt, Rinehart and Winston, Inc., 1967), p. 4.

STUDENT John Wilson GRADE LEVEL 8th

FACULTY SPONSOR Mr. William Boyce DEPARTMENT Social Studies

PROJECT TITLE: The Role of United Fund Agencies in the Community.

OBJECTIVES:

1. To identify specific United Fund Agencies in the community.
2. To outline the services of each of the above agencies.
3. To identify the specific community problems to which each agency addresses itself.
4. To present available evidence as to the success of agencies in helping to solve community problems.
5. To produce a report detailing the above information.

PROCEDURES:

1. Conduct necessary library and other research activities to investigate the history, organization, and component agencies of the United Fund.
2. Devise appropriate questionnaires to be mailed to United Fund Agencies.
3. Conduct personal interviews with directors of sample United Fund Agencies.
4. Organize and detail information obtained, draw appropriate conclusions, and detail in a final report.

DESCRIPTION OF FINAL PRODUCT:

A written report detailing the history, organization, component agencies, services, and evidence of effectiveness of United Fund Agencies and appropriate conclusions based on the data produced by the study.

EVALUATION:

Conferences with the sponsor and the content of the final report will be used to provide specific evidence of the degree to which stated objectives of the project have been realized.

PROJECTED SCHEDULE:

An anticipated period of fifteen weeks will be scheduled as follows:

4 weeks — Begin library research and devise and distribute questionnaires.

6 weeks — Continue library research and arrange for and conduct interviews with selected agency directors.

3 weeks — Organize all information from library research, questionnaire returns, and interviews and develop conclusions.

2 weeks — Produce final report and evaluate results.

APPROVED ______________
Sponsor's Signature

Figure 6–2. Independent Study Plan

Finally, there will come that moment when the student is ready to culminate the activity. At this time, the teacher helps clinch the educational objectives by discussing certain questions with the student. Have you accomplished what you set out to do? In what ways have you fulfilled the original intentions and in what ways have you been unable to do so? What are some of the outcomes that were not foreseen when you began? What difference has the project made in your thinking? In your life? What can we do with it now? Are there next steps? By means of such queries, the teacher helps to unify the entire experience, bring closure, and lay the basis for future learning activity.

There are numerous means for individualizing instruction and learning other than those described in this chapter. Mini-courses as described in the previous chapter are an example, as are the technological ideas put forth in the following chapter. When organizing or reorganizing a school for individualization, one must begin by examining the program of studies. Which learning experiences are best accomplished in which particular setting? How much of the instructional time will it be necessary to devote to each instructional setting? When these determinations have been made, then particular strengths and interests of the teachers involved can be analyzed, in order to attempt to utilize them to best advantage. The characteristics of the student body to be served can be studied; class and instructional groups can be formed in order to enhance the learning opportunities for each individual. Having analyzed the activities involved in the program of studies, having looked at staffing considerations, and having taken the characteristics and needs of the students into account, one can develop schedules that will provide the time and space allotments necessary. Of course, all of this is easier said than done; it will require honest devotion to the task and considerable effort. Any dedicated group of staff members can generate the specific activities that will accomplish each of the tasks above. At least a year of planning should probably precede any operational program, but with a carefully constructed base from which to operate, a staff can successfully change the educational system.

Learning programs, organized as discussed in this chapter, make it possible to promote successful achievement for each student. There is no repeating of grades or even of learning experiences. Reports and evaluations of learning progress can be related to specific learning achievements at specific levels of development. Children who need repeated exposure to particular concepts can become involved with another curriculum unit dealing with the same concepts. The opportunities for outright failure are almost completely eliminated, and the natural momentum of most learning experiences is directed toward some degree of personal development and, thus, toward success. It is the teacher's responsibility to determine which instructional techniques to use with particular children at a particular time.

READINGS FOR TEACHERS

Curtis, Thomas E., and Wilma W. Bidwell, *Curriculum and Instruction for Emerging Adolescents.* Reading, Mass.: Addison-Wesley Publishing Co., 1977.

Musgrave, G. Ray, *Individualized Instruction: Teaching Strategies Focusing on the Learner.* Boston: Allyn and Bacon, Inc., 1975.

Talmage, Harriet, ed., *Systems of Individualized Education.* Berkeley, Calif.: McCutchan Publishing Corp., 1975.

Trump, J. Lloyd, and Dorsey Baynham, *Focus on Change: Guide to Better Schools.* Chicago: Rand McNally and Co., 1961.

Chapter 7
Technology in the Middle School

Many advances in educational technology hold exciting promise for the middle school. A number of these innovations relate in some way to an instructional systems approach to learning. As a result, they are especially applicable to middle grades. These innovations are not only useful as component parts of an integrated learning system; they also have great capability for enhancing individualized instruction, considered by many educators to be the heart of the middle school instructional process.

Among the innovations discussed in this chapter are learning packets, instructional systems approaches, new trends in audio and visual instruction, the latest developments in computer equipment and software use, and the emerging role of the media center.

Although all of these innovations relate in some way to advances in technology, their successful inclusion in the instructional process will be, as always, dependent on farsighted, inventive teachers and administrators.

DIFFERENTIATED LEARNING PATHS

The varied interests and capacities of middle school students can be best met through the use of many different kinds of educational media and through constant evaluation. The learning packet or system must provide for the use of different media for learning and, when evaluation indicates that the student fails to achieve or comprehend, for alternative paths or tracks for learning.

Constant evaluation of student progress must be structured into the learning packet or instructional systems approach. By testing the student prior to the learning experience, the teacher ensures his or her proper placement in the program material. In fact, more pretesting with increasingly difficult graded tests allows the individualized learning process to become effective, since the teacher can then prescribe paths for learning, either direct or alternative.

Testing the student after the learning process has taken place allows the teacher to determine if the learning objective has been achieved. A low test score indicates nonlearning and prompts the teacher to prescribe alternative learning paths. These can include different media, different materials, reteaching, or any other proven remedy for nonlearning.

The philosophy that there can and ought to be differentiated learning paths changes the roles of the student and the teacher. The program rather than the teacher's manual or guidebook contains the structure of the discipline. The teacher becomes a facilitator or a prescriber of learning paths. The student, according to this theory, becomes more independent, since the process of learning becomes an individual responsibility, with expert help and advice readily available.

Contrast these programs with the middle-grades programs of the past two decades in which groups were taught en masse, regardless of prior learning or nonlearning, and the teacher, even if he or she was so inclined, was incapable of diagnosing and prescribing on an individual basis for the needs of two dozen or more children in six or more subjects. Is it any wonder that educators, by necessity, looked for structured programs that could pace, place, evaluate, diagnose, prescribe, and provide for differentiated learning paths when nonlearning occurred? Thus the learning packet and instructional systems approaches were born.

LEARNING PACKETS

One of the most promising breakthroughs in the movement toward individualized instruction for middle schools has been the development of the learning packet, or learning cell. Simply defined, a learning packet is a structured learning program developed around predetermined instructional objectives. It allows a student to proceed independently yet with direction through a sequential learning experience.

The desired result of this experience is that the ten- to fourteen-year-old student will learn the process of researching and how to apply that process in other situations. The program content allows the student to acquire the intended learnings in a predetermined sequence so that higher-order learning skills can be developed from lower-order learnings.

The development of individualized learning packets, or cells, has progressed during the 1970s from the infancy stage to widespread acceptance and use. During the past ten years, the repertoire of instructional materials has advanced from a disorganized collection of heterogeneous, single-dimension learning activities to a well-ordered, multidimensional approach to learning. What were once isolated teaching units have become complete learning systems, structured and sequenced from low-order learning to higher-order cognitive and affective learning experiences. In the 1980s we will certainly see the development of complete series of sequenced learning packets in most of the major disciplines, especially in the middle grades, where the obvious enthusiasm of the student creates an atmosphere receptive to individualized projects.

Middle schools contemplating the use of either teacher-prepared or commercially available learning packets should apply certain criteria in the development or selection of new learning packet materials. These would include the following:

1. The packets selected for use should be part of a sequential program articulated with the preceding elementary program and with the secondary program that follows.
2. The program packets should employ a strategy for mastery and learning easily understood by both the teacher and the student.
3. The materials should employ diagnostic procedures early in the program, with periodic evaluations of achievement during the learning process.
4. The packets should attempt to develop sequential learning toward a predetermined series of instructional or behavioral outcomes, carefully selected for the ten- to fourteen-year-old.
5. The individual abilities of students should be carefully considered in the development or selection of materials in order to provide for the wide range of student capabilities.
6. The material should be relevant to student interests from preteen to emerging adolescent.
7. The process of learning is equally as important as content retention, if not more important. The packets should relate to the acquisition of library skills, research skills, and organizational skills, all of which the student will require in secondary school.
8. The packets should attempt to provide mastery in a relatively short period of time in order to promote a sense of success. Properly developed learning packets guarantee the achieving or learning of the predetermined instructional objective.
9. Learning packets should employ all of the VAKT (visual, auditory, kinesthetic, and tactile) approaches recognized as important to the psychology of learning for ten- to fourteen-year-old students.
10. Learning packets should be open-ended, since some students might be stimulated to explore other related subjects using the processes learned in the structured materials. Avenues for further study should be stressed.

11. Whole kits of varied learning materials and allied equipment should be available to supplement the learning packets. These materials should relate directly to the packets and should be available as a resource when the packet directs the learner to specific new sources of information.
12. Alternative paths for learning should be structured into the packets when evaluation reveals that intended learnings are not occurring.
13. Since the life process itself is not completely individualized, but a shared experience with others, the packets should provide for group, as well as individualized, learning. A program based completely on individualized learning packets would lose impact and student interest.

INSTRUCTIONAL SYSTEMS

A logical extension of the concept of learning packets is the development and use of an entire system for learning. Learning packets can be successfully used for short-term projects within well-defined parameters, but a more exciting idea is that of structuring a complete new approach to learning an entire discipline through a long-term instructional systems approach. Basically, an instructional system can be defined as a complete program for individualized learning, with accompanying resources and materials, sequentially developed to cover a number of years of study in one discipline.

Whereas learning packets adapt to a unit study of learnings for which limited, predetermined objectives have been drawn, the learning system extends over a number of years, embodying more extended objectives. These extended objectives are carefully sequenced to ensure retention through constant maintenance and reinforcement of skills acquired in the program.

Certain subjects seem to lend themselves to the learning packet or short-term approach. These include social studies, health, and language arts. Mathematics, reading, and possibly science could be approached through the instructional system or long-range approach. These subjects require extended study and are sequential in their learning process.

Advances in the technology of educational hardware are beginning to be evident in currently available and well-developed instructional systems. We are now seeing the introduction of complete learning systems in reading, mathematics, and science for middle grades.

All of the recommended criteria from the previous section on learning packets are also applicable to instructional systems. Learning systems already being used give middle schools the opportunity to approach individualized instruction through a carefully researched, long-range program of instruction, using a number of components over an extended period of time. A discussion of several such programs follows.

INDIVIDUALLY PRESCRIBED INSTRUCTION SYSTEM The IPI system is one of the pioneer projects started as a cooperative venture of the University of Pittsburgh and the staff of the Oakleaf Elementary School. The work was taken over and extended by Research for Better Schools, Inc., the Philadelphia-based, federally funded regional laboratory.

Individually Prescribed Instruction provides for planning and carrying out with each student a program based on his or her particular learning needs and characteristics as a learner. The learning materials in each individualized program will conform to the following characteristics:

1. The rate of speed at which each child progresses depends upon his or her capacities. Initial placement on the continuum is determined by both placement tests and pretests.
2. The curriculum material is arranged in a sequential order called a continuum. Assignments are given by a prescription to fit individual needs. (A prescription is an individual lesson plan for each student each day.)
3. The student's mastery of the curriculum is judged by curriculum-embedded tests and post-tests. He or she is required to perform at a level of 85 percent.
4. The child works independently in most cases, thus building up a sense of responsibility and a confidence in his or her own knowledge. He or she begins to know that learning is a process that is dependent on his or her own participation and initiative.

IPI programs of study are built upon very specific and detailed learning objectives, such as the following:

1. Identify synonyms for specified words when these words are presented in a sentence.
2. Distinguish between a word that names a group and a word that identifies a member of that group.
3. Select, from choices, the meaning of a specific word in a sentence when the meaning of that word is included as part of the sentence.

Each objective is stated so that it communicates to teacher and student exactly what the individual who has mastered the skill or content can do. The objectives are grouped together in meaningful units of content, which are arranged sequentially so that skill development or content mastery proceeds on a continuum from lower to higher abilities. In Table 7–1, for example, skills in the various competencies are sequenced from simple to more complex through eleven developmental levels, designated A through K.

All IPI lesson materials are related exactly to the objectives and are presented in such a way that the student can proceed with a minimum of teacher direction. The following four types of instruments are utilized to diagnose student needs and monitor their progress:

1. Placement instruments are tests used to assess mastery of units of work along the learning continuum and to indicate the entering level of the student in the continuum.
2. Pretest instruments are used to discover which specific objectives within a unit and level a student knows or does not know.
3. Post-test instruments, alternative forms of the pretests, are given at the end of each unit of work to determine the student's mastery of the unit.
4. Curriculum-embedded tests are short tests of a student's progress toward a particular objective within a level and unit of work. Each test has two parts: the first measures progress toward a particular objective, and the second serves as a pretest of the ability to achieve the next objective within the unit and level of work.

Table 7-1

COMPETENCIES	DEVELOPMENTAL LEVELS (A B C D E F G H I J K)
Visual discrimination	A → B
Auditory discrimination	A → B
Literal comprehension	A → K
Interpretive comprehension	A → K
Evaluative comprehension	A → K
Vocabulary development	B → K
Structural analysis	C → K
Library skills	A → J
Reference skills	B → K
Organizational skills	F → K
Related reading	A → C

Written lesson plans, called prescriptions, are prepared individually for each student. They provide the means for guiding the student through the learning sequences. Figure 7–1 diagrams the process through which students proceed in the IPI program. Figures 7–2A and 7–2B illustrate a reading prescription sheet.

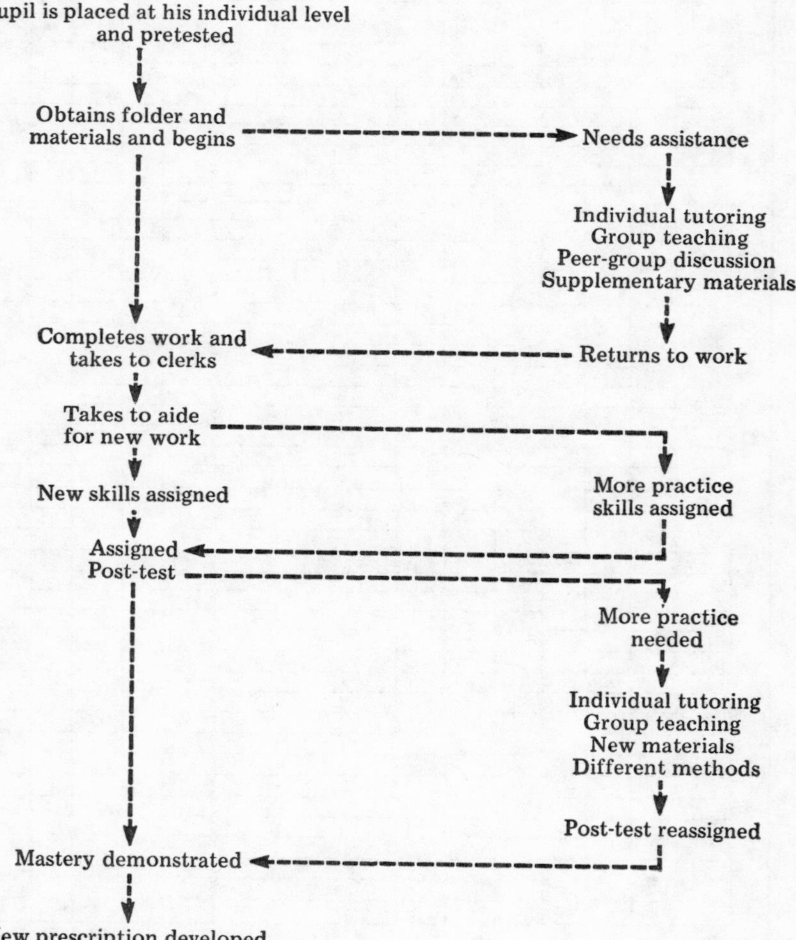

Figure 7–1. Flow of the IPI System (Source: Reprinted from "A Progress Report: Individually Prescribed Instruction," Research for Better Schools, Inc., Philadelphia, (1973).

READING PRESCRIPTION SHEET

_______________ STUDENT NAME _______________ UNIT PAGE ____ OF ____

TASKS								CURRICULUM TEST				DAYS WORK-ED
								PART 1		PART 2		
DATE PRES.	PRES. INIT.	SKILL NO.	PAGE NO.	TOTAL POINTS	NUMBER CORRECT	INST. TECH CODES	INSTRUCTIONAL NOTES	NO. OF POINTS	%	NO. OF POINTS	%	

Figure 7–2A. Reading Prescription Sheet, Page 1

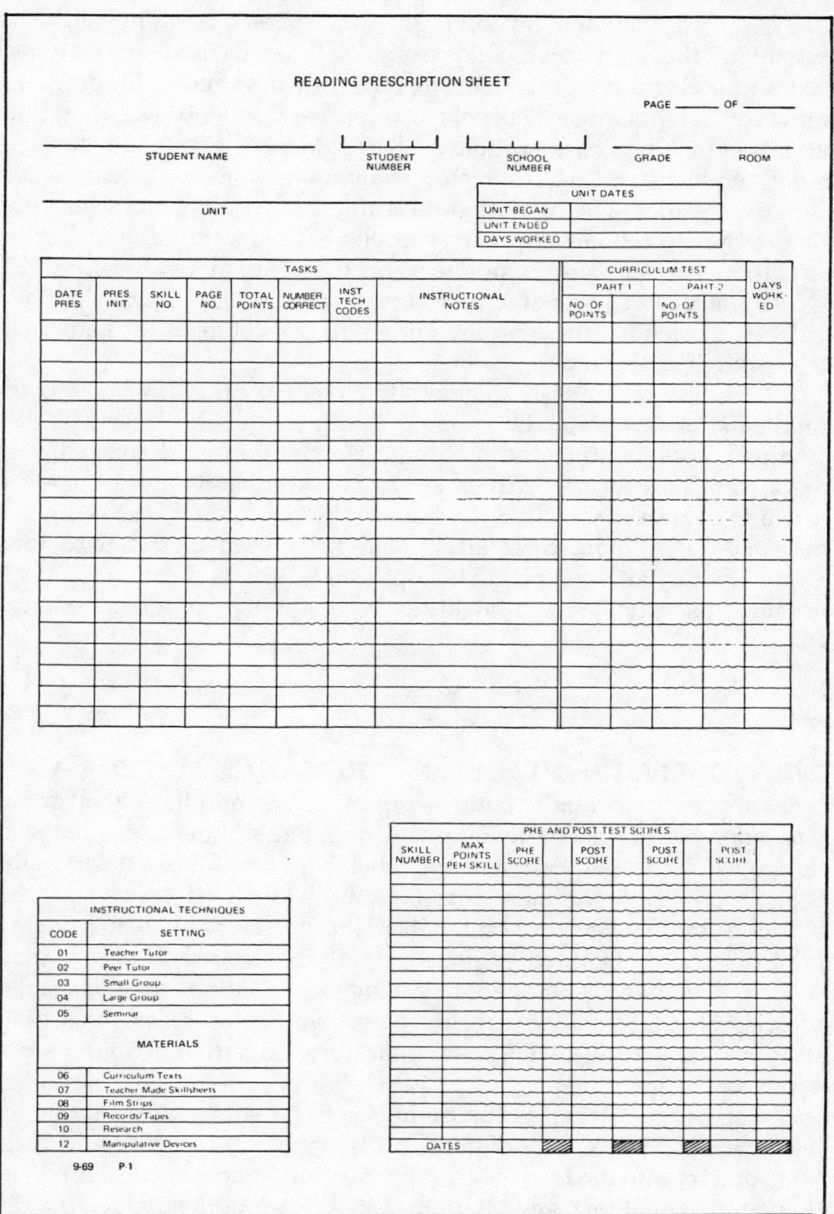

READING PRESCRIPTION SHEET

PAGE ______ OF ______

STUDENT NAME | STUDENT NUMBER | SCHOOL NUMBER | GRADE | ROOM

UNIT

UNIT DATES	
UNIT BEGAN	
UNIT ENDED	
DAYS WORKED	

TASKS								CURRICULUM TEST				
								PART 1		PART 2		DAYS WORKED
DATE PRES.	PRES. INIT.	SKILL NO.	PAGE NO.	TOTAL POINTS	NUMBER CORRECT	INST TECH CODES	INSTRUCTIONAL NOTES	NO OF POINTS		NO OF POINTS		

INSTRUCTIONAL TECHNIQUES	
CODE	SETTING
01	Teacher Tutor
02	Peer Tutor
03	Small Group
04	Large Group
05	Seminar
MATERIALS	
06	Curriculum Texts
07	Teacher Made Skillsheets
08	Film Strips
09	Records/Tapes
10	Research
12	Manipulative Devices

PRE AND POST TEST SCORES								
SKILL NUMBER	MAX POINTS PER SKILL	PRE SCORE		POST SCORE		POST SCORE		POST SCORE
DATES								

9-69 P-1

Figure 7–2B. Reading Prescription Sheet, Page 2

INDIVIDUALLY GUIDED EDUCATION SYSTEM The Individually Guided Education System (IGE) was designed as a total education system at the University of Wisconsin's Research and Development Center for Cognitive Learning. The IGE provides a model for programming for individual learners based on rates and styles of learning, with attention to other considerations such as guidance, curriculum development, educational measurement, evaluation, and home and school communications. The first program is aimed at reorganizing school personnel to help schools improve their curriculum and individualize instruction. Another program, the Wisconsin Design for Reading Skill Development, was prepared as a management system to expedite individually guided instruction in reading skill development for kindergarten through sixth grade.

One portion of IGE that is often used in middle schools is the mathematics program Developing Mathematics Processes (DMP). Completely sequential, the program extends from grade one through grade six. The entire DMP program has been built around specific learning objectives. Closely related objectives and the activities designed to promote their attainment have been clustered to form approximately ninety topics. The topics have been grouped into units to organize materials and to facilitate the continuous progress design of IGE.

INDIVIDUALIZED MIDDLE MATHEMATICS SYSTEM A systems approach to mathematics instruction for middle school grades was adopted in the basic rationale of another innovative program developed by the government-funded laboratory Research for Better Schools (RBS), in Philadelphia. The Individualized Middle Mathematics System (IMM) contains all of the necessary elements: behavioral objectives, planned sequence, tightly controlled structure, diagnosis and evaluation, individual pacing, remediation through teacher prescription, alternative learning paths, and multi-sensory learning. It is a complete VAKT (visual, auditory, kinesthetic, and tactile) approach to learning.

The program divides the middle school mathematics curriculum into seven topics: (1) foundations, (2) integers, (3) rationals and reals, (4) geometry and measurement, (5) probability and statistics, (6) equations and inequalities, and (7) applications. Each of the topics is divided into levels of difficulty. At each of these levels, there are a number of skills that must be learned. For each skill, there is a folder of from four to twelve teaching pages.

SOURCES FOR MORE INFORMATION

Wisconsin R & D Center News, 1025 W. Johnson Street, Madison, Wis. 53706
Sources on Individualized Systems/IGE Instructional Systems.

Cemrel Newsletter, 3120 59th Street, St. Louis, Mo. 63139
Math Instructional Systems—C.S.M.P. (Comprehensive School Math Program).

Educational R & D Report, CEDAR (Council of Educational Development and Research), 1518 K Street, N.W., Suite 206, Washington, D.C. 20005
National reporting systems for programs developed by federally funded regional laboratories.

Curriculum Review, Curriculum Advisory Service, 500 S. Clinton Street, Chicago, Ill. 60607
Review evaluations of programs, systems, textbooks, etc. Published bi-monthly.

PROGRAMMED MATERIALS

Programmed materials are the learning components of programmed instruction. They are designed so that a learner attends to a very limited amount of material at one time, making a response to each segment of the sequence, after which he or she receives immediate feedback concerning the adequacy of his or her response. The cycle is repeated throughout the program; each student proceeds at his or her own pace. New developments in audiovisual-based, self-instructional programs also permit students to move at their own individual rate, but with that the similarity ends. Programmed materials are developed with much more attention to the behaviors intended as outcomes of instruction, with a more sophisticated psychological analysis of behavior, and with a more rigorous experimental approach used in sequencing the learning segments.

The underlying principles of programmed instruction, then, are the following. Instruction is goal-oriented and organized into effective sequences. Materials present one simple increment of learning at a time. Students are actively involved in the learning process, receive immediate knowledge of results, and proceed at their own pace.

There are four major steps involved in developing a program, each of which requires skills and understandings for its accomplishment: (1) goals are specified as particular tasks that students must master; (2) the material leading to the accomplishment of these tasks is broken down into small units and ordered into individual frames; (3) each frame is a unit which the learner must focus on and respond to; and (4) the initial program is a fully developed learning system providing learning and evaluation.

Programmed materials are presented in a variety of formats. Many are published in written and audiovisual format, with various devices used to present the learning sequences and provide for the immediate reinforcement. Most are developed to be used with particular mechanical aids.

One of the excellent systems of individualized instruction is the Tutor Systems Programs, developed and marketed by Sargent-Welch Scientific Company. Over one hundred programs are available in English, reading, math and science. All programs are designed for use on a solid-state, audiovisual machine called the Auto-Tutor. The programs can be used by both advanced and remedial students. These teaching devices combine various components of audiovisual machinery into one system.

COMPUTERS

The use of the computer in education has shown a rapid and continuous growth in the past decade. As price and size of computers have decreased, their use in American schools has increased proportionally.

Computer use in schools has generally been concentrated in the four areas of (1) computer-assisted instruction, (2) computer management of instructional systems and programs, (3) instruction in the programming and use of computers, and (4) administrative chores.

A number of middle schools have begun successfully to use computers "in-house" in all of the four areas. As the cost of purchasing equipment and software has decreased, as more trained personnel have become available, and as the national use of computers, both large and small, has grown, schools have increased their use of computers for both instruction and administration. More and more schools have begun to lease terminal time and to purchase equipment and software.

Computer-assisted instruction (CAI) is a two-way interaction system—between computer and learner—that results in learner behavior modification. It is a highly sophisticated application of the principles of programmed instruction to machine technology, utilizing the computer as its central component. It is based on behavioral objectives and provides a well-tested system for achieving specific learning goals. It individualizes instruction by varying the rate of learning as well as the pathways of learning. The systems now available have the capability to keep accurate records of students' progress and to make available summarized data for research purposes.

How does CAI happen? A programmer takes the material for a given course of study, identifies the behavioral objectives involved in the learning, and develops a learning program compatible with a given computer. The program is entered into the computer and is then available for use from any properly connected remote terminal. A terminal usually consists of a typewriter-like keyboard which the student uses to interact with the computer program. Messages to and from the computer appear on a cathode ray tube, or TV screen, which is incorporated into the terminal unit. Some systems have also included print devices for the presentation of hard-copy material. In some installations, displayed problems can be responded to with electronic pens. In the circuit between the terminal and the computer, an electronic switching device, called a multiplexer, makes it possible for the computer to handle communications with many terminals.

Computer-assisted instruction has not spread as rapidly as was anticipated. The problems inherent in the initiation of computer-assisted programs can mainly be classified under the following categories:

1. Cost problems in using a main frame or large computer.
2. Lack of worthwhile software or programs, although more and more programs are becoming available.
3. Tie-up of terminals by one student, with a resultant lack of flexibility.
4. Opposition to a stimulus-response instructional approach.
5. Lack of conclusive research to demonstrate that computers were cost-effective in terms of learning growth for students.

Computer-managed instruction deserves a closer look than it has received to date. As individualized programs of instruction become more available, and the educational systems approach to learning becomes more common, the problem of management of the programs becomes more pronounced. Scoring, record keeping, branching, and alternative tracking for each student can easily be programmed and managed by computer systems, which allow teachers and administrators instant access to student record data.

Instruction in the use and programming of computers was once limited to high school and college students; it is now being mastered by the middle school child. Mastery of computer language and understanding of program design, as well, are achievable by middle school students.

Administration at all levels has made increasing use of the computer to assist in administrative chores, scheduling, class listing, reporting and grading, and attendance. As costs continue to decrease, more use of the computer can be anticipated in middle schools, enabling administrators to instantly retrieve data for current and future planning needs.

CONTROL DATA PLATO PROGRAMS PLATO computer-based education programs, available in almost every subject, provide a versatile and cost-effective approach to instruction. Unlike programmed instruction that simply feeds out information, PLATO individualized computer-based instruction creates a constant dialogue with the learner.

Control Data Corporation, the developer of PLATO, designed the computer system to provide an individualized learning experience for the student using a terminal with keyboard and display screen. In some cases the screen is of the type that allows students to touch it with an instrument to record input. Errors are immediately flashed on the screen, and alternate learning paths are presented. Students can repeat key exercises as often as desired, or "freeze" a situation at a certain point for review of performance. A total record of performance is available from the computer upon demand of the instructor or the student.

Students can operate simultaneously at different places in any program; each can proceed at any rate of speed, based on successful performance. Students are also involved in determining their learning needs; they may work only on that material necessary to attain competency.

Research for Better Schools, the Philadelphia-based regional educational lab, has been working with Control Data Corporation in the Baltimore public schools, at the middle school level, to develop programs in intermediate-level basic skills areas. These federally funded efforts have proven successful and represent the next step forward in the development of a meaningful use of computer technology in computer-assisted instruction.

DIGITAL EQUIPMENT COMPANY PROGRAMS (DEC) DEC computer equipment and software programs are available for middle school use in either instructional or administrative areas. The relatively inexpensive DEC PDP11 packaged computer systems allow middle school students to program in a variety of computer languages, or to use an extensive variety of educational software made available through DECUS (Digital Equipment Corporation Users Society).

Up to four terminals can input into this small packaged computer, and a variety of low- or high-speed printers can be used for data output.

One middle school in Massachusetts is using a PDP11 system for basic instruction for students in computer programming. The school is also using available software in a variety of computer programs in the environmental science area. An instructor in the computer program reports that most of the students have responded well to the challenge of programming and using a computer. Many eighth graders can write programs and run the equipment with skill and understanding.

HOME COMPUTERS FOR SCHOOL USE For those middle schools whose budget will not provide for the purchase of a packaged computer system, a relatively modest expenditure will allow for the purchase of a desk-sized, surprisingly sophisticated home computer. Radio Shack Corporation markets a small computer with a central processing unit of 4,000 to 16,000 bytes, a terminal for input, a cathode ray tube for viewing, and a cassette tape recorder for storage of programs. Other companies in this rapidly growing field are manufacturing comparable units. A mini-system such as this can be used to teach programming, as well as to run software usable in many instructional areas.

SOURCES FOR MORE INFORMATION

EDU Magazine, Digital Equipment Corporation, Education Products Group, 146 Main Street, Maynard, Mass. 01754
The education magazine of DEC—listing programs, classroom resources, and software.

IDEAS, Digital Equipment Corporation, 146 Main Street, Maynard, Mass. 01754
An index and description of educational-application software.

Courseware Catalog and Subscription Courseware Catalog, Control Data Corporation, 8100 34th Avenue, North Bloomington, Minn. 55440
Catalog of educational-application software.

TELEVISION AND VIDEO CASSETTE RECORDERS

The latest news in the field of educational technology is that television is being reinvented. The television set is rapidly being transformed from an infrequently used information source to what will be the primary visual teaching tool available in schools. The era of the relatively expensive 16mm motion picture film is drawing to a close. The reason for the change is the video cassette recorder (VCR), which allows schools to record up to four hours of full-color programs for later replay, and which can also be used with commercially available, pre-recorded cassette tapes. In addition, 35mm slides or 16mm electronic film can be transferred onto VCR cassettes, allowing schools to standardize the medium of reproduction and to eliminate the use of many of the slide, sound, and film projectors now in use.

The middle grades possess particular potential for expanded use of "reinvented" television with its components. Among the best-known and recognized stimuli for learning among ten- to fourteen-year-olds are those projecting through the visual and auditory senses, yet these stimulus techniques have not been fully exploited in education.

A large number of schools have purchased video cassette equipment and have begun to make increasing use of these systems in instruction. VCR equipment has been used by ingenious teachers and media specialists in every subject area. Schools have assembled collections of cassette tapes by recording from TV broadcasts and purchasing from commercial sources. Thus, they have many worthwhile shows available for future individual or class use, as program needs require.

VCR systems generally use one of two standards of technology. The Beta system, first introduced by Sony, is also the basis of VCR equipment marketed by Sanyo, Toshiba, Sears, and Zenith. The second system is called the Video Home System (VHS) and is marketed by Japan Victor Company, Hitachi, Panasonic, RCA, and General Electric.

Both Beta and VHS formats provide equal quality in color reproduction. The differences are that the Beta format is a single-speed system and can record and play back up to three hours of tape on each cassette, while VHS is a dual-speed system and can record and store up to four hours of tape on each cassette. Either system is ideal for school use. The major criteria for selection should be the cost of purchase of "software" for use in the players and the availability of libraries of cassettes for school use.

SOURCES FOR MORE INFORMATION

T. H. E. Journal (Technological Horizons in Education), Information Synergy, Inc., 409 Massachusetts Avenue, Acton, Mass. 01720

Video Corporation of America, Consumer Video Division, 231 E. 55th Street, New York, N.Y. 10022

Time-Life Video Corporation, Time-Life Building, New York, N.Y. 10020

Catalogs of prerecorded video cassettes.

Popular Video, Inc., P.O. Box 2269, G.P.O. New York, N.Y. 10001

Video newsletter with more than 100,000 video programs available.

Video Magazine, 235 Park Avenue South, New York, N.Y. 10002

Magazine about equipment and cassettes, etc.

Video Tape Network, 115 E. 62nd Street, New York, N.Y. 10021

Catalogs of programs and prerecorded cassettes.

CAMERAS Every available Beta or VHS system video recorder is equipped not only to record television programs, but also to allow students to produce their own videotapes by use of inexpensive black-and-white or more expensive color cameras. Schools can currently purchase new-technology color camera equipment, which will promote even greater use of the VCR sets. It is possible to add optional rechargeable battery equipment, which makes the camera more portable and thus usable in many locations.

DIAL ACCESS AND RETRIEVAL EQUIPMENT Many new middle school plants are being designed to allow teacher or student dial access and retrieval of off-the-air, cable television or video cassette programs on television screens in classrooms or media centers. The designs of many new types of study carrels permit students to dial a program for listening or viewing. Programs originate from the media center, or some central station in it, and are available upon request by telephone or cable. As video cassettes become more plentiful, the use of this dial-access capability will grow, especially as more instructional systems require integrated program use of many forms of media.

The design of the retrieval system should provide instant, individual, and remote access to video cassettes. Specifications required for a topnotch dial-access retrieval system would be:

1. Random access to stored materials must be provided. That is, each request for materials must be honored upon presentation. Materials in the system must never be "not available now" or "now in process."
2. Access must be provided for both audio and visual materials.
3. The individual user must have full control over the selection and use of the instructional materials.
4. Remote access to the materials in the system must be supplied on the widest possible scale. Individual carrels, conference rooms, classrooms, other schools, and private residences must be potential receiver points.
5. The efficiencies of a single, central storage and control facility must be provided.

Middle schools of the future can look forward to functional new ways to store and use information and materials. As these systems become more plentiful, the price will probably be reduced to the point where they become economically feasible for most school districts, and the software necessary to complement the hardware will become more generally available and better oriented to integrated learning systems.

VIDEO DISCS Many video industry leaders predict that eventually the VCR equipment will be totally replaced by video disc players, which will resemble a phonograph and deliver up to two hours of programming from a single, low-cost, twelve-inch record.

The major reason for the eventual replacement of VCR equipment by the video disc players centers around the cost. Discs should sell for about 25 percent to 40 percent of the cost of similar tape programs and could be played on equipment selling for half the price of a VCR player.

The state of the art is changing rapidly; it is possible that the video disc player will use a low-power laser beam to deliver the picture and sound from the disc to the viewer.

INSTRUCTIONAL MATERIAL MEDIA CENTERS

A necessary and vital part of the middle school is the instructional material media center. In order to support individualized learning, the middle school program requires a strong and well-supported instructional material center. The physical environment, and the variety and the quality of materials and media available, must be determined with the ten- to fourteen-year-old in mind.

One of the major weaknesses of many new material media centers has been the lack of vision of the personnel who run the centers. They tend to be librarians from the "old school," trained in the tradition of books rather than of media. Most of these librarians, untrained in the use of machines, cassettes, and video equipment, have forced administrators to place the care and feeding of these vital tools into the hands of another person, who is generally designated the audiovisual coordinator. This results in a chaotic, uncoordinated program for utilizing instructional materials, books, equipment, and films. Untrained teachers only add to the confusion because they do not or cannot look beyond the medium of a textbook as a means for acquiring knowledge.

The choice of an undertrained media center specialist incapable of coordinating and advising on the use of all types of media will result in a less than complete and less than satisfactory program. Since a variety of media and materials are crucial to individualized learning, the media specialist must have depth and breadth of vision.

The following outlines the criteria that are considered important to the evaluation of the media program.

A. Personnel Criteria

1. Is the media specialist knowledgeable about all phases of the program from books and films to television, cassettes, and microfiche, and can he or she relate these to the middle school curriculum?
2. Can the specialist relate well enough to his equipment to lead in the use of the materials rather than react passively, as most school librarians do?
3. Has the librarian image been erased, or do the administration and faculty view the media center as a library?

B. Program Criteria

1. Does the program require specific use of varied media and materials at designated points in the instructional system?

2. Can the students manipulate the audio equipment, slide projector, film loops, television tapes or cartridges, audio cassettes, and reference collections in order to enhance individualized learning?
3. Does the planning process involve the media specialist in continued planning with the instructional teams, or is the typical pattern of sporadic or periodic involvement the only contact between the program and the media center?

C. Facilities and Equipment Criteria
1. Is the center carpeted for acoustical control?
2. Does the environment attract, or does it have the stereotyped library image?
3. Can one study individually? Work in a group? Confer one to one? Read for fun? Browse? Listen? View a visual? Relax? The physical design should permit all of these without disturbing the other necessary functions.
4. Is equipment available for individual student use in the following areas:
   a. Microfilm and microfiche viewers?
   b. Television tape, cassette, and broadcast reception capability?
   c. 16mm, super-8mm, reel, and loop film?
   d. Audio tapes and cassettes for instruction?
   e. Record and tape cassettes for music listening?
   f. Filmstrip viewing with audio capability?

SCIENCE LABORATORIES

In addition to an instructional media center, a middle school should have a science laboratory. The advent of packaged science programs and National Science Foundation–sponsored science programs has radically changed the teaching of science in the intermediate grades. Longstanding programs such as the AAAS (American Association for the Advancement of Science), ESS (Elementary Science Study), SCIS (Science Curriculum Improvement Study), and QAESS (Quantitative Approach in Elementary School Science) have been published commercially by various textbook companies. These elementary programs, in conjunction with already existing intermediate-grade programs such as ISCS (Intermediate Science Curriculum Study), IPS (Introductory Physical Science), and ESCP (Earth Science Curriculum Project), have changed the dimensions of middle school science instruction.

Certain recurrent educational themes are typical of these programs. They include the following:

1. Stress on the process-of-science approach.
2. Laboratory experimentation.
3. Development of student learning through inquiry.
4. The need for and use of science-trained teachers.
5. Use of science equipment and apparatus.
6. Use of multi-media for instruction.
7. Integration, where possible, with other disciplines.

Thus these science programs are generally designed to utilize as much laboratory space and equipment as can be obtained. As the middle school idea grows, the use of science laboratories will grow with it.

CONTRIBUTIONS OF REGIONAL EDUCATIONAL LABORATORIES

The Elementary and Secondary Education Act authorized, and provided funds for, fifteen regional educational laboratories to operate throughout the United States. These laboratories were instrumental in developing and disseminating educational ideas and programs to local school systems. However, cutbacks in funds and duplications of effort have caused the federal government to close some programs and to curtail others. Thus the number of labs and centers serving under the auspices of the National Institute for Education (NIE) has been reduced dramatically. Among those regional laboratories and centers developing usable programs for middle grades were the following:

1. Research for Better Schools, Philadelphia, Pennsylvania—developer of Individually Prescribed Instruction (IPI) in reading, math, spelling, and science.
2. Southwest Education Development Laboratory, Austin, Texas.
3. Northwest Regional Laboratory, Portland, Oregon—developer of teacher training programs, videotaped math programs, and Patterns in Arithmetic (PIA).
4. Mid-Continent Regional Educational Laboratory, Kansas City, Missouri—developer of program for dropout prevention in inner-city schools.
5. Appalachia Education Laboratory, Charleston, West Virginia—developer of programs in reading, language development, and media.

6. Central Midwestern Regional Laboratory, St. Louis, Missouri—developer of programs in aesthetic education and the arts, lab theater, and instructional systems for students with learning disabilities.
7. Far Western Laboratory for Educational Research and Development, San Francisco, California,—developer of a teacher training program using micro-teaching and mini-courses.

The laboratories were charged with the responsibility of innovating through research on a large scale and of diffusing the programs once models were developed. Curriculum planners recognize that for the first time coordinated research did effectively cut the lag time from development to implementation and did speed up the process of improving education, and the regional laboratory system certainly deserves a large part of the credit.

Chapter 8
The Activity Program

Many activities that were once outside the regular school program have been integrated into the curriculum. Schools should pursue this course with caution, however, for it is probably desirable that certain activities remain outside the structured curriculum; otherwise, they might not be as attractive to the students. At as early an age as twelve or thirteen, a student needs to begin to practice self-direction, and the balance between student initiative and direction by the teacher becomes very important. There are many educational benefits to a well-organized, comprehensive activity program. For this reason, a major objective of any program must be widespread participation with a high level of student involvement.

A PROGRAMMATIC APPROACH

Student activity programs can be traced back to the academy of Benjamin Franklin's period. Originally, they were probably started as a means of providing recreational activities for students, since schools were mainly residential. Sports and forensics were the activities in early programs. It was not until after 1900 that student activities were really acknowledged by educators, whose viewpoints advanced from ignorance to toleration and, finally, to acceptance.

The term extracurricular belongs to the period when activities were the stepchildren of the school program. It implies that they were beyond the scope of the curriculum, even though some might have developed from subject-area interests. They were looked upon as a source of entertainment or as a means for providing structured recreational opportunities for children. At times, the term "extra-class" was used. This had the same implication—not part of the regular program as provided in classes. If activities are essential to the pupil's education (and we believe they are), the terms extracurricular and extra-class are obviously not appropriate.

Cocurricular, a term applied later and still used today, seems to give more status to the program; it still implies that the activity program is separate, but it indicates that the program is of an importance equal to that of the regular curriculum. Cocurricular is no longer a completely accurate term, however, since some program activities such as band and chorus have become an integral part of the regular curriculum in many schools.

Student activities is a much more comprehensive term. It implies that the activities are part of the regular program, and it avoids the distinction between curricular and extracurricular. Now, student activities are another important means of achieving educational objectives rather than being a recreational pastime. The term also implies that there is no regular pattern or uniform program for all schools or students.

GOALS

Curricular Improvement. As has been stated, school programs should provide for self-development, exploration, and individualization. From a curricular viewpoint, these objectives apply to the more informal activity program as well as the more formal program of studies. A well-designed activity program will provide opportunities for the development of those cognitive, affective, and psycho-motor behaviors that cannot be learned as well within the more structured framework of the curriculum. An activity program also provides opportunities to practice skills introduced in the formal classroom setting. Democratic principles learned in social studies class should be applied to develop democratically organized activities, while skills carried over from music and art classes should be used in activities in those areas.

It should be obvious that the student activity program can be a valuable supplement to the usual classroom program. It assists students in exploring various interests, talents, and abilities. It provides opportunities for students to apply fundamental skills and knowledge acquired in the classroom program. It provides as well for a gradual transition from preadolescent activities to the types of activities, education, and specialization appropriate for older adolescents.

Middle school personnel who administer and implement student activity programs must be firm believers in student-centered learning if programs are to be successful. By application of new theories of learning and development and an awareness of the implications of earlier adolescence, personnel can make the activities an effective supplement to the more formal educational program.

Student Development. Participation in a student activity program can have positive effects on the development of student interests. The program extends the academic curriculum and furnishes a broad, exploratory experience. For some students, it provides the motivation needed to keep them interested in school. For others, it offers opportunities to develop creative abilities and to gain satisfaction from doing things that they enjoy and find interesting. Although students frequently participate in activities for fun and personal enjoyment, they find that activities also satisfy other individual needs and interests, of a recreational, emotional, social, and academic nature.

In addition, a good student activity program should satisfy psychological needs, such as the needs for recognition and approval. Cooperation, responsibility, and respect for others can develop along with social competence. There is an opportunity for a constructive release of youthful energy that might otherwise be turned into less productive channels. A good, vital program arouses and takes advantage of natural youthful spontaneity and enthusiasm in ways that will benefit its participants in other facets of their school life.

Still pertinent today, despite the fact that it was developed by Miller, Moyer, and Patrick over twenty years ago, is the following comprehensive outline of the values and contributions of student activities.

A. Contributions to Students

1. To provide opportunities for the pursuit of established interests and the development of new interests.
2. To educate for citizenship through experiences and insights that stress leadership, fellowship, cooperation, and independent action.
3. To develop school spirit and morale.
4. To provide opportunities for satisfying the gregarious urge of children and youth.
5. To encourage moral and spiritual development.
6. To strengthen the mental and physical health of students.
7. To provide for a well-rounded social development of students.
8. To widen school contacts.
9. To provide opportunities for students to exercise their creative capacities more fully.

B. Contributions to Curriculum Improvement
   1. To supplement or enrich classroom experiences.
   2. To explore new learning experiences which may ultimately be incorporated into the curriculum.
   3. To provide additional opportunity for individual and group guidance.
   4. To motivate classroom instruction.

C. Contributions to More Effective School Administration
   1. To foster more effective team work between students, faculty, and administrative and supervisory personnel.
   2. To integrate more closely the several divisions of the school system.
   3. To provide less restricted opportunities designed to assist youth in the worthwhile utilization of their spare time.
   4. To enable teachers to understand better the forces that motivate pupils to react as they do to many of the problematic situations with which they are confronted.

D. Contributions to the Community
   1. To promote better school and community relations.
   2. To encourage greater community interest in and support of the school.[1]

ORGANIZING THE ACTIVITY PROGRAM No two schools will have identical student activity programs. Each program should be tailored to meet the needs of the particular student body it serves. However, in general, a well-developed activity program provides each student with an opportunity to experiment or explore in a nonthreatening atmosphere. He or she has new experiences, has new interests aroused, and develops new abilities. Sometimes new subject areas can initially be made available for exploration through the activity program. Certain types of language and science clubs fall into this category. In one school, an English teacher with foreign language training conducted a language club after school hours. Because the club interested students very much, the language became part of the regular curriculum one year later.

An effective program should provide desirable activities that might not be possible in the regular classroom. These may offer students an

---

1. Franklin Miller, James Moyer, and Robert Patrick, *Planning Student Activities* (Englewood Cliffs, N.J.: Prentice-Hall, © 1956), pp. 13–19. By permission of Prentice-Hall, Inc.

opportunity to discover or identify special abilities and may smooth the gradual transition from preadolescent education to the specialization required of older adolescents.

Balance among the various activities must be maintained. Athletic or music programs must not be permitted to overshadow the other areas. The contributions of each activity to overall educational objectives must be studied, and, on this basis, the priorities of staffing, financing, facilities, and time determined. The activity program must be a balanced offering that supplies students with educational experiences that have not yet become part of the regular curriculum.

The first step in developing a comprehensive program is preparation of a list of potential activities. Suggestions should be obtained from students, faculty, other schools, and professional publications. John Frank suggests forming a committee of teachers, students, and administrators to represent all interests. Student representation is particulary important since

> activity events are designed for students and they should have sufficient committee representation to insure parity. Students provide valuable insights into the types of school-wide activities that interest the student body; their presence stimulates greater overall student interest in the program.[2]

While the reference is to development of school-wide activities, the concept is also applicable to the general activity program.

The next step is development of a complete description of each activity. The following elements should be included:

Name of activity
Objective of activity
Description of experience
Facilities, equipment, and materials needed
Activity rules and guidelines
Student selection
Miscellaneous[3]

John Frank's book also contains more details about developing both the descriptions and an activity course guide as well as suggestions for publicizing the program from a community relations point of view.

---

2. John Frank, Jr., *Complete Guide to Co-Curricular Programs and Activities for the Middle Grades* (West Nyack, N.Y.: Parker Publishing Co., 1976), p. 82.

3. Ibid., p. 107.

SCHEDULING Some schools use an extended day to provide time for activities even though they are regarded as part of the curriculum. Ideally, activities should be scheduled as an integral part of the daily schedule. If the program is truly to meet the academic, social, recreational, and emotional interests and needs of students, and to emphasize participation, responsibility, cooperation, and leadership, it must be conveniently available. Scheduling some activities around the noon hour provides a welcome break for teachers and students alike.

Students should have the opportunity to participate in a variety of activities throughout the course of the school year. If there is more than one activity period per week, the scheduling should make it possible for any interested student to participate in a different activity during each of the periods. (One to three activity periods per week is recommended.) Also desirable is allowing repetition of student selection processes halfway through the school year to accommodate students who wish to make a change.

PROGRAM EVALUATION Continuous evaluation of the activity program is just as important as continuous evaluation of any other aspect of the total educational experience. The program must be assessed in terms of the needs and interests of individual students and of the community. The program as a whole and each of its parts should be examined by a representative committee including students, faculty, administrators, and community representatives. A variety of techniques, including teacher observation, check lists, questionnaires, and self-evaluation, might be utilized.

Some of the factors to be considered include:

1. Appropriateness of the objectives
2. Consistency of offerings with the objectives
3. Comparison of offerings with expressed student needs and interests
4. Determination of the amount and pattern of participation in individual activities
5. Evaluation of contributions by faculty and community sponsors
6. Study of the relationship between the activity program and the regular classroom program
7. Study of individual activities
   a. Identification of objectives
   b. Chief accomplishments as related to the objectives
   c. Major difficulties preventing achievement of objectives
   d. Principal projects of the group
   e. Recommendations for improving a particular activity

8. Surveys of use and availability of school and community facilities
9. Cost studies of the activity program

Clark and Starr suggest the following criteria or standards by which the program may also be assessed:

1. It is planned so as to contribute directly to the educational aims of the school.
2. It supplements and reinforces curricular activities. It does not repeat classroom activities. Rather, it introduces learning approaches and materials not available in regular courses.
3. It is pupil-centered, and in so far as feasible, pupil-planned and -directed.
4. It provides every pupil ample opportunity to participate up to the limits of his abilities and interests. No one is eliminated because of race, religion, financial ability, social position, or academic standing.
5. It provides enough different activities to allow every pupil to participate in something he finds congenial.
6. It provides pupils with adequate opportunities to develop leadership and "followership" abilities.
7. It fosters the development of healthy attitudes, ideals, and value systems and avoids the development of false and inadequate attitudes, ideals, and value systems.
8. It is flexible. It is easy to add new activities and drop old ones that are no longer useful.
9. It is adequately supported by competent, sympathetic faculty sponsors or advisors.
10. It is adequately funded.
11. It is recognized by being properly scheduled.
12. It is constantly being evaluated and reevaluated.[4]

Again, a truly adequate activity program must reflect the needs and interests of the students in a particular school. Evaluators must determine whether or not there is provision for the less talented to participate in the skill activities such as music, dramatics, and athletics. The extent of student participation must be examined by comparing the

---

4. Reprinted with permission of Macmillan Publishing Co., Inc., from *Secondary School Teaching Methods*, 3rd ed., p. 42, by Leonard H. Clark and Irving S. Starr. Copyright © 1976, Macmillan Publishing Co., Inc.

number of boys and girls who participate with the total enrollment of the school, with the goal being participation by each student in at least one activity. The other extremes, overemphasis and overparticipation, must be examined. Is there guidance available to ensure against overparticipation by some individuals? The extent of the influence of the expectations of the senior high school on the activity program must be assessed. The middle school must not become a training ground for high school activities, as has occasionally happened in the past, particularly in athletics.

The evaluating committee should also examine the relationship between the activity program and the regular instructional program. There should be apparent similarities, and both programs should be consistent with the school's philosophy and objectives.

An important question is the cost of participation to the student. If the activity program is important, with specific educational objectives, there should be no cost to the student, just as there is no cost for participation in an English class. While the financing is being examined, a study should be made of how program money is handled. Is the accounting system an accepted one? Are students involved in the handling of money? If not, they should be.

TYPES OF ACTIVITIES

Student activities are necessarily of various types. Some are related to the curriculum in that they extend or enrich the content found in the formal instructional program. Some activities are related to physical development; they are an extension of the gym program. Others might be termed interest activities; they offer physical and emotional release. Two additional types are service and social activities, which are important means of improving interpersonal relationships, enhancing an individual's self-perception, and increasing self-confidence.

CLUBS A very common form of activity is the club. Most often, it is a local group, not part of a national organization. Clubs should meet no more than a single period a week. Planning for several types of clubs is recommended to ensure a well-rounded program. Representations from the following types would provide adequate coverage: interest, subject-related, and service.

Clubs that focus on special interests might utilize common hobbies as a theme. A small school could have one hobby club where its members pursue their hobbies on an individual basis and acquaint others with them, but a large school should have a variety which could include the following:

Marionette Making	Hiking
Wood Carving	Chess and Checkers
Photography	Arts and Crafts
Sketching	

Hobby clubs are frequently more popular than subject-related clubs because the student gains satisfaction from working on or completing a project or task that is self-selected.

Subject-related clubs help motivate the development of skills. Students should be able to select from a range of these clubs. Possibilities include language clubs, a science club (which is more appropriate for the middle school than a very specialized club in biology or chemistry), a home economics club, and, perhaps, a local history club. Besides supplementing and enhancing basic skills and knowledge taught in the classroom, these activities also provide an opportunity for the academically talented to concentrate more intensively on a particular subject interest.

Service clubs are oriented to school or community needs. They offer an opportunity for practical experience and participation in projects defined by a group. One kind of service activity is the student council, which will be discussed as part of the larger question of student decision making. Escort-service groups that provide student hosts and hostesses for school visitors are a possibility. Library and office assistants are another. Other common groups include stage managers, audiovisual equipment assistants, and traffic control personnel. Students frequently consider it an honor to be part of such groups.

Community-oriented service groups might focus on a project such as converting a local lot into an attractive play area for neighborhood children. Assisting at local nursing homes, working at child-care centers, and providing tutoring services at local community centers are other possibilities.

Julia Thomason describes some interesting alternative activities through which students offer services. Among these is a babysitting exchange whereby students receive training in child care and first aid. A fringe benefit here is the career-education aspect of the activity. Another possibility is a record exchange. Students frequently tire of the records and tapes they seem to buy in great quantity; a formalized exchange operation based on some of the same principles as a library could be attractive. The operation, if successful, could be extended to books and posters. As the writer says, "the rule to remember is . . . Transescents Are Capable Kids."[5]

5. Julia T. Thomason, "The T.A.C.K. Approach to Belonging," *Middle School Journal,* Vol. 9, August, 1978, pp. 17–18.

ATHLETICS Most educators agree that participation in highly competitive interscholastic athletic programs is undesirable for middle school boys and girls. In 1952, a joint committee of representatives (from the National Education Association, the Department of Elementary School Principals, the American Association of Health, Physical Education, and Recreation, the National Council of State Consultants in Elementary Education, and the Society of State Directors of Health, Physical Education, and Recreation) issued a statement disapproving of sports programs involving intense competition for children prior to the ninth grade. Later, the Educational Policies Commission of the National Education Association and the American Association of School Administrators issued a strong statement recommending that varsity-type interscholastic athletics not be permitted for junior high boys and girls. This recommendation was based on the opinions of 220 physicians who were consulted about the suitability of interscholastic competition for boys between the ages of twelve and fifteen. Growth during the middle school period is rapid and uneven, and one of its by-products is low endurance. Because of low endurance, intense competition may be damaging to the individual.

In contrast to interscholastic programs, a strong intramural program makes it possible for all students, regardless of the degree of their ability or talent, to participate in sports activities if they wish. It also allows for the unequal rates of development in boys and girls, and for the uneven opportunities they might have experienced during their earlier school years to develop athletic skills. A sound intramural program begins within the framework of the regular physical education classes and is then extended to other periods, such as before and after school and during the lunch periods. This kind of program nurtures a healthier spirit of competition, sportsmanship, and teamwork than does the high emotionalism of interscholastic activity.

Another advantage of a strong intramural program is that it provides equal opportunities for boys and girls, in contrast to the usual senior high school situation where the activities for boys tend to overshadow those for girls despite the mandates of Title IX. Boys and girls can participate together (or separately) in sports such as tennis, badminton, volleyball, bowling, and table tennis, and even croquet and horseshoes. Other sports, including touch football, track, softball, wrestling, basketball, and soccer, are more appropriate for separate participation.

Rather than interscholastic programs, many schools find the field day to be a suitable way of encouraging community interest in athletic programs and of increasing students' motivation as a result of the chance to perform in public. Three or four times a year, several schools join together in athletic events that provide an opportunity for each individual to objectively evaluate his or her own performance and that of others. Good sportsmanship and fun are emphasized more than competition.

Such programs will arouse recreational interests and be an educational experience for their participants if they are carefully organized and supervised. They provide an opportunity to learn sports rules and sports appreciation. Teams can be developed according to weight, age, or grade, depending on the type of activity and the situation. For example, a grade organization might be preferable for basketball, whereas weight should be the guiding factor in wrestling.

DRAMATICS Many young people have a natural flair for the dramatic. Given ample opportunity to develop, it can become the base for a marvelous learning opportunity. As in the athletic program, participation by many is preferable to professionally executed performances by a selected, talented few. Skits and short plays presented by one sixth-grade class for the other sixth-grade students are one way of achieving this. A half-hour play involving as many members of a class as possible might be presented to parents early in the evening, with refreshments served afterwards by the participants.

Creative drama should be completely student-oriented; middle schools should not follow the lead of senior high schools in using commercially prepared plays, since many original ideas can and should come from the regular instructional program. The culmination of a unit in social studies, science, or any other subject area can be a satisfying production in which the students not only write the script but also prepare their own costumes and scenery. The assistance of the art and music teachers will help the students to recognize the integration of various components of the instructional program. Writing even short skits for presentation can be exciting. They may be inspired by a poem, a song, or a work of art.

Plays provide many opportunities for students to work together toward common objectives. The quality of the end product is not as important as the experience of those involved in producing it. An added understanding of self, other people, and concepts confronting students can all be developed through original dramatic productions.

PUBLICATIONS As in other activities, the major objective in the production of various kinds of publications should be widespread participation. The slick, high-cost, professional-looking newspaper or magazine is most inappropriate for the middle school. A mimeographed newspaper issued frequently can keep students aware of school events, give recognition to students, groups, and classes for their particular achievements, and make the community aware of what is happening in the middle school. This kind of publication makes it unnecessary to depend on local businesses for the advertisements that are so often needed to subsidize the high cost of high school papers.

The same principle should be applied to any kind of literary publication. With a little thought, students can produce attractive publications of excellent quality. Any kind of colored stencils might be used to produce a booklet containing writing efforts. There should be at least one contribution from each child. Contributions might range from a simple haiku to a short story. Each child might make his or her own stencil by printing, typing, or handwriting stories and illustrating them with simple, suitable artwork.

One English teacher introduced a project in which she and a panel of students selected what they considered to be the best short essays, stories, and poems produced by the seventh-grade students and had them reproduced in a mimeographed magazine. The art teacher assisted students in preparing appropriate artwork and attractive covers. The result was a production that aroused great interest throughout the school.

School publications can exert a strong influence on the student body. They can be produced on a school-wide basis, by departments or clubs, or by classes—either grade-level or individual. No matter what form the publications take, they provide a real opportunity and incentive for an expression of student ideas and accomplishments.

MUSICAL ACTIVITIES Disagreement often arises among music educators and administrators regarding the major objectives of musical activities. Should only the talented participate or should such activities be open to all interested participants regardless of ability? Should musical activities focus on fostering school-community relationships through entertainment value, or on the enjoyment and personal development of the participants? In keeping with the middle school philosophy, musical activities must focus on the development of the individual student and on the pleasure he or she can gain from participation.

Development of a prize-winning marching band should not be a major goal. In addition to the regular band organization, a small feeder band might be organized for beginners and less advanced students. Instruction must be available at least for beginners and intermediate students. Most school districts anticipate that parents will finance advanced instruction if and when a child becomes ready.

Exploratory opportunities with musical instruments are just as important in the middle school as other kinds of exploratory experiences. Some of the less common instruments, such as oboes and bass clarinets, should be introduced even if it is necessary to borrow them or to share them with a local high school. Experiences with stringed instruments are also essential.

In some situations, full-fledged bands and orchestras may not be possible because the level of achievement is inadequate. Small ensembles are then appropriate, and possibly even preferable, because they increase opportunity for individualized instruction. In addition, the small-group situation gives the participant a feeling of security.

A variety of vocal music activities is also desirable. Small and large groups, boys' and girls' groups, plus mixed groups from duos to large choruses, make it possible for each and every child who so desires to participate. Participation in choral singing gives much enjoyment and is within the ability of everyone. In one instance, so many girls wanted to join the girls' chorus that it was impossible to accommodate them in the choral room. The teacher initiated a policy that no girl in her final year in that school would be turned away. Thus, everyone eventually had an opportunity to participate. Even "monotones" were accepted and then placed in the alto section between the strongest singers. The elementary school child's natural love for singing should be fostered in the middle school and encouraged in every way.

Competitive situations and contests involving musical performances should be discouraged, since they serve to limit participation to only the most talented, as well as to create undesirable pressures upon the participants. Two long-range goals of any music program are listening enjoyment and participation in adult life. The joy of performance and creative production should also be emphasized. Music can be fun; this should be the main objective stressed, whether it be through the standard bands, orchestras, and choirs, or through jazz and dance bands, guitar groups, kitchen bands, or barber shop vocal groups.

OUTDOOR EDUCATION As national and international interest continues to focus on environmental problems, increased attention is being given to opportunities for outdoor education. These range from ongoing activities on school grounds to weekends or several weekdays spent away from school.

Some school boards have purchased sites outside the school district to provide natural areas for fairly extensive programs. In other instances, outdoor facilities are available for overnight use for a very minimal fee. Occasionally, a nearby park or vacant lot might be used as a site. Worthwhile programs on the school grounds are possible as well.

Some school boards budget funds which enable all students to participate in two- or three-day away-from-school visits at some point in their educational program. Outdoor activities, related arts and crafts, and science activities form the nucleus of the program. Parents assist by chaperoning and even by instructing if they have some expertise in a particular area.

Donald Daugs recommends "hitting the streets" for field studies, as well as making maximum use of school grounds and facilities. For example, he suggests installation of flower and vegetable beds, planters, hanging pots, cold frames, and bird feeders. A rather unique idea is the use of inexpensive wading pools as aquatic sites on roof tops, on school grounds, or even in classrooms.[6] The possibilities are myriad.

Outdoor education encompasses opportunities for social development as boys and girls share duties at mealtime, clean-up periods, etc. They learn to develop give-and-take relationships. A good program also fosters closer relationships among parents, faculty, and students.

SCHOOL-WIDE ACTIVITIES In addition to numerous special-interest activities, there should be a number of general events in which whole grades or even the entire school population may participate. The previously described field days and intramural programs fit into this category. These activities give students something to look forward to and encourage a feeling of cohesiveness among the student body and staff.

One other possibility is establishing a game room available to students before and after school as well as during lunch periods. Sufficient community interest could lead to having volunteers monitor the facility in order to make it available during evening hours and weekends as well. Chess, checkers, other board games, table tennis, and shuffleboard are just a few of the activities that might be pursued at such a facility.

Other popular school-wide activities include skating parties, open bowling, ski trips, recycling projects, international fairs, decoration contests, and fund-raising activities.

SOCIAL ACTIVITIES Social activities in a school program provide opportunities for boys and girls to work together. These should be group-type activities that do not stress boy-girl pairings. Their major

6. Donald R. Daugs, "Urban Outdoor Education," *Clearing House*, Vol. 51, March, 1978, pp. 319–21.

objectives should be development of personality, self-confidence, and skill in social behavior.

Many boys and girls do not know how to act in social situations and need to learn the social amenities in a low-pressure setting. Square dances, large circle dances, and games such as table tennis and shuffleboard are possible activities for social gatherings in the middle school. Grade-level socials including some kind of instruction by faculty members before the social event itself are recommended. Previously described school-wide activities provide additional opportunities for socializing.

Some students are eager to have dances. A limit of two during the year is recommended for the eighth grade, one of which might be scheduled in the evening. One afternoon dance should be sufficient for the seventh grade; younger students should participate in a social activity that includes games and group dances. Regardless of the kind of event, students should assume responsibility and leadership in planning, decorating, and implementing their plans.

HOMEROOM ACTIVITIES A school needs to be humane. One means of accomplishing this is to provide a home base for each student. A homeroom can be a place where each student feels secure because the teacher recognizes and is concerned about each individual. The most extensive participation involving all students takes place at the homeroom level.

Care must be taken that the homeroom does not become merely an administrative convenience for making announcements and taking attendance or even an extension of the study hall. Time and attention must be given to extensive planning of a program that is an outgrowth of the needs of the students. The program should range from an orientation for new middle school students to an introduction to the senior high school for those who are ready to be transferred.

Unfortunately, orientation programs have too often been a half-day experience comprising perhaps a large-group meeting and a whirlwind tour of the building. Much more appropriate is immediate assignment to a homeroom teacher who then undertakes to provide a well-planned program that might extend for several weeks. Topics for the orientation program and experiences, such as becoming acquainted with the building, should be sequential. For example, the first homeroom meeting might include an introduction to the functions of the homeroom, assignment and discussion of the class schedule, and a guided tour limited to the areas and rooms on the class schedule. A tour of the entire building is more appropriate for a later meeting when students have a partial knowledge of the layout and are therefore less apt to become confused.

Additional topics for subsequent homeroom periods might include: policies and procedures for the homeroom and the school, curricular opportunities (including required and elective courses), opportunities available in the school activity program, how the middle school differs from the elementary school, objectives of the middle school, development of objectives for the class and by each individual in the class for himself or herself, and effective study habits.

One school has developed a rather unique homeroom activity. Because the school is small, only one lunch period is needed. Just prior to lunch, all students return to their homerooms for a fifteen-minute silent reading period. Both teachers and students spend the time reading material of their own selection. Besides encouraging the concept of reading for enjoyment, this period creates a feeling of togetherness between teacher and students as well as furnishes a "winding-down" prior to lunch.

When a class enters its final year in the middle school, visits to the senior high school and reports on the events there by individuals and small groups of students are appropriate. Even a visit by an entire class might be desirable. Also, senior high school representatives should be invited to the middle school. Some excellent programs result when the high school wrestling team provides a demonstration or high school newspaper editors discuss their publications with groups of interested middle school students.

PRACTICAL POLICIES

The student activity program must serve the students. Each student should have an opportunity to succeed at something, whether it be giving a good performance or chairing a meeting. Each needs an opportunity to participate without worrying about a grade or about reaching a certain level of achievement. In order for every student to gain maximum benefit from participation in activities, a clear set of policies governing activity operation should be established.

PARTICIPATION IN POLICY MAKING Too often, policies are established but become obsolete because they are not frequently reviewed and revised. Rapidly changing circumstances—which influence education directly and indirectly—mandate an annual review of all school policies and appropriate revision where needed.

Policy making should be a mutual effort involving staff, community, and students. Addition of parents and other members of the community to the policy-making body is a most appropriate means for enabling them to become part of the school situation, view it firsthand, and, perhaps, better understand student concerns and reactions. And what better way is there for students in a middle school to learn how to develop effective and appropriate policies that they and their peers will accept?

In many instances, student councils have not been an effective instrument for student involvement in governance. The day of the faculty-sponsored student council with its token decision-making process has passed. No longer will students accept a situation where their recommendations are forwarded to the principal by the faculty sponsor, ignored by the principal, and then forgotten.

Students want to discuss issues much more crucial than the date of the next social event or how to decrease the noise in the cafeteria. From the issues of long hair and dress codes, students have progressed to demanding opportunities to participate in the determination of policies for day-to-day administration and even for the curriculum.

The flow of information once moved in one direction—from teacher to student. Now, communication must flow in many directions. Adults can learn from and with students. Parents, teachers, and administrators must all develop sensitivity to student feelings and perceptions. They must learn to see the world as their students do. Some teachers and administrators feel threatened by these developments, but nevertheless they must work toward a situation where teachers and students are involved together in appropriate decision making.

The homeroom is an ideal place to assist students in developing the skills needed for worthwhile participation in governance activities. Development of policies and procedures for homeroom activities provides preparation for participation on a school-wide basis, in addition to producing input for school-wide governance deliberations.

Participation in a governance structure can provide opportunities for students to develop good habits, responsibility, and self-identification. As their responsibilities are gradually increased, they will develop increased competence, receive a psychological lift, and become more self-disciplined. Growing up in today's society is difficult and demanding. Responsible participation by students in the fixing of the policies affecting them can be of immeasurable value to them in their growth. For their own best interests, then, the capabilities of students must not be underestimated.

FACULTY AND ADMINISTRATIVE INVOLVEMENT The student activity program is a vital part of the educational program. The degree of its effectiveness is dependent upon the philosophy, enthusiasm, and competence of the staff. All staff members should be involved with the program in some way and should fully understand its objectives.

Members of the school staff have a critical role to play in encouraging students to join activities, helping students to formulate policies concerning their activities, establishing meeting dates, and determining the qualifications for membership. Even more important is their role in assisting students in establishing goals for their activities, in developing ways of achieving these goals, and, then, in planning programs based on the established goals. Throughout, they must encourage group control while gradually reducing their own control.

The role of faculty members in school activities is not very different from their role in the classroom. They must facilitate the learning experiences, fitting the program to the interests and needs of the students. They must be willing to give time and effort to planning and working with groups. They must make special efforts to stimulate student groups to organize their own programs. Teachers must develop student self-direction rather than exercise arbitrary controls.

An effective activity program requires time and effort from staff members. Their organizational role might include calling members together for their first meeting, assisting in the election of officers, starting a discussion of the kind of organization that would be the most appropriate for the situation, assisting student leaders in conducting meetings, helping in the formulation of objectives, or providing needed information.

Both faculty and administrators play an important part in the success of any school-wide program, particularly in policy-making bodies. There must be an openness to student participation, as well as a willingness not only to listen to students but also to take their contributions seriously. There is another very important responsibility. Students are learners; they do not possess the background nor have they had the experiences necessary for fruitful participation in decision making. Faculty and administrators must be willing to spend the time and effort necessary to give students adequate information and guidance to sustain their role in the process.

The staff must provide the necessary direction where needed, and they must determine when students must be allowed to proceed on their own, even if they make mistakes. Effective staff members will encourage the development of leadership. They will be concerned with the personal and social development of each student and will continually guide students in their realization of established educational objectives.

Staff members associated with middle school activities must understand the age group with which they are involved. They must thoroughly understand how they grow, their likes and dislikes, their problems, and the reasons for their various kinds of behavior patterns. They must be a constant source of counsel, influencing attitudes and behavior without coercion. A command of the techniques of group-work approaches to learning is essential.

Staff members must want to be effective in whatever roles they play in the total activity program. Their participation must not become a burden added to an already heavy teaching load. The activities in which they are involved must be of interest to them if their enthusiasm is to be a factor in the successful operation of the program.

It is also important that involvement with an activity not overshadow the teaching assignment. The coach who relegates everything but coaching to a lesser degree of importance is regrettably all too familiar. The music teacher who views the annual concert as the only important event of the year is also undesirable. An appropriate balance between involvement with activities and teaching must be maintained. Ideally, the activity program should be viewed as an aspect of the teaching situation and involvement in activities should be viewed as part of the individual staff member's teaching load.

It must be remembered at all times that the activity program is for the students and should focus on their needs and interests. Unfortunately, this does not always happen. Sponsors of musical and athletic activities particularly have been accused of furthering their own careers by means of overemphasized activities in their area. Staff members from middle school athletic departments often view their assignments as steppingstones to high school coaching jobs; they encourage participation in interscholastic competition as one means of achieving this goal.

No staff member should ever be permitted to take over a student activity to the extent that it is viewed as his or hers alone. Care must be taken that each activity be viewed in proper perspective as part of the total activity program and, most important of all, as part of the total educational program.

USE OF COMMUNITY RESOURCES In the early history of school activities, it was not uncommon for a school to employ an individual who was not a regular staff member as sponsor of an activity. In fact, sponsorship was considered to be a nonprofessional task unbefitting a teacher. As the educational value of activities became increasingly apparent, their sponsorship shifted to the regular teaching staff.

A reverse shift has ensued. In many situations, teachers are not interested in the additional burden of involvement with an activity. In fact, many do not have the particular skills required to be effective. As a result, some schools are utilizing individuals from the community who are qualified by interest and training. The local resident who makes jewelry from polished stones and the dramatic coach from the local community theater organization can make valuable contributions to a school's activity program.

In addition to parents and other community resource personnel, some schools have found interest and talent among office, maintenance, and security staff members. When these individuals are assimilated into the activity program, students gain both insights into the functions of these individuals and a better relationship with them. Students may even gain a new respect for the physical plant itself when they find that members of the maintenance, custodial, and security staffs are interested enough in students to participate in the activity program, and this can lead to a decrease in vandalism.

Community and school personnel of various kinds might prove to be the ideal individuals to encourage students to participate in very satisfying activities that can become lifetime hobbies.

INTRAMURAL VS. INTERMURAL The advantages of intramural over intermural activities were discussed in an earlier part of this chapter. A firm policy establishing an intramural program must be developed. The same policy should exclude intermural or interscholastic athletics, for the existence of such policies will make it more difficult for community members to press for an intermural program, as they unfortunately tend to do. The pressures of Little League competition with the attendant parental emphasis on winning must not be permitted to become part of the middle school sports program.

EXPENSE As was mentioned earlier, there should be little or no cost to the participants for student activities. Membership dues, high admission fees to athletic events, and excessive costs for rental of musical instruments prevent participation by some. A school must constantly examine its program to make certain that excessive costs are not hindering student participation. Since the activity program must be looked upon as an integral part of the ongoing educational program, fees could be looked upon as discriminatory.

Each activity that in any way involves expenditures must have an operating budget. A budget review committee is recommended not only for the essential function it might serve, but also because it provides an excellent learning opportunity for its student members.

Where money is involved, accepted accounting procedures must be followed. A central treasurer for the entire activity program is recommended. Although all activities money should be in a common bank account, a definite budgetary allowance must be made for each activity. Where disbursements are made by check, at least two signatures, possibly the principal's and the faculty sponsor's, should be required for authorization. Clark and Starr make the following recommendations concerning the handling of money:

1. Set up a system of accounting for funds before collecting any.
2. Give receipts for all money received. Be sure to keep a duplicate or stub.
3. Record all transactions immediately.
4. Deposit all funds with the school treasurer, safe, or bank immediately after receiving them. Get a receipt.
5. Do not keep money in your desk or on your person.
6. Do not keep school money with your personal money.
7. Do not commit the school or extracurricular activity to any indebtedness without official approval.
8. Do not authorize payments of any bills until they have been approved.
9. Do not pay any bills by cash. If possible, always pay by school check. Be sure to get receipts for any payments made.
10. Always follow to the letter school regulations concerning handling of funds.[7]

EQUAL OPPORTUNITY Participation in the activity program is a right, not a privilege. Every student must have an equal opportunity to participate if activities are to have educational value. Race, sex, religious belief, economic status, and scholastic standing must not be criteria for membership. A possible exception is the honor society, but it is questionable whether such a group should be part of a middle school activity program.

The time of day at which activities are scheduled must encourage, not discourage, participation. As discussed in the section on scheduling, time should be allotted within the school day. If too many activities are offered outside normal school hours, some students will be ineligible because they are unable to remain for various reasons.

Effects of Title IX. For many years, educators advocated equal opportunities for all students for participation in school activities. In actual practice, this did not occur; discrimination existed particularly in the athletic programs, where opportunities for male students traditionally exceeded those for female students.

---

7. Reprinted with permission of Macmillan Publishing Co., Inc. from *Secondary School Teaching Methods,* 3rd ed., p. 260, by Leonard H. Clark and Irving S. Starr. Copyright © 1976, Macmillan Publishing Co., Inc.

The passage of Title IX, the Education Amendment passed in 1972, has done much to eliminate discriminatory situations. In many instances, remedial action has been necessary. Because of the salary and budgeting requirements, the athletic program has been the most difficult with which to deal.

Ronald Schnee describes an extensive Title IX self-study. Among the five areas included in the outline for the study, the two below are related to school activity programs and provide an excellent starting point for self-examination.

A. Athletics
   1. Sports activities availability
      a. sports available to male students
      b. sports available to female students
      c. determination of interests and degree of accommodation
   2. Facilities, equipment, and supplies—determination of the equality or inequity of equipment and supplies available for boys' and girls' interscholastic athletic programs
   3. Organization of athletic activities
      a. facilities available for boys' and girls' practice sessions
      b. scheduling of facilities for practice
      c. scheduling of facilities for games
      d. the schedule of game times and days for boys' and girls' events
   4. Opportunities to receive equal coaching
      a. coaches available for female sports
      b. coaches available for male sports
      c. coaches available for coeducational sports
      d. coaching salaries for boys' and girls' sports
   5. Equality concerning publicity
      a. adequacy of publicity for girls' interscholastic athletics as well as that for boys'
      b. methods that may be utilized to work toward equity in publicity
   6. Equality of travel and meals for boys and girls on trips
   7. Awareness of sports that are available—methods utilized or planned to be utilized to make students, especially girls, aware of athletic activities available to them

B. Extracurricular Activities
   1. Organizations and clubs
      a. sponsors—sex, method of assignment and interest, pay for services

b. examination of all organizations and their constitutions
   1) philosophy
   2) dues
   3) membership: sex and race
   4) meeting time, place, and date
   5) leadership participation
c. interest of both sexes

2. Course-oriented extracurricular activities, e.g. band, chorus, cheerleaders, yearbook, etc.
   a. sex of sponsor and pay
   b. membership requirements
   c. skill requirements
   d. honors and awards[8]

Affirmative action efforts must be supported by board of education members, faculty, administrators, parents, and students. If the program is properly carried out, the benefits to students will be well worth the effort.

PROTECTION OF STUDENTS The ultimate value in an activity program is the benefit it provides to the participants. The welfare of the individual is of the utmost importance. Students must not be permitted to become so extensively involved that their health becomes endangered or that their academic progress is detrimentally affected.

The amount and type of participation by individual students should be determined in a counseling situation. Each student should participate in at least one activity; some are eager to become involved in several and are capable of doing so in combination with their academic programs.

The physical well-being and the emotional stability of each student are the basic considerations. An emphasis on competitiveness and finished performances has no place in the middle school. The shy, quiet girl must be encouraged to be an active member of an activity rather than a silent observer. Aggressive students who tend to "run the show" must be counseled carefully concerning this so that other students have an equal opportunity. No group of students should ever be permitted to form a clique that takes over the program. Officers of various organizations should rotate; no one should serve successive terms.

---

8. Ronald G. Schnee, "Frying Pan to Fire: School Advocacy of Title IX," *Phi Delta Kappan*, Vol. 58, January, 1977, p. 424.

Each student's total participation should be limited by the time required for each activity, the difficulty of his or her academic program, individual interests and abilities, and demands on time and energy by non-school activities. It is recommended that a maximum of five hours per week be devoted to middle school activities.

Occasionally, it is desirable to schedule programs outside school hours so that parents and community members can attend. However, these should begin early in the evening and they should be no more than one to one and a half hours in length. Students must be able to return home at a reasonable hour to be rested for the next day in school. At all times, the educational value of the activity and the welfare of the students it serves must be more important than the performance value for the community.

Chapter 9
Staff Organization and Utilization

Staff organization and utilization in a middle school may follow numerous patterns. There may be, for example, the line and staff arrangements with which most people are familiar—arrangements that typically feature the principal at the top, the department head in the middle, and the teacher at the bottom. Although line and staff arrangements have merit if the roles and relationships of personnel are defined functionally, this chapter considers other ways of organizing and using staff in schools geared to youngsters ten to fourteen years of age. An accountability model for determining the effectiveness of staff organization or reorganization is also discussed.

TEAM TEACHING

Many changes in the techniques of grouping and regrouping students have occurred during the past ten years. Some have been masquerading as team teaching. Ask any group of educators to define team teaching and you will hear a variety of definitions that relate to large-group instruction, small-group instruction, or shared planning.

Simply stated, team teaching is the cooperative or collaborative effort of two or more teachers who share in both the planning and the conduct of instruction. The term team teaching is a misnomer. A better titular description would be team organization or team planning.

A major problem with team teaching has been the tendency for the teachers comprising the team to "turn" teach rather than team teach. This practice has done much to diminish the positive effect that cooperative-collaborative teaching and planning has on the improvement of instruction.

An open-plan, multi-graded, flexible middle school program will be more successful if it stresses cooperative planning and teaching. A middle school organizational plan stressing the team approach has a more cohesive curriculum and a more integrated approach to instruction from both the teacher's and the student's viewpoints.

Some educators in middle schools advocate cooperative-collaborative arrangements whereby teachers in a single discipline plan and teach a block of instruction for two or three classes at the same time. Another variation is the assignment of an interdisciplinary or cross-discipline team to plan and teach interrelated subjects. Here the teachers generally represent all major subject areas and are concerned with planning for and teaching the same group of students. Imaginative middle school staff designs encourage interdisciplinary planning and teaching by allowing teams the authority to rearrange blocks of time to suit instructional needs.

Inherent in any successful design for cooperative-collaborative teaching are the following criteria:

1. The group is able to set long-range and short-range goals and to develop the techniques for meeting these goals.
2. A climate exists that encourages the team to become involved in curriculum decision making.
3. Authority for rearrangement of instructional groups of students is given to the team.
4. Adequate time is scheduled for team planning.
5. Leadership potential is placed in each team.
6. Personalities, potentialities, and abilities of teachers are considered in organizing the team.
7. Various disciplines are represented on the team planning the instructional process.
8. Communication channels with the administrative team are built into the structure.

If these criteria are successfully applied to the staff design for middle schools, the goals of a student-centered middle school can be met. Time, space, and personnel can be rearranged by cooperative-collaborative planning, allowing for the full flexibility that best serves the needs of instruction. Of the possible patterns, three will be discussed next because it is felt that they are best adapted to the implementation of the curriculum in a dynamic middle school.

THE LEADERSHIP-TEACHER TEAM A leadership-teacher team, with an organizational arrangement similar to that shown in Figure 9–1, has a definite place in middle schools and offers excellent opportunities for strengthening the instructional program. Before discussing the

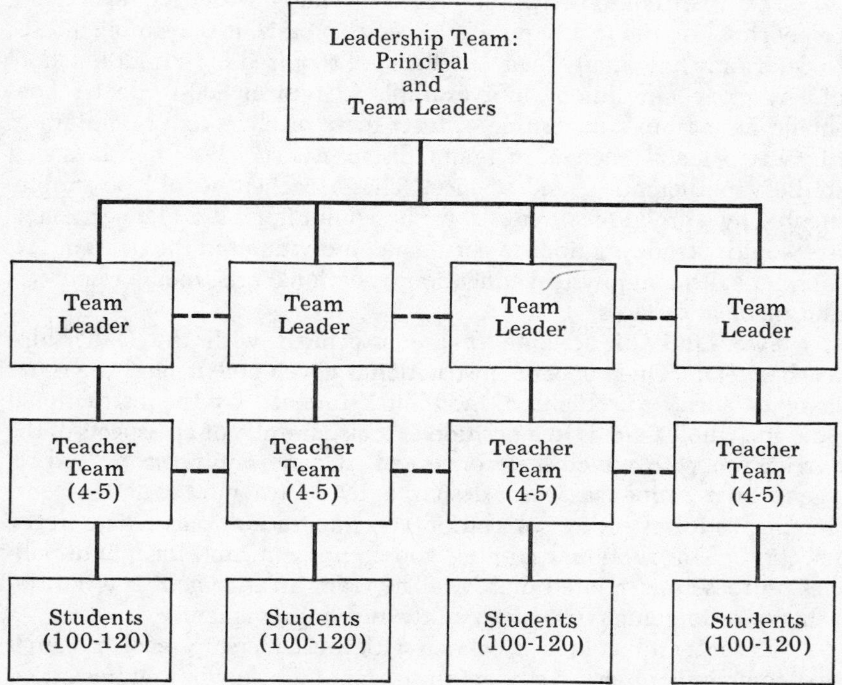

Figure 9–1. The Team Approach to Middle School Organization

advantages it provides, we will look at the composition and organization of a team and the number of staff members involved.

Each teacher team is headed by a leader who chairs team meetings, arranges agendas for meetings, establishes contact with resource people, and performs such other activities as are deemed essential to the successful operation of the team. The leader is usually a teacher in one of the major disciplines.

As depicted in the diagram, all team leaders constitute a leadership team or a steering committee which meets regularly with the principal. In these meetings, questions of policy are discussed, needs defined, procedures worked out, resources determined, and any related questions considered. In this respect, the leadership team or steering committee serves as a clearing house. Ideas and suggestions offered by the principal and team leaders are discussed and evaluated. Those that are thought to have merit are taken by the team leaders back to team members for review and judgment. In turn, the ideas and opinions of team members are presented to the steering committee by team leaders. This setup permits an easy two-way flow of information which helps to weld each team into a strong unit.

Teams are composed of four or five teachers, with each team being responsible for 100 to 120 pupils. Given this basis, it is a simple matter to determine how many team teachers are required for a middle school of any given enrollment. For example, a typical 800-student school should have from a maximum of forty team teachers to a minimum of thirty-two team teachers in major disciplines such as English, social studies, mathematics, and science. These teachers would be supplemented by a group of specialists, as shown in Figure 9–2. These specialists would include a guidance person and individuals in the fields of art, music, health and physical education, vocational arts, media resources, and medical services.

Two kinds of advantages are associated with the leadership-teacher team. One concerns instructional development, and the other involves learning problems of individual students. On the instructional side, the whole team is in a position to look carefully at all aspects of the curriculum with which it is concerned. It can examine scope and sequence, determine curricular design, agree on teaching strategies, outline means for effecting correlation and integration, participate in the selection of instructional supplies and equipment, and formulate policies on these and related matters. The team arrangement is a natural vehicle for ongoing curriculum study and improvement.

The other advantage associated with the leadership-teacher team is that commonly observed student problems and behavior manifestations can be identified and shared by teachers and other staff. Decisions can

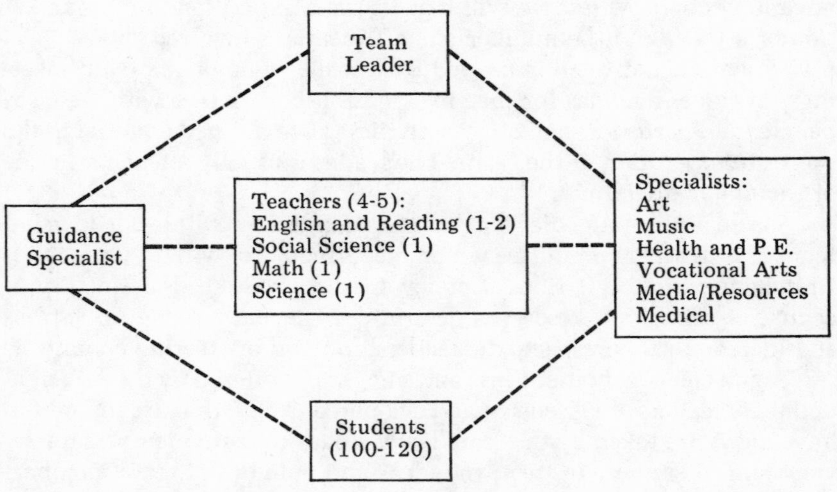

Figure 9–2. The Teacher Team

then be made regarding remedial or corrective actions. The efforts of the entire team can be concentrated on observing and evaluating progress or the extent to which action taken has been successful. Without doubt, the efforts of four or five teachers can have a more salutary effect than the efforts of a single teacher in dealing with either a learning or a behavior problem.

Professional assistance from a psychologist, social worker, learning disability specialist, or counselor should be available to the team upon request. These specialists broaden the talents brought to bear on a problem and can often produce a more tenable working hypothesis or solution. When necessary, parents should be invited to meet with the team and exchange ideas as to causative elements and possible ways of dealing with a troublesome question. This type of cooperative approach gives parents the feeling that the school is genuinely interested in the welfare of their children.

Another positive aspect of team-directed guidance is the possibility of having one team member serve as the primary counselor to each individual student. Each team member, then, is responsible for counseling twenty-five to thirty students. This counseling approach necessitates the development of a rapport between teacher and student, if students are expected to entrust their personal problems to their teachers. Children of middle school age must feel comfortable with and trust the adults to whom they look for understanding and guidance.

Role of the Principal. If the concept of the leadership-teacher team is to be realized properly, then it must be backed by dynamic, democratic, and constructive leadership on the part of the school principal. Although he or she undertakes administrative responsibilities in such areas as management, school-community relations, child guidance, and plant supervision, his or her primary task is that of instructional leadership; this encompasses a number of activities directed toward the steady and continuous improvement of the educational program within the school. It is through these activities that the principal facilitates the tasks of leadership-teacher teams in their work of helping students to learn.

Although the principal is responsible in the final analysis for the educational program, he or she shares this authority and responsibility with team members. In so doing, the principal operates under the assumption that staff personnel should have a voice in making recommendations and arriving at decisions that concern their work. He or she believes that the quality of recommendations and decisions is much higher when they are developed jointly. This does not preclude making solitary decisions based on established policies or on the need for arriving at quick judgments when circumstances dictate immediate action.

Team members should understand what the principal must do to handle administrative matters so that they do not feel he or she is working in an authoritarian way.

The middle school principal's role is that of a change agent and a facilitator of services performed by members of the staff. As a change agent, a principal exercises his or her talents to create a tone or a climate in the school that fosters open, cooperative relationships among staff members. He or she knows that unless people are free to speak their minds on professional matters, feel good about themselves and others, and have a sense of personal worth and dignity, change is not likely to occur. Change requires an environment that encourages people to exchange views, examine ideas, study innovations, and experiment with new ways of thinking and acting.

As a facilitator of services performed by staff personnel, the principal arranges for materials and resources when they are needed. He or she is concerned with doing everything possible to enable the staff to achieve the major purposes of the school. This calls for ready assistance in solving problems that staff members think are important and in expediting actions that contribute to the smooth operation of the teaching-learning process.

The middle school principal should be a communications expert. He or she needs to know what people in the organization think and feel, whether or not they are experiencing a sense of progress in their work, and if they have job-related desires and frustrations. Both as a listener and a communicator, a principal establishes channels for the two-way flow of information and ideas. He or she encourages feedback to his or her own proposals and suggestions and those of colleagues. He or she tries to make certain that staff members possess the understandings and have the perceptions required for sound decision making. A good principal is fully aware that the method of operation in listening and communicating is a vital factor in the success of the leadership-teacher team.

Responsibilities of Team Members. All members of the teacher team must possess certain attitudes and understandings, along with a willingness to accept responsibility, if the group decision-making process is to be successful. There must be a genuine desire on their part to cooperate fully in attacking problems—studying the implications of events occurring in school and community, framing and receiving propositions to be tested, making recommendations, and formulating policy statements based on rational review and assessment of pertinent information.

At the same time, team members must feel a strong sense of individual and group accountability for the decisions made and the actions that follow. They must take it upon themselves to help define the purpose or purposes for which they are meeting and to acquire an adequate knowledge of the subject under discussion. Once decisions have been reached, they have a moral obligation to implement assigned duties to the best of their ability even though they may disagree with the decision. Loyalty in this instance is to the group and not to oneself, the leader, or the principal.

The effectiveness of the team approach to decision making rests largely upon the members' ability to adapt themselves to the group process. Members must acquire skills in the identification and understanding of problems and in the use of democratic methods for their solution. They must know the limits within which the group can function, including the nature of the decisions to be made and where the line is to be drawn between their authority and that reserved for the principal. They must learn to empty themselves of pride in their own points of view and to eliminate the conviction that they alone know the whole truth. Group process calls for a spirit of give-and-take, an atmosphere that is appropriate for exploring problems, and a method for testing for consensus without creating pressures for uniformity. If these conditions prevail, then both productivity and member satisfaction will be achieved in a minimum amount of time.

Parent and Student Involvement. Parents and students also have a role to play in decision making by members of the leadership-teacher team. When a particular issue or problem concerns them, they should be invited to take part in the study and deliberation. Generally, parents and students are willing to participate if it appears that the final determination of an issue or a problem may affect them in some significant way. For example, they would have a natural interest in such matters as a change in homework policy, a reorganization of graded instruction programs, or a new system of reporting student progress. There are times, however, when they do not feel strongly about a proposal and are rather indifferent about their involvement in it.

In selecting parents and students to take part in team discussions, every effort should be made to secure those who have the most to contribute. The real challenge is to involve them in ways that will satisfy them and, at the same time, enrich the decision-making process.

HOUSE PLAN ORGANIZATION In order to provide maximum focus on the needs of each student in a guidance-centered middle school, it is possible to divide the school organization into discrete grades or "houses" with individual administrative leadership, team leadership, and staff personnel.

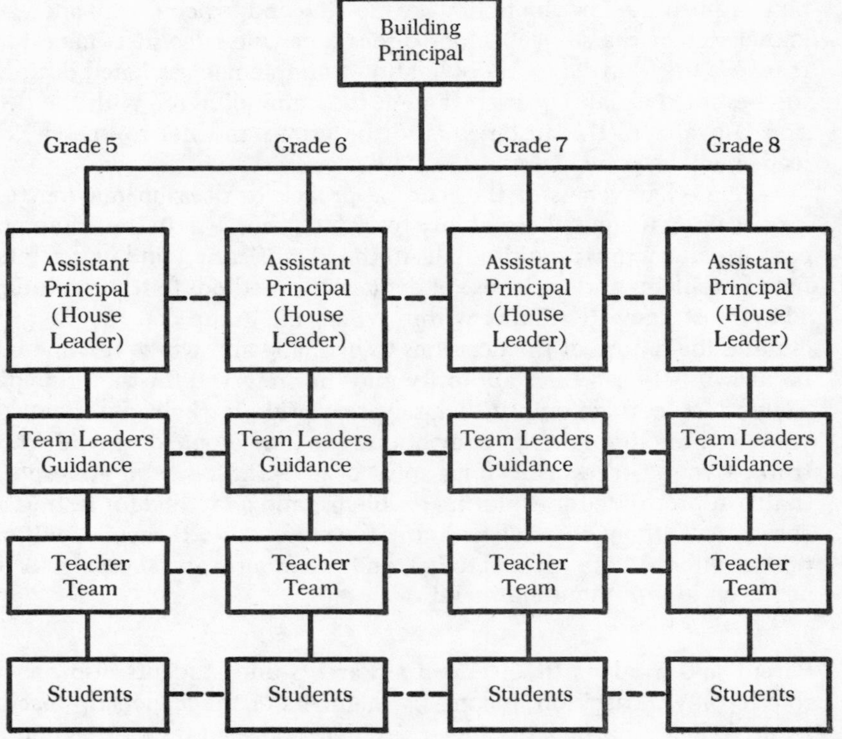

Figure 9–3. Middle School House Plan

What makes the house plan different from the regular team approach described above is that each house or grade leadership team has greater administrative responsibility for controlling the instructional, cocurricular and guidance programs.

The house plan can be superimposed on any organizational pattern of staffing middle schools, including the teacher team plan, the differentiated staff team, or even the old-fashioned line and staff organizational pattern.

The house plan organizational pattern can be varied to fit the size of the student population. In small schools, one assistant principal or house leader can be assigned to two or more grade levels. Guidance counselors can also work across two or more grade levels.

The major advantage to using the house plan organizational pattern is that a smaller group of students will receive the undivided attention of an administrator, guidance counselor, and a teaching staff whose sole responsibility is the instructional and personal welfare of the individual students within the smaller, more manageable group.

DIFFERENTIATED STAFFING Another pattern of staffing somewhat similar to the leadership-teacher team is differentiated staffing. Differentiated staffing is an organizational arrangement in which various levels of teaching responsibility are designated. Teachers within a team are assigned in a way that matches their talents to the needs of students. There are many definitions of differentiated staffing, but almost all of them divide the professional staff into levels and include teaching aides.

Figure 9–4 shows how this level idea works. At the top is a team leader. This individual heads the team and provides the expertise needed to stimulate and give direction to team efforts. Next, in descending order, are staff teachers, or teachers who perform a variety of services that are in keeping with their specialties, such as curriculum study, curriculum guides, activity packages, testing programs, programmed materials, and audio tapes. Assistant or apprentice teachers constitute the next level of personnel. As their title implies, they assist the staff teachers in various ways and frequently assume responsibility for lecturing, small-group instruction, remedial tutoring, translating goals and curriculum units into lesson plans, and devising tests. The various kinds of aides or paraprofessionals depicted in the model work with all team members in taking care of routine matters and noninstructional activities so that professionals have more time available for their specialties.

Figure 9–5 shows the relationship of the instructional team to students and instructional support centers.

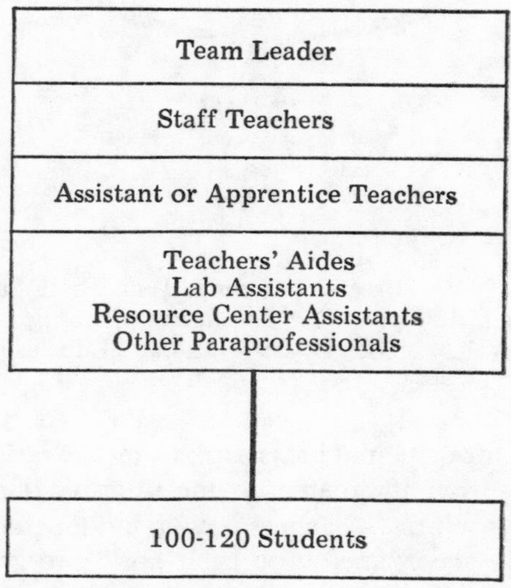

Figure 9–4. Differentiated Staffing Team Approach

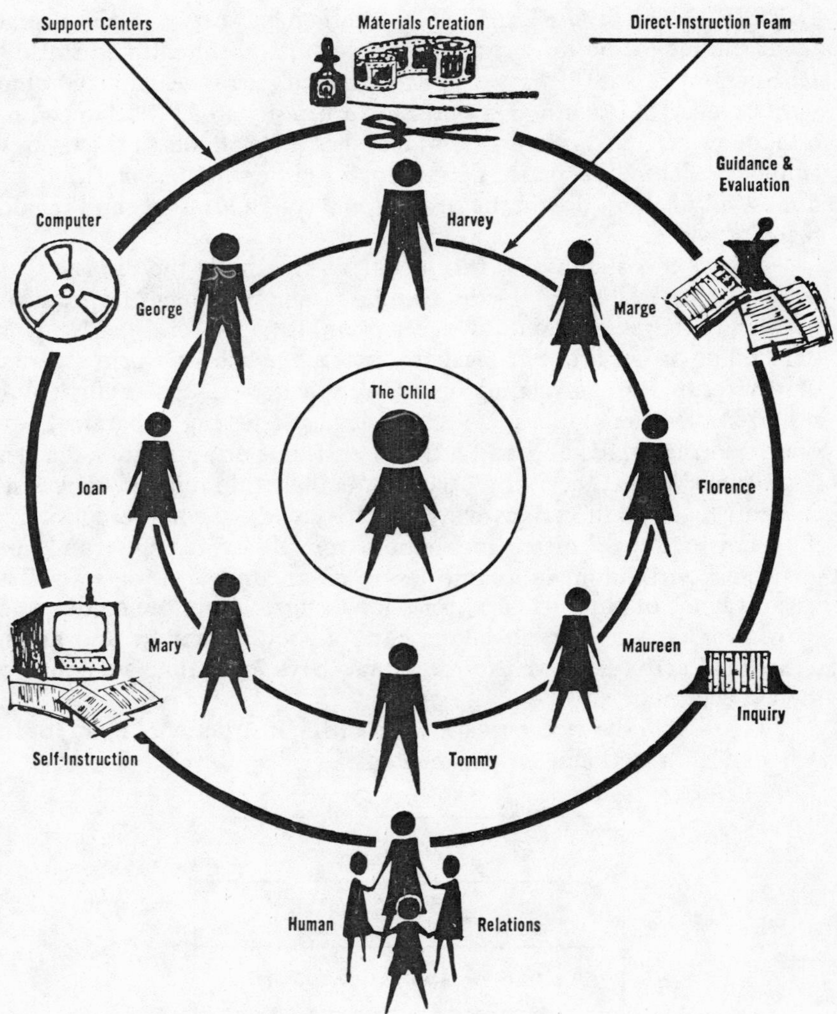

Figure 9–5. The Direct-Instruction Team and Support Centers (Source: Bruce R. Joyce, *The Teacher & His Staff: Man, Media & Machines* [Washington, D.C.: National Education Association, 1967].)

There are four principal ideas composing the rationale for differentiated staffing. First, it creates an incentive system which places a career label on teaching. Teachers have a ladder they can climb; they make progress in accordance with their ability to grow and improve. Second, financial rewards are in keeping with responsibilities at different levels in the organizational structure of the team. Third, differentiated staffing fosters a climate that stimulates teachers to discover their own strengths and weaknesses and to move into new areas of interest and competency. And fourth, it embodies a team approach to instruction, underscoring the development, implementation, and evaluation of the educational program.

Characteristics. The following is a quick review of the more outstanding characteristics attributed to differentiated staffing:

1. A larger number of adults are available to provide for the instructional needs of students.
2. Better opportunities are created for the individualizing of instruction.
3. More efficient use is made of teacher time, teacher talent, school facilities, and other resources.
4. Greater job satisfaction is derived by teachers who put their talents to use.
5. The staffing pattern is flexible and can easily be correlated with the introduction of new instructional systems.
6. Talented teachers are kept in the classroom and receive additional compensation for leadership roles.
7. New avenues are created for developing concepts and for experimenting in ways that help to bring about essential changes in education.

Tied in with these characteristics is recognition of the fact that the development of new kinds of curriculum materials and systems will shift the emphasis away from a teacher-centered program to one in which a well-defined structure of both material and process is built into student learning experiences. As these changes occur, the teacher will become more and more of a diagnostician, a facilitator, and an evaluator of individual student progress.

Problems. Like other innovations adopted by middle schools, differentiated staffing in a variety of patterns has given rise to a few problems. Among them is the attitude of teachers and of the professional organizations to which they belong. They oppose the idea of paying salaries according to the levels on which teachers are functioning. Such a plan, they fear, will destroy the concept of the single-salary schedule and result in the allocation of good salaries to only a few good people at the top of the team. They view the differentiated-salary plan as a disguised merit rating and would prefer to have all teachers receive higher salaries so they can afford to stay in teaching.

Another problem emerges when schools look upon differentiated staffing as a cost saver. Existing models in such states as California,

Florida, and Kansas do not indicate any real savings. In fact, the opposite is more apt to be the case, because more professionals and paraprofessionals are used than in conventional staffing patterns. To meet increased costs, schools using differentiated staffing may find it necessary to raise the number of students assigned to a team. Even so, it is likely that the ratio of staff to students will still permit greater individualization of instruction.

Effective use of differentiated staffing presupposes the availability of learning materials and systems to provide for the articulation of content and process on both an individualized and a group basis. Without these materials and systems, the end products of instruction will probably fall short of established goals.

One other problem sometimes develops in schools using differentiated staffing. With new roles for team members and new patterns of interpersonal relationships, the chances of personality conflicts are greater than normal. Their severity can be controlled if the principal sets a wholesome tone in the school and if the team leader is sensitive in identifying trouble spots and taking constructive action to control them.

Overview of Differentiated Staffing. The important advantages and disadvantages of differentiated staffing are summarized in the following lists.

Advantages

1. Differentiated staffing allows for more efficient and effective use of teacher/specialist time since assistants/apprentices/aides can perform many nonprofessional tasks.
2. It increases the number of adults available to help students.
3. It enhances individualized instructional and management systems since teacher/specialist can assign assistants/apprentices/aides to work with students having problems.
4. It leads to better management of student progress in learning when correlated with individualized instructional system.
5. It allows for paying top salaries based on the performance of talented teachers/team leaders.
6. It makes better use of teacher/staff salary budget than does a single-salary schedule.
7. It is a vehicle for a continuous program of curriculum development and staff development.

Disadvantages

1. Differentiated staffing may be opposed by current staff if they construe it as a "merit-pay" program.

2. It may be opposed by teacher unions that do not wish to break the lock-step, single-salary schedule.
3. It requires talented leadership to cope with inevitable personality conflicts among members of large teams.
4. It is not easily implemented in a traditional school or school district.
5. It is generally adaptable only where instructional systems are used; it will be of little or no benefit unless the team's efforts are enhancing an instructional management system.

STAFF ORGANIZATIONAL DESIGN Whatever form of team teaching is chosen, appropriate planning of the organization of the staff is necessary if a middle school program is to be truly effective. As a point of departure for designing or evaluating a staff organizational chart, one should apply the following criteria:

1. Is the principal released from administrative tasks so that the instructional program can be a primary responsibility?
2. Are job descriptions available to spell out in detail each person's area of responsibility?
3. Are team leaders and other staff personnel able to become involved in decision making? How close or accessible to the principal are these people?
4. Does the organizational chart help or hinder communication flow?
5. Is the organizational chart geared primarily to facilitating instruction and secondarily to administration areas?
6. How can communication occur between teams? Between disciplines? Across disciplines?
7. What is the role of the student in the whole organizational pattern?
8. Is the community involved in organizing the school? If so, how?
9. Is the organizational scheme flexible enough to allow change to occur?
10. Are planning and evaluation built into the organizational chart? Into the job descriptions?

USING SPECIALISTS AND AIDES

The advent of any form of staff reorganization allows the school to look closely at the feasibility of using a larger number of adults in the learning process.

SPECIAL RESOURCE PERSONNEL The teacher alone cannot completely individualize instruction for all students. Such an expectation would be professionally naïve. There are a significant number of children whose development deviates in some way from the normal so that they are considered exceptional. When learning is not progressing normally for a particular child, it is essential that the teacher be able to call upon the services of specialized personnel to help pinpoint the exact nature of the problem.

The group of specialists whose particular skills are necessary to identify the physical and/or psychological impairments causing underachievement and to devise an appropriate strategy for removing or circumventing these problems is the diagnostic team. Because there will be various specialties represented, and because it is necessary that their work be coordinated and integrated to be effective, these professionals must operate as a team. The actual composition of the diagnostic team will vary, depending on the particular nature of each case. The school principal or counselor, the teacher, and the school psychologist would be a basic nucleus for all such teams. Other possible team members would be drawn from such specialties as pediatrics, neurology, psychiatry, and social service. It is also likely that where circumstances warrant, various specially trained personnel from areas such as reading, speech, vision, hearing, adaptive physical education, and special education might become a part of the team.

A constant effort must be made in every school to prevent serious long-term consequences that can and do occur in the lives of children because of unrecognized physical and psychological problems.

The teacher is perhaps one of the most important people in the child's life when it comes to the early recognition of such problems. Although perceptive parents and medical personnel sometimes discover impairments, it is often in the school situation under the eye of a professional teacher who knows normal developmental patterns that the first evidence of a problem is detected. It is the teacher's keen sensitivities that are important in noting early difficulties, alerting others, and initiating the process of diagnosis and remediation.

It is also the teacher who will carry out with the child many of the prescriptions that grow out of the diagnostic team's efforts. When the classroom teacher follows the advice and direction of these specialists, he or she makes a unique contribution to improving the impaired child's ability to function normally. By utilizing the special competencies of professionals on a diagnostic team, the teacher gains command of new information about specific children and thus increases his or her ability to provide a meaningful and effective individual program for learning for each student.

INSTRUCTIONAL AIDES Teacher aides or instructional assistants should be employed by school districts to perform those nonprofessional tasks that can be economically taken over from teachers. The term "economically" must be considered, because the employment of aides, as recommended by teacher unions or associations, does not relate directly to increasing the professional efficiency of the teacher. Many teacher groups advocate employment of aides in their negotiations without having preplanned the effective use of these paraprofessionals in instruction.

The decision to employ instructional aides should derive directly from the following criteria:

1. The amount of scoring or record keeping required for material used in individualized instructional programs.
2. The number of large-group and small-group instructional situations.
3. The size of the team.
4. The number of students needing individual help that could be supplied by a nonprofessional.
5. The possibilities for differentiated staff assignments in the school district staffing pattern.

REMEDIAL/TUTORIAL PERSONNEL The advent of Title I, Elementary and Secondary Education Act, as well as the many state-sponsored compensatory education programs brought about by declining test scores in reading and mathematics, gave birth to a proliferation of tutorial projects in schools throughout the country. The lack of individual achievement in reading, mathematics, and other disciplines could be remedied, it was felt, if the nonachievers could receive tutor-to-student assistance on a one-to-one basis or in small groups. Schools have used various kinds of tutoring arrangements: paid adult tutors, adult volunteers from the community, and, in many cases, student tutors, both paid and volunteer.

Many schools have found that student tutors are effective in the one-to-one tutoring arrangement. In fact, use of older student tutors who are themselves experiencing difficulty in a subject to tutor younger students helps both students to learn and to achieve.

Middle school staff designs should include personnel to assist in remedial or compensatory tutoring. Benefits accrue not only to students, but to the school itself, as more of the community becomes involved in helping the school to achieve its instructional goals.

CLERICAL AIDES AND PRODUCTION PERSONNEL Middle school teacher teams need clerical and production assistants in order to perform their tasks efficiently. Assistants do not necessarily have to be provided to each team; they can be centrally located to perform similar services for all teams in the school.

The larger the number of available instructional systems, the more clerical help is required for scoring, record keeping, production of allied materials, mimeographing, photocopying, and the myriad of other necessary services. These should be performed by nonprofessionals when possible, leaving teachers more time for instruction and their students.

QUALIFICATIONS OF STAFF

ADAPTABILITY TO STUDENTS OF MIDDLE SCHOOL AGE Coping with the ten- to fourteen-year-old is not always as easy as many adults imagine. The junior high child has always been considered the most difficult to handle by teachers who have taught a wide range of ages. Teachers find the naïveté and enthusiasm of the ten- to fourteen-year-old to be most delightful when harnessed purposefully, and most demanding when left undirected.

Teachers of the middle grades, then, must be warm, capable, child-oriented, subject-knowledgeable leaders of youth. It is far easier to teach high school students than it is to teach the ten- to fourteen-year-old who is looking for an identity. Some teachers of the ten- to fourteen-year-old ultimately tire of the challenge and request a transfer to the high school.

One of the major factors causing staff mobility at the middle school level is the lack in most teacher-training institutions of programs to prepare future teachers for middle grades. The common practice of state departments of permitting either elementary or secondary training as an acceptable preparation program for the middle school generally leaves us with a neither-fish-nor-fowl arrangement for staff training. This problem will continue until something is done to change it. Accordingly, we believe that standards such as those below should be adopted by state education departments and used for the approval of preparation programs for middle school teachers. Certificates for teaching in the middle school should be issued only to those individuals who have attained the competencies implied.

Standard I. Knowledge of the developmental stages of late childhood and early adolescence in the physical, intellectual, psychological, and social-emotional areas.

Standard II. Knowledge of the learning processes appropriate to the above stages.

Standard III. Understanding of the nature and objectives of the kindergarten-through-twelfth-grade curriculum with emphasis on the place of the middle school in its sequential development.

Standard IV. Fundamental knowledge of curriculum construction and its bases.

Standard V. The ability to work with children at many different reading levels.

Standard VI. Depth in two content areas (combined time should equal about one-quarter of the total time spent in the program of preparation).

Standard VII. Completion of a methods course based on methods common to good teaching rather than on specific content areas.

Standard VIII. Observation of and participation in middle school situations as part of professional courses.

Standard IX. Student-teaching experience in a middle school unit.

BALANCE ON THE TEAM Schools function best when the leadership team can draw on the talents and enthusiasm of a faculty with both experience and recent training. A well-balanced staff with levels of both experience and inexperience adds to the potential for inspired instruction.

The placement of "has-been" or "never-was" teachers on faculties was one of the major reasons why the junior high school never reached its full potential. Teachers assigned to junior high schools were often unwanted high school teachers or new teachers training or waiting for high school placement. The problem was sometimes further complicated by the assignment of elementary teachers who also did not fit into the pattern. All of these factors together helped to diminish the effectiveness of junior high schools.

It is obvious that if the personnel for the middle school are selected as haphazardly as were those in the junior high school, the success of the new model can be no greater than that of the one it replaces. The ultimate weapon in the army is the infantry soldier; in education, the teacher makes or breaks the program and the school.

The planning process in which the instructional team engages is strengthened by careful selection of that team, particularly when teachers who comprise the team are able to relate to both materials and systems in more than one discipline. A mix of talent should step up the quality of the planning almost in proportion to the number of disciplines represented on the team. This conjecture has been borne out in the work done by outstanding teacher teams.

STAFFING SCHEDULES

How can the talents of both the professionals and the nonprofessionals be utilized to provide the most meaningful educational program? There are many answers to this question, all dealing in some way with, or at least related to, how well the school district can afford to support the program.

OPTIMUM USE OF TEACHER TIME AND TALENTS Where resources are available, the leadership-teacher team or differentiated staff team can be assigned to work exclusively with one group of students. Where resources are limited, it might be best to explore the possibility of assigning each team two groups of students, possibly smaller in number. It might also be remembered that some part of the student day must be reserved for individual or small-group work.

Schedules must allow for group planning, both for instruction and for problems related to students. These meetings should be scheduled and all personnel required to attend. The effectiveness of the team is related directly to the outcomes of these team meetings. Therefore, the leadership-teacher team must keep abreast of developments within each team.

The teacher's program in Table 9–1 shows one possible program or schedule that could effectively serve the needs of the student-centered middle school. The schedule allows for large-group and small-group instruction, individual study and counseling, as well as for team planning for both instruction and pupil personnel study. The time distribution may vary from week to week.

The effective use of teacher time can be evaluated best by the faculty, since they are most closely connected with the problem.

Table 9-1 TEACHER'S PROGRAM

ACTIVITY	FRACTION OF SCHOOL DAY
Instruction	½ – ⅝
Team planning for instruction	⅛
Team planning for pupil personnel study and problems	⅛
Individual counseling—independent study preceptor	⅛ – ¼

Effective programming allows the teacher time to prepare for instruction, to consult professionally with other teachers, and to meet individually with students needing personal guidance. If teachers feel that their program offers opportunities for a professional challenge and a sense of accomplishment, then the program has a better chance for success.

OPTIMUM USE OF STUDENT TIME As students progress from one level to the next, the amount of time spent in self-contained or block-of-time instruction in skills and general studies should begin to decrease. Older students should be able to spend more time in meaningfully structured independent study with less direction from the teacher team. A typical program of student time utilization in middle schools is shown in Table 9–2.

Modular scheduling could be utilized by the teacher team in planning the student's schedule and in tailoring the time required for instruction as necessary. Modular scheduling can be defined as a method of flexible scheduling that allows for the utilization of short modules of time, normally twenty to thirty minutes, rather than the more convenient and rigid periods of forty-five to sixty minutes found in most secondary schools.

The teacher team, during its daily planning sessions, can rearrange the modules as needed for effective instruction, since all those involved teach the same group of students. This flexibility offered to the team of teachers to rearrange instructional time should make their instruction even more pertinent. When necessary, the team can combine the talents of a number of adults for instructing or divide the group of students for learning.

Table 9-2 STUDENT'S PROGRAM

ACTIVITY	FRACTION OF SCHOOL DAY (BY GRADE) 5	6	7	8
Block-of-time instruction in skills and general studies	½ – ⅔	½ – ⅔	⅓ – ½	⅓ – ½
Specialized instruction and independent study	⅓ – ½	⅓ – ½	½ – ⅔	½ – ⅔

The possibilities for more effective instruction are limitless when flexibility and decision-making power are provided to the teacher team. When instruction time is needed, it can be allotted. When instruction requires different modes of grouping, they can be arranged. When added staff is required, differentiated staff aides are available. With all of these advantages, combined with effective and approachable leadership, the middle school of the future could indeed become a real student-centered environment for learning.

AN ACCOUNTABILITY AND MANAGEMENT MODEL FOR REORGANIZING

Low test scores in reading and mathematics, plus poor performance in College Board scores and general public dissatisfaction with the observable accomplishments of students in reading, mathematics, and other basic skills, have aroused a hue and cry for school improvement.

The practice in business and industry of seeking better management procedures has led to a similar demand for better school management and for schools' accountability for improved performance by students. This is, in essence, the bottom line.

Among the most widely accepted and rapidly spreading tools for defining accountability for staff personnel, as well as for better defining school management, is the business practice of setting goals and assessing accomplishments. The business management terminology for the goal-setting design is "managing by objectives."

Schools have begun to institute accountability and improvement programs for both management and teaching personnel, whereby goals are set, based on observable and definable needs, and then procedures are devised by which the goals can be met. Staff reorganization has been a natural outgrowth of the pressure to improve student achievement. Inherent in all of these procedures is the designing of measures by which school and student accomplishments can be measured or evaluated. The process of measuring accomplishment is defined at the same time that goals are set, then the objectives based on these goals are determined.

The entire process of reorganizing staff and determining the best methods of utilizing staff from the viewpoint of both efficiency and cost-effectiveness requires careful business management procedures, for it is incumbent on any person or group charged with the responsibility of reorganizing the staff structure of a middle school to spend the resources of the district wisely and to the best advantage of the students

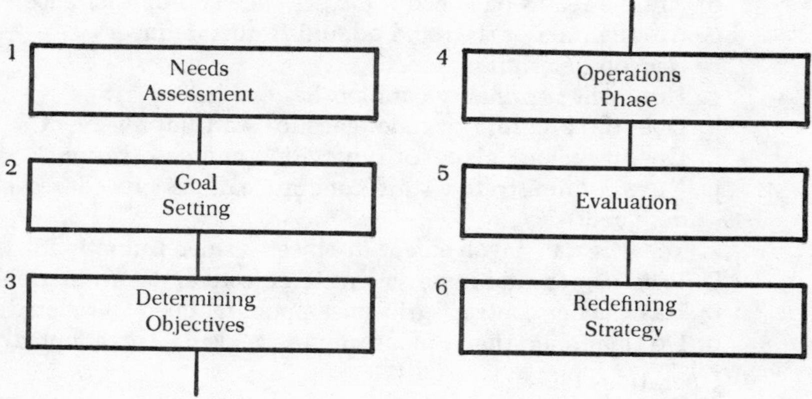

Figure 9–6. Accountability Model for Staff Organization

and the taxpayers. The following staff-organization management model, whose elements are depicted in Figure 9–6, could be considered:

1. Needs Assessment
   a. What are the staff needs in terms of optimum student-teacher ratios?
   b. In terms of curriculum additions or deletions?
   c. In terms of program changes?
   d. In terms of demographic data?
   e. In terms of the district master plan?
   f. What is the staff involvement in determining needs?
   g. What is parental involvement in determining needs?
2. Goal Setting
   a. Define all possible staff models.
   b. Develop plans for organizing teams using models based on school philosophy and instructional effectiveness.
   c. Assess the effectiveness of each model—its advantages and disadvantages.
   d. What is the staff involvement in the goal stage?
   e. Are staff goals based on data from needs assessment?
   f. What is parental involvement in goal stage?
3. Determining Objectives
   a. Select the most logical staffing pattern.
   b. Relate present and future staff costs to district budget projections and tax revenues.
   c. Will staff program model work operationally?

d. Are the teams balanced for experience and inexperience?
e. Are the roles of staff and administrators defined?
f. Are job descriptions clear?
g. How will personality conflicts be resolved?
h. Does the program include plans for staff improvement?
i. Does it include plans for supervision and observation?
j. Have administrative/staff communications procedures been designed?
k. What is staff involvement in objectives determination?
l. What is parental involvement in objectives determination?
m. Has teacher contract-grievance potential been considered?
n. Do final operational plans support goals set and adopted?

4. Operations Phase
   a. Does the model work?
   b. Is support for the teams functioning?
   c. Are the communications lines working?
   d. Do all staff members understand the philosophy and their roles?
   e. Is the in-service program for staff improvement working?
   f. Are the students in tune with the program—are they achieving?
   g. Is the program design simple enough for anyone to define and for everyone to understand?
   h. Are any changes needed and, if so, when?
   i. Is the evaluation procedure in place and functioning?
5. Evaluation
   a. What have we accomplished after a year's operation?
   b. Did we meet our goals and objectives?
   c. What are the student achievement results?
   d. What is the staff evaluation at this time?
   e. What is the parents' evaluation?
   f. What is the administrators' evaluation?
   g. What has been the effectiveness of guidance?
   h. Have we adhered to the design?
   i. What are the most notable successes and failures?
6. Redefining Strategy
   a. What changes are needed as a result of all evaluative data?
   b. What is the best strategy to effect these changes?
   c. What effect will the changes have on students, parents, and staff?
   d. How do changes relate to program needs?
   e. Should we reassess needs and begin change process again?

COMMUNICATION

A very important element in the effective operation of the leadership-teaching team or in a differentiated staffing arrangement is communication. Although there are a variety of meanings connected with this term, as used here it will refer to the free flow of information and ideas among staff personnel and the resultant degree of understanding.

An efficient communications system is crucial to a middle school for several reasons. The primary one is to facilitate consistent action on the part of all individuals within the institution toward the achievement of educational goals. Another reason is that of bringing about the unity of thought and feeling, the sense of cohesiveness, that is so essential to the maintenance of harmonious interpersonal relationships among members of the group. Clear-cut and efficient channels of communication are necessary for the transmittal and receipt of the orders, directions, and requests that serve as command messages. Failure to communicate efficiently within the school system and within an individual building usually gives rise to poor work performance, unhealthy attitudes, misunderstandings between administration and staff, and lack of serious concern for the attainment of educational goals.

A good communications system is one that employs various channels—up, down, and horizontal—that are both formal and informal. Messages are sent through formal channels from one part of the institution to another. They may pertain to routine matters, important information, new procedures, personnel decisions, and the like. Associated with the formal network are individuals who decide when a message should be transmitted, what its content should be, who should receive it, and the form in which it should be dispatched and recorded.

Informal communication is carried on largely through face-to-face relations among teachers, principals, supervisors, and other employees. It is more characteristic of the way ideas and information are exchanged in an individual school. Often this method of communication revolves around the analysis and interpretation of messages received through formal channels. Much of the time, it concerns speculation about people, policies, and consequences of anticipated action as well as the discussion of rumors. The latter is especially common in school systems where little has been done to set up formal means of establishing a two-way flow of information. It is the job of the superintendent and his or her staff, including the middle school principal, to integrate the formal and informal channels of communication. By doing so, they improve the chances of increasing unity of understanding, cooperation, and the satisfaction of individual needs.

Four principal means of communication are used for the transmission of messages. They are writing, reading, speaking, and listening.

However, more is needed to impart information, attitudes, and interests. The unspoken part of the message that is conveyed by facial expressions, physical gestures, tone of voice, small favors, and implied suggestions means a great deal in the communication of a whole message and the effect that message has on the behavior of an individual or a group.

In order to create an atmosphere in which the middle school principal can communicate freely with teachers, teachers with the principal, and teachers among themselves, the principal must have a fairly good understanding of how the communication process operates. This calls for the setting up of channels through which feedback can be received. The principal needs to know how his or her messages are being interpreted and what co-workers are thinking. For this process to operate efficiently and effectively the principal must have the ability to listen, read, speak, and write. He or she must be open to persuasion by staff personnel and be competent in the art of persuasion.

Chapter 10
Evaluating Performance and Program

This chapter is concerned with the place of evaluation in the middle school program. Attention is first directed to the meaning of the term and the need for evaluation. This is followed by a section dealing with the evaluation of student performance and a description of the instruments available for the task. Marking student performance and communicating these marks to both students and parents are then discussed. Last is a brief treatment of curriculum or program evaluation.

THE RATIONALE

Evaluation as a process is no different for the middle school than for any other school. It is a very complicated process, which can be described with misleading simplicity. It assumes that one begins with some sort of goal, makes efforts to reach that goal, observes the results, introduces appropriate changes in the light of observations, makes further efforts to achieve the goal, again observes the results, and so continues to repeat the refinement process indefinitely or until such time as further refinement for practical purposes is unnecessary.

The evaluation process involves both measurement (the collection of relatively precise data by testing, measuring, etc.) and assessing the collection of data by more subjective means. Data from all sources are put together to make judgments concerning the degree to which stated objectives, purposes, or goals have been met.

It is clear that systematic evaluation must be a part of any middle school program. In brief, the tasks of evaluation include helping pupils and teachers:

1. To discover the levels of student achievement in a given area.
2. To ascertain the quality of student achievement in a given area.
3. To communicate information to students so that they may judge their own progress toward personal and school goals.
4. To provide a data base for individualizing instruction.
5. To aid in the diagnosis of learning difficulties.
6. To furnish data for reporting student achievement to students, parents, and other schools, particularly the high school.
7. To determine how well the program is meeting the instructional and social goals of the middle school.

Reflected in these tasks of evaluation in the middle school is the emphasis placed upon the individualization and humanization of the total program. The diagnosis of student performance in the classroom may be undertaken by the teacher, by the student himself or herself, by small groups, or by entire classes.

TEACHER EVALUATION A familiar approach to the evaluation of student performance is centered around the teacher. The teacher may be in charge of a self-contained classroom or of instruction in a single subject in a departmental organization, or he or she may work with one or more other teachers in a block-of-time, interdisciplinary, or team-teaching arrangement. No matter what the instructional arrangements may be, the teacher has unique perceptions of learning and employs whatever diagnostic devices he or she knows how to use to reach judgments about student performance and to decide what steps should be taken to further the learning process.

But before the teacher can undertake a diagnosis of student performance, either alone or with other teachers, he or she must have a well-defined series of goals. These goals should be peculiar to student needs in a particular area of the curriculum as well as consonant with the self-determined goals of individual students and the group, and the goals of the school. It does not matter whether the teacher's goals are worked out before or after those of the individuals and the group. Preferably, they should be stated in terms of terminal behavior or of changes desired in students as a result of teaching-learning activities. For example, one way of stating behavioral objectives is as follows: "The student will be able to distinguish between the actual and the implied meaning in magazine advertisements." Or an objective might be worded in the following way: "At the end of the course, the learner will be able to engage in a foreign language conversation with a native speaker of the language." There are other patterns for expressing behaviors that are specific, measurable, or observable, but these two are sufficient for illustrative purposes.

In middle school education, the goals today are not limited to the dispensing of subject matter and the teaching of subject-matter skills. They are concerned also with such matters as the development of attitudes, ideals, interests, and critical thinking, with writing and speaking competencies, work habits, and acceptance by peers, with the personal-emotional, personal-social, and personal-physical aspects of daily living, and with problem-solving abilities, the making of intelligent choices, and the reaching of logical conclusions.

Evaluation of students by the teacher ought to be done on an individual basis. In this way, the teacher is in a position to note changes that have occurred from one period of time to another. Sometimes it is advisable for the teacher to administer pretests and so establish a baseline against which progress can be judged. For example, a student could be asked to use the facilities and resources of the library for preparing a paper or report and a careful record would be kept of these activities. This record may then serve as a base for comparing with performance on a similar assignment sometime later in the year.

Almost total dependence was formerly placed upon pencil-and-paper tests to assess student performance. Today, teachers still rely on this type of measurement, but supplement it with a broad assortment of instruments, devices, and procedures that deal with other aspects of learning. For example, by arranging pertinent situations and then observing and recording behavior, a teacher is able to judge with a respectable degree of accuracy how well a student can plan, engage in critical thinking, or follow the steps in problem-solving. Or, if the teacher wants to find out how well a student attacks a social problem, he or she selects and administers instruments that yield measures of the student's ability to gather information and use it in dealing with the problem. Or, if the teacher is interested in knowing whether or not a student is acquiring a particular skill or a particular understanding, he or she uses appropriate instruments to sample the relevant aspects of the skill or the fundamental ideas of the concept.

The former dependence upon pencil-and-paper tests rested upon the idea that all students could be handled at the same time, with a consequent saving of teacher time and labor. Saving time certainly has merit, but it is also possible to accomplish the same thing by testing and interviewing only a sample of a class. By testing six students from a class of thirty, the teacher can obtain a useful picture of the learning that is taking place in the group and the attitudes that are being developed.

Team teachers, and those in block-of-time and interdisciplinary classes, are in a position to pool information about individual students.

Even though their observations and judgments are subjective in nature, they have a real place in evaluation since they represent a team conclusion. It seems likely that in many instances the collective judgment of team members is more valid in assessing student progress than a battery of pencil-and-paper tests.

The collective contribution can be improved when teachers apply suitable instruments and devices to their appraisal of student performance. If appraisal is carried on over a considerable period of time, the accumulated findings enable team members to identify more accurately the students with problems that call for the services of counselors, nurses, home and school visitors, and other specialists.

All middle school classroom teachers must decide what techniques to use for evaluative purposes. Although variations in objectives, situation, and facilities will result in different procedures, nevertheless there are many techniques that appear to have rather wide application. Some of these are as follows:

1. The initiation of an individual student record system that permits the continuous recording of data concerning such items as standardized test results, performance patterns, and samples of classwork.
2. The creation of special situations in classes that enable the teacher to observe and appraise progress in specific areas of learning—responses to suggestions, the application of correctional measures, etc.
3. The comparison of teacher and student ratings of progress in specific aspects of learning.
4. The discussion of papers by the student and the teacher when the pupil is satisfied with his or her work; otherwise, grading of the papers by the teacher.
5. The development of pencil-and-paper tests that reflect the objectives of teaching and the work done in class.

STUDENT SELF-EVALUATION A defining purpose of a student-centered middle school is that of encouraging and assisting the individual to evaluate his or her own progress. It is believed that through self-evaluation each student can develop a healthy self-image as well as the ability to undertake self-direction. This process means that the individual student, with teacher assistance, establishes personal learning goals and then ascertains how fully they are achieved. In the course of doing this, the student makes a systematic analysis of personal strengths, weaknesses, assets, and learning deficiencies, and plans a program of action. He or she may either emphasize the further improvement of those aspects of learning that are handled well or adopt measures, within the limits of his or her capacity, for overcoming deficiencies.

In helping the student to establish goals, the teacher must ascertain that the goals are reasonable ones, that they are compatible with what is known about the learning process, that they are consistent with each other and with the goals of the class and the school, and that they are appropriate for the student. With respect to this last point, it should be recognized that students not only acquire similar concepts, attitudes, or bodies of information at widely different rates, but also acquire readily only those ideas, attitudes, and bodies of information that are in keeping with chosen goals and learning capabilites.

It has been demonstrated consistently that the kind of feedback a student receives from systematic self-evaluation is significant in directing future learning. For example, if a student discovers that an inability to read well is due to a limited vocabulary, he or she may then decide to start listing words that are unfamiliar and looking up their meanings, thereby compiling and mastering a more extensive vocabulary.

To be comfortable with the self-evaluative process, students need teacher assistance as well as a sturdy self-concept. It is the teacher's role to encourage each student to assess his or her own competencies. As a diagnostician, the middle school teacher should be seriously concerned with the behavioral characteristics of each of his or her students and should direct students' efforts into areas where a need for improvement is indicated. Usually, the teacher helps a student identify a weakness and stimulates the student to choose a plan to deal with it, meanwhile reserving recommendations until they are called for. At the same time the teacher makes it a point to help the student overcome any fear of failure he or she may have. In all this, the emphasis should lie in promoting individual achievement of self-selected goals rather than in comparing one student's progress with that of others in the class. The self-evaluative process is facilitated by this emphasis on a noncompetitive standard, since it engenders self-respect and the satisfied feeling that accompanies perceived progress.

Reference has been made in the discussion of student self-evaluation to the necessity for gathering reliable evidence concerning progress or lack of progress toward goal achievement. So far, not much has been said specifically about the means for undertaking this task. Although the general methodologies of evaluation will be dealt with in a subsequent section of the chapter, a few procedures suitable for students' self-evaluation will be described next.

A device that has proven useful for directing student self-evaluation is the checklist. The checklist consists of a sequential arrangement of the activities included in a given assignment or a given unit of study.

When the assignment or unit has been completed, the student checks off the activities in which he or she has been engaged. If devised properly and adapted to a particular group or situation, the checklist helps to inform the student of progress made in specific areas of growth and development, such as participation in class discussions, assumption of particular responsibilities, cooperation with other members of the group, preparation of particular reports, and the like.

Other self-evaluative devices include: questionnaires that require the student to react to his or her own classroom performance; descriptive statements that characterize qualities of personality, social attitudes, and emotional controls; tape recordings that may help a student to evaluate speech performance; folders that contain samples of written work enabling the student to compare present with past efforts; and special self-evaluative report cards on which the student records in sequence the grades received for work corrected and marked by the teacher.

GROUP EVALUATION In addition to individually defined goals, teachers and students must establish group goals. Common agreement on the ends toward which work should be directed may be reached in a single class, by a team arrangement, within an interdisciplinary program, or through some other plan or organization. Generally, once these group goals are agreed upon, they are then compared with those of the school and any inconsistencies eliminated. Not only are the goals that are arrived at through teacher-student planning taken seriously by members of the group, but also the process of developing them provides a valuable learning experience.

Once goals are mutually acceptable and consistent with those of the school, it is possible to make provision for group evaluation of learning outcomes. Plans may be developed to gather evidence in order to find out how the group as a group, not as individuals, performed with reference to its objectives. The concern is that of finding answers to such questions as the following: How close are we coming to the goals we set up? In what areas did we make our best gains? Where did we fall short? How can our performance be improved?

Evaluation procedures are usually selected by the group on the basis of teacher-student discussions of the best ways to secure the information needed for assessment and appraisal purposes. Sometimes the group decides to convert its statement of objectives into rating scales or checklists that can be used by both teacher and students in determining progress. Peer evaluation may be employed by asking for written judgments from the whole group about committee reports and related matters. These appraisals may then be reviewed critically through oral discussion. Other tools adaptable for group evaluation are selected tests, questionnaires, informal discussions, and structured observations.

EVALUATIVE INSTRUMENTS

Though applications of some evaluative instruments and techniques have already been described, we will now undertake to arrange a more extensive array of instruments in a systematic order, to describe them in more detail, and to impart more information about how each is best used.

SELF-REPORTING DEVICES Included in this category of instruments are questionnaires, checklists, rating scales, autobiographies, and sociometric tests. They are self-administered by students and, with the exception of autobiographies, may be referred to by teachers in their appraisal of performance. They assist the teacher in better understanding the student as a person. They help in problem situations by providing clues both as to student reactions to particular issues and as to student convictions. They are valuable in assessing progress toward objectives when progress is difficult to appraise by other means. Some of these devices enable the teacher to determine that things are accomplished according to a fixed schedule or sequence.

OBSERVATION Observation is used by all teachers in the evaluation of student performance. It may be done informally, formally, or in a combination of the two ways. If done informally, it takes place during regular class activities and is, for the most part, unplanned. However, the wise teacher always keeps careful notes describing the behavior of the students observed. The perceptive teacher also tries to interpret the behavior of various students. For example, noted observations may lead to a careful analysis of student participation in class work and to certain conclusions about some members of the group. The teacher may become aware that a few boys and girls are experiencing real difficulties in handling particular assignments but are trying to conceal their lack of understanding. Through ongoing observation the teacher may develop a sensitivity to the nature of interpersonal relations among students, then he or she can search for the ensuing effect on learning outcomes.

Informal observation frequently creates the need for a more formal type of observation in order to acquire more precise information about a student. A previously identified situation may be watched more carefully for patterns of student behavior, or new situations may be created as a means of determining how a student reacts to or deals with a different set of conditions. Usually, the teacher keeps a running record of the student's actions—how long it took to accomplish a particular task, what sort of difficulties were encountered, what degree of intensity characterized the workings, whose help was sought, and so on. Obviously, this detailed record-keeping will probably have to be limited to students with particular difficulties. After the teacher has accumulated enough data, he or she then analyzes the findings, draws conclusions, and plans what should be done to overcome learning obstacles or to raise the quality of the next assignment.

SITUATIONAL TASKS Complementary to observation as an evaluative technique is the use of situational tasks. Developed by the teacher, they are practical tests of how well a student can apply the information, skills, and concepts that have been studied. The nature of this technique and the ease with which it can be utilized are brought out in the illustrations that follow.

If reading and interpreting graphs has been a subject of class work, a simple test of these skills would consist of exposing students to a new set of graphs with instructions to write out the story they depict. Or students could be given a set of facts with the directive that they develop a graph and an accompanying interpretation.

Assuming that one or two fundamental scientific principles were dealt with in a unit under study, their application could be tested by presenting students with a situation or a problem that called for the use of these principles in resolving a difficulty or in reaching an acceptable conclusion. In similar fashion, the ability to arrive at valid generalizations based on evidence could be tested by creating a situation involving the analysis of historical data. Students' reactions to a wide variety of situations may be tested through presentations by means of films, slides, filmstrips, recordings, sociodramas, or stories told by the teacher.

WORK SAMPLES Analyzing sequential samples of a student's work is an excellent means of finding out how much progress is being made toward particular objectives. The samples may be taken at any time. Their selection will vary with the area of study and the amount of information needed for assessing performance. They may include special homework assignments, oral reports, panel discussions, essays, research papers, dramatic sketches, letters, etc.

From these samples, it is possible to determine, among other accomplishments, subject matter assimilation, application of knowledge, organizational ability, logical thinking, depth of understanding, nature of attitudes, and skill in oral and written expression.

The findings from sample analysis constitute a valid reason for the teacher to confer with the student. Together they can review the quality of the work and decide how to go about a similar task in the future. The point of the conference is the mutual sharing of something that each regards as being important.

If grading the sample is necessary, it can disturb the teacher-student relationship unless the purpose of grading is understood and accepted by the student ahead of time. Not only should the purpose of grading be explained before the sample item is prepared, but also the criteria for grading should be reviewed so that the student knows what the teacher will be looking for in the work. Preferably, grading should be avoided in the evaluation of individual work samples; rather, the entire sequence of samples should be judged for overall progress in specified areas.

CONFERENCES Conferences can be used as devices in evaluating student performance. Unfortunately, their use is limited in many schools because teachers do not have time during the regular day to schedule conferences with students. If conferences are held in these cases, it is necessary to schedule them either before or after school. Increasingly, however, schools are providing a daily period during which a teacher and student may confer about a topic related to the student's welfare. This is especially true in modern middle schools, where time is provided for teachers to meet with students and their parents, including specialists in the meetings when their services are needed.

Conferences become diagnostic devices when they are directed toward the satisfaction of an evaluative purpose. The purpose may be reviewing an analysis of work samples, discussing difficulties experienced by a student in everyday class activities, comparing teacher and student ratings on a scale for assessing student performance, working out remedial procedures for dealing with a learning problem, or trying to pinpoint the causes for conflicts in interpersonal relations in school and family.

Achievement of its evaluative purposes depends to a large extent upon the skill of the teacher handling the conference. The teacher must be able to establish rapport with the student, to assist in the identification of the problem, to offer suggestions without suppressing thinking, and to help the student to reach conclusions and to decide upon future courses of action.

CUMULATIVE RECORDS The cumulative record is regarded as an essential tool in the evaluation of student performance at all levels. It is a record that follows a student through his or her entire school career. Each year new information is added so that the record becomes a resource file of fact and opinion as well as the most comprehensive record maintained about the student during his or her school career.

Although variations in the content of the cumulative record exist from district to district, most records include data relating to family background, test results, health examinations, previous academic grades, interests, correspondence, special awards, cocurricular activities, conferences, learning problems, and anecdotes about classroom experiences. The inclusion of other items depends upon the needs of personnel who use the record or the purposes to which it is applied.

The information in the cumulative record is particularly helpful in the evaluation of students' progress. By bringing past achievement into the foreground, the teacher can often determine whether or not a student is living up to his or her achievement expectancy level. If special learning problems arise, then an analysis of the contents of the record can be made for information that may bear upon the problem. Such analysis also aids the teacher in getting a better understanding of any special needs that require immediate or long-range attention. The information in the cumulative record frequently puts the teacher in a better position to plan individualized learning situations and to work with the student more constructively on self-evaluation.

TESTS AND INVENTORIES When mastery of subject matter and related skills was the main purpose of education, tests were the principal devices for evaluating pupil progress. They were used for arriving at marks, issuing progress reports, and determining promotion. Today, tests still have a primary place in the evaluative process, but their use should be a diagnostic one. They, along with special inventories, can be used to reveal several facets of an individual's growth and development, such as academic achievement, special aptitudes and interests, personality factors, and vocational skills and preferences.

For convenience, the discussion here of tests and inventories will be divided into two parts. The first part will deal with standardized instruments, the other with those that are constructed by the teacher.

Standardized Instruments. A standardized instrument is one that is commercially prepared and has norms. Before the instrument is placed on the market, it undergoes systematic study to determine its reliability, validity, and usability. The norms are the product of careful experimentation with either a nationwide or a regional sample of students; they represent the distribution of scores made by members of the sample group. The norms make it possible to compare performance of a student—or group of students—with that of the larger sample group with reference to age, grade level, percentiles, intelligence quotients, or standard scores.

The middle school teacher should become acquainted with the various types of standardized instruments with which he or she is apt to have contact. They have a significant place in the evaluation of student performance, particularly in diagnosing strengths and weaknesses. Following are the types of tests and inventories administered most frequently in middle schools.

The *general intelligence test* is also known as a scholastic aptitude test or a mental ability test. It is administered on a group basis. It purports to measure how easily an individual can learn —now and in the future. In this respect, it identifies students with either high or low learning ability. This information is valuable to the teacher in planning educational experiences for and with a student. However, there is considerable skepticism regarding the validity of this test when a student has low reading ability, an apparent emotional disturbance, or a cultural background at variance with that of the group.

Achievement tests are designed to measure how thoroughly students have assimilated various outcomes of instruction. Traditionally, achievement tests were limited to the measurement of knowledge and skills pertaining to specific subject areas in the curriculum. But in recent years they have been broadened in scope, and they now provide measures of achievement in general areas such as problem-solving, critical thinking, application of principles, logical reasoning, propaganda analysis, and evaluation of factual data. Although the results of achievement tests can shed light on only a small part of an individual's growth pattern, nevertheless they are valuable diagnostic tools for determining specific learning difficulties, discovering the nature of learning gains and losses, planning appropriate learning activities, channeling students into proper groups and into challenging situations, and relating performance and abilities to defined behavioral objectives.

An *interest inventory* is an instrument that is designed to survey a student's interests in various fields of work. It differs from a test in that there are no right or wrong answers. The answers given by the student merely indicate a preference for something—a part of a personality pattern. Although interest inventories are used largely to suggest possible occupational fields for eventual exploration, they are also important in helping the student to gain insights into his or her interests and to see relationships between what is being studied and various vocational fields.

Personality inventories, like interest inventories, have no correct or incorrect responses. The choice made among the items comprising the inventory are assumed to indicate gradations in personality structure. Differences are revealed in such characteristic ranges as extroversion/introversion, masculinity/femininity, and tolerance/intolerance. Neither teachers nor administrators should attempt to administer or interpret the various personality inventories unless they have received rigorous training in the administration and interpretation of such instruments. To protect the student's privacy, the results of such inventories should not be included in the cumulative records, although a notation may be made on the record that such data exist. The teacher and the proper specialists should consult concerning any students who appear to have problems. However, teachers and administrators must keep in mind that they are not therapists.

Teacher-made Tests. Student progress is more often monitored with teacher-made tests than with those that are standardized and sold commercially. Standardized tests are usually viewed as periodic supplements to teacher-devised and teacher-administered instruments. This is because teachers can construct tests that reveal more directly the kind of progress students are making toward the particular goals they are trying to reach. They can construct the tests in light of immediate classroom experiences and intimate knowledge of the students themselves. There are usually two types of tests built by teachers—essay tests and objective tests. Each type will be reviewed briefly.

An *essay test* is made up of one or more questions that must be answered in sentence form. The answers cannot be given with a check mark, a single word, or by filling in blanks on an answer sheet. The essay test requires that the student express the answer in his or her own words after deciding on the correct response and organizing its elements to best advantage.

Essay tests have characteristics that make them valuable for evaluating student performance. They can be used to gain insight into a student's ability to organize material, to analyze and synthesize factual data, to transfer concepts from one situation to another, and to arrange ideas in logical sequence.

The drawbacks associated with essay tests relate to their lack of high validity and reliability—subjectivity in scoring; possible bias on the teacher's part due to illegible handwriting, poor use of English, or knowledge of previous student performance; and limited sampling of knowledge about a subject.

Essay questions designed for middle school students should require only a one- or two-paragraph response. Remember that many sixth-graders and almost all fifth-graders are either still in the stage of concrete operations or just moving into the period of formal operations. (See Chapter 3.) Therefore, essay questions for grades five and six should generally be short and concrete; questions for grades seven and eight may be somewhat longer and a little more abstract.

Objective tests consist of a series of items—of various kinds arranged in various ways—for which the answers are very specific. These tests are classified according to their arrangement as recall, completion, alternate response, multiple choice, matching, or rearrangement.

Generally, the advantages claimed for teacher-made objective tests are that they sample a wider scope of knowledge than do essay tests, are consistent in the results produced, are accurate in measurement, can be scored rapidly, and are not as affected by teacher bias as far as scoring is concerned. However, the disadvantages of these tests have been recognized for many years. Critics point out that they invite the guessing of answers, take too much time and thought to construct, require unusually precise use of language, measure retention of facts more than application of knowledge, focus more on details than upon generalizations and understanding, and place a greater premium on memory than upon reasoning.

READINGS FOR TEACHERS

Ahmann, J. Stanley, and Marvin D. Glock, *Evaluating Pupil Growth*, 5th ed. Boston: Allyn and Bacon, Inc., 1975. A comprehensive work on evaluation, useful to the teacher.

Karmel, Louis J., and Marilyn O. Karmel, *Measurement and Evaluation in the Schools*, 2nd ed. New York: Macmillan Publishing Co., Inc., 1978. In addition to the usual coverage, useful material is provided on informal techniques: observation, self-reporting, anecdotal records, rating scales, etc.

Wood, Dorothy, *Test Construction: Development and Interpretation of Achievement Tests*. Columbus, Ohio: Charles E. Merrill Publishing Co., 1974 (paperback). Designed especially for use by classroom teachers.

MARKING AND REPORTING STUDENT PERFORMANCE

Perhaps one of the things teachers most dislike about teaching is marking or grading student performance, especially at report card periods during the school year. Some teachers strongly oppose this practice and would like to see it eliminated entirely. There are others who feel that marking is necessary and should be continued. In any event, some sort of system is needed to convey an appraisal of student achievement to the student, to parents, to successive teachers, and to the next school. Marks or their equivalent are one such system. Report cards, letters, checklists, and teacher-parent-student conferences are among the means available for reporting marks.

MARKING IN THE MIDDLE SCHOOL Teachers in most middle schools are required to rate student performance periodically and then to report their ratings to students, parents, and school officials. If the procedures by which teachers judged a student's performance were analyzed, the analysis would undoubtedly disclose the presence of many subjective factors. Some teachers are influenced strongly by deportment, physical appearance, and native endowment, whereas others let class activities, cooperativeness, and family background play a part in their decisions. These and other subjective elements can be partially controlled if a school adopts a basic marking policy that spells out the guidelines for teachers to follow. Such guidelines do not restrict the teachers' freedom to supplement or to implement the policy in their own ways. Guidelines merely bring about a necessary consistency in marking and reduce elements of subjectivity. The teacher still has the right to follow a personally chosen grading system by supplementing the school's system; however, the position he or she takes on marking must be consistent with the school's position.

A marking system that uses a single symbol for reporting various kinds of growth runs counter to the objectives of middle school education. It is out of line to establish uniform standards of accomplishment for all students of middle school years, when only some are at the same level of development. The real purpose of grading students is not to compare their performance with some external standard or to establish their relative positions in an internal competitive situation; it is to indicate how well a student has determined his or her own objectives and moved toward them. It seems likely that a consideration of individual differences will reduce and even prevent some of the anxieties tied in with a period in life that is replete with concerns and doubts about personal worth and identity. Thus, the middle school should certainly employ an individualized approach in its system of marking.

An individualized marking system obviously should take the utmost consideration of the uniqueness of the individual. To this point the student has been regarded as a person in his or her own right. He or she has been encouraged to use individual capabilities and to develop them as much as possible in a consistent way. In carrying through with this standard, the teacher has the responsibility to understand the student, to render help as needed, and to evaluate and mark the student as a person apart from the group. When this approach to marking is implemented fully and correctly, instruction ties in more closely with the nature of the middle school child. Unfortunately, this type of marking procedure is not used as widely as it should be in schools today.

The introduction of such an individualized approach to marking is certainly not easy; established practice is strong and cumbersome to modify. However, in systems where tradition blocks major changes in marking, improvements nevertheless can be brought about by combining parts of absolute and comparative systems with elements of the individualized method. Some suggestions for such improvements follow:

1. Place descriptive comments on work done by students rather than just one-symbol marks. Descriptive comments on term reports, special projects, regular themes, and oral presentations not only tell the student more about the quality of the work but also reduce the emotionalism often connected with the single-symbol system of marking. A similar method can be used in reporting to parents on a student's performance at stated intervals during the year.
2. Define the competencies that an "A" student, a "B" student, etc., should be able to demonstrate. For example, an "A" student should be able to organize work carefully, show superior study habits, participate constructively in class discussion, and so on.
3. Employ a split-grade system when a letter mark is required. In this system, a mark is given for each objective or point that is stressed in class work. For example, a report in social studies might be marked for originality, accuracy of content, organization of material, and clarity of written expression. A combination of such points can be included in the periodic reports that go home.
4. Assign grades in accordance with different standards, and define the competencies each grade measures in relation to each standard. Assign one grade for achievement compared with an absolute standard, one for achievement relative to other members of the class, and one for achievement based upon personal ability.

It is possible to make other modifications in conventional marking practices in order to place more emphasis upon clinical approaches to the evaluation of student performance.

READINGS FOR TEACHERS

Gronlund, Norman E., *Improving Marking and Reporting in Classroom Instruction.* New York: Macmillan Publishing Co., Inc., 1974 (paperback). Prepared by an expert and geared to the needs of the classroom teacher.

Karmel, Louis J., and Marilyn O. Karmel, *Measurement and Evaluation in the Schools,* 2nd ed. New York: Macmillan and Co., Inc., 1978. See Chapter 17 for grades and report cards.

National School Public Relations Association, *Grading and Reporting: Current Trends in School Policies and Programs.* Arlington, Va.: NSPRA, 1972 (paperback). Brief but very useful survey of current trends.

REPORTING STUDENT PERFORMANCE The purpose of reporting on student performance is simply to inform those concerned about an individual's progress. Reporting informs both the student and his or her parents as to how well he or she is doing. If necessary, they can then seek help or undertake constructive measures for bringing about improvement. Reporting also sets the stage for closer home and school cooperation. Often a report card or other reporting form serves as a motivational force for a student. The student works harder and makes gains that otherwise might have taken longer to accomplish. Formal reporting is also a means of recording information that is necessary for administration and counseling, especially when the information is incorporated into the student's permanent record.

Whatever form reporting takes, it should be consistent for the whole school and there must be agreement among staff members on the purposes and content of the reports. If the school is concerned only with recording scholastic achievement based on an absolute standard of marking, then the report form will express that narrow purpose. If the intent of the report is that of comparing the relative standing of a student with that of other members of the group, it should be designed to provide for this end. If progress toward stated behavioral goals is the purpose, then the report form should carry descriptions of behavioral goals and indicate where the student stands with respect to them. In essence, the report form reflects the educational beliefs and practices of the school.

It is important that parents receive a careful explanation of the reporting system. Unless parents understand the procedure, trouble is bound to result. One way of obtaining better parental understanding is to involve them in the development of the reporting form. As a rule, they have many excellent ideas, particularly with reference to which method of reporting they think most useful to them. Students also have fine contributions to make in shaping a reporting system; they should be involved as well.

It is standard practice for schools to make formal reports to parents four to six times a year, usually by means of printed report cards. The level of performance is communicated most often by means of symbols on a five-point scale of letter grades (A, B, C, D, F) or less often by means of three letters (O, S, U—for outstanding, satisfactory, unsatisfactory). A small amount of space is provided on the card for both teacher and parent comments. The student's attendance record is also shown for the period covered by the report.

An example of the card used at Hill Middle School (see Chapter 5) is shown in Figure 10–1. This is a very conventional report card with standard provisions for letter grades in subject areas and appraisals of conduct recorded numerically (1 = good; 2 = fair, improvement needed; 3 = unsatisfactory). Space is provided on the back for teacher or parent comments. Interestingly, Hill Middle School formerly used a much more "modern" report form which included a great deal of detail and employed a system based on student progress in relation to ability. The "modern" report form was dropped in favor of the one illustrated for three reasons: (1) parents, according to a survey, had difficulty understanding it and did not like it, (2) the clerical burden placed upon teachers was backbreaking, and (3) it was inconsistent with the report cards used in the two other middle schools in the district.

It was obvious to the Hill Middle School staff, however, that the "new-old" card did not convey to parents all the information teachers and administrators believed they should have. Consequently, teacher-parent-student conferences were instituted; the school administration is satisfied that they have been quite successful. Ninety percent of the parents participate in the conferences; in 80 percent of the cases students are present. Communication between school and parents has been greatly improved and a source of irritation removed. Of course, to obtain the maximum benefit from parent conferences in a reasonable period of time, teachers must plan and prepare very carefully for them.

No middle school should depend solely upon the type of report card shown in Figure 10–1. It must be supplemented in some fashion. Schools that have been unable to schedule conferences have found it expedient to develop supplemental report forms to provide parents and students with more detailed and varied information. Supplemental

HILL MIDDLE SCHOOL

Name ______________________________ Grade ________

H.R. Teacher ______________________________ Year ________

SUBJECT	MARKING PERIOD								FINAL GRADE
	1		2		3		4		
	Gr.	Con.	Gr.	Con.	Gr.	Con.	Gr.	Con.	
ENGLISH									
READING									
BASIC SKILLS — READING									
COMMUNICATIONS/ CAREERS									
SOCIAL STUDIES									
SCIENCE									
MATHEMATICS									
ALGEBRA I									
BASIC SKILLS — MATH									
FRENCH I									
SPANISH I									
PHYSICAL EDUCATION									
HEALTH									
MUSIC									
ART									
INDUSTRIAL ARTS									
HOME ECONOMICS									

ATTENDANCE	Sept.	Oct.	Nov.	Dec.	Jan.	Feb.	Mar.	Apr.	May	June	TOTAL
DAYS ABSENT											
TIMES TARDY											

Figure 10–1. Conventional Report Card

reports may be distributed with the regular report cards, at irregular intervals as need dictates, or upon the completion of a particular unit, as in the following example.

The supplemental report card shown in Figures 10–2A and 10–2B is designed to provide detailed background for the single letter grade for mathematics on the standard form. Space is provided for assessing "mathematics skills" and "classroom skills." In both instances the skills are stated in terms of desirable behaviors. There is a code (1, 2, X, no mark) for reporting student performance in relation to each skill. In addition, space is provided for teacher comments. Probably the most effective use of the supplemental report is as a basis for a teacher-parent-student conference.

Another form of supplemental report, which could also serve as a basis for a teacher-parent-student conference, is a letter containing a series of brief paragraphs describing a student's performance, and perhaps also including standardized test scores. If a conference is not feasible, the letter is sent directly to the parents. Since writing individual letters is time-consuming for the teacher, this procedure is best-suited to small groups or perhaps alternative types of programs.

An example of a "modern" report card is reproduced in Figures 10–3A and 10–3B. This card reports on specific behavioral outcomes. Check marks are entered in appropriate columns, but no provision has been made for recording comparative levels of achievement. The format of this card suggests lines along which reporting practices in middle schools could be strengthened.

In addition to the previously noted reasons for schools' dropping this type of advanced report card and returning to the conventional type, another is the frustration occasioned among teachers when the card calls for judgments in areas where there is confusion concerning goals or for judgments of behaviors for which no data have been collected. For instance, many new report cards ask for a judgment concerning the student's cooperation. In newer programs, cooperation refers to students working well with each other. In more traditional classrooms, cooperation may be judged in terms of how well the student gets along with the teacher; in fact, student cooperation with other students may even be viewed as cheating. Again, if asked for judgments of problem-solving, teachers find it difficult to assess a student's performance and arrive at a grade when neither the content of the curriculum nor instructional practice make provision for observing the student engaged in it.

This discussion is not intended to discourage the use of newer and more up-to-date reporting procedures. Rather, its purpose is to emphasize the fact that evaluation must be consistent with curriculum content and instructional practice. The middle school cannot report to parents on student behaviors not actively fostered.

HILL MIDDLE SCHOOL
MATHEMATICS ASSESSMENT REPORT

Teacher ______________ Student ______________ Team ________ H.R ________

Explanation:

The following key was used by your child's teacher in completing the assessment report:

Key: 1 – Student demonstrated acceptable performance of the skill according to his/her ability.
2 – Student did not demonstrate acceptable performance of the skill according to his/her ability.
X – Student demonstrated acceptable performance of the skill prior to this school year.
No mark – Skill was not focused on during the report period.

MATHEMATICS SKILLS	1st Report Period	2nd Report Period	3rd Report Period	4th Report Period	MATHEMATICS SKILLS	1st Report Period	2nd Report Period	3rd Report Period	4th Report Period
Adds whole numbers. (20 skills)					Demomstrates an understanding of:				
Subtracts whole numbers. (10 skills)					Numbers and Sets (5 skills)				
Multiplies whole numbers. (16 skills)					The Language of Algebra (6 skills)				
Divides whole numbers. (11 skills)					Axioms of Closure and Equality Commutative and Asociative Axioms				
Factors (3 skills)					Adding Real Numbers Absolute Value				
Adds fractions. (4 skills)					Distributive, Multiplication, Reciprocals Axions				
Subtracts fractions. (7 skills)					Transforming Equations (5 skills)				
Multiplies fractions. (8 skills)					Using equations to solve word problems				
Divides fractions. (12 skills)					Solving Inequalities (4 skills)				
Interprets decimals. (7 skills)					Solving problems: integers, angle measurement, uniform-motion, mixture				
Adds decimals (2 skills)					Addition and subtraction of polynomials				
Subtracts decimals. (2 skills)					Multiplication of polynomials (5 skills)				
Multiplies decimals. (2 skills)					Division of polynomials (3 skills)				
Divides decimals. (4 skills)					The Distributive Axiom in Factoring (2 skills)				
Rounds off decimals. (1 skill)					Binomials and quadratic trinomials (9 skills)				
Demonstrates an understanding of ratio and proportion. (2 skills)					Applications of factoring (3 skills)				
Demonstrates an understanding of percentage. (3 skills)					Defining and reducing algebraic fractions				
Demonstrates an understanding of percentage. (1 skill computational)					Multiplying and dividing fractions (3 skills)				
Demonstrates an understanding of sets & symbols					Adding and subtracting fractions (3 skills)				
Demonstrates an understanding of subsets					Solving fractional equations and inequalities (2 skills)				
Demonstrates an understanding of operations and properties					Functions, relations and graphs (7 skills)				
Demonstrates an understanding of integers. (4 skills)					Systems of open sentences in two variables (5 skills)				
Demonstrates an understanding of operation of rationals. (4 skills)					System of rational and irrational numbers (5 skills)				

Figure 10–2A. Supplemental Mathematics Assessment Report

MATHEMATICS SKILLS	1st Report Period	2nd Report Period	3rd Report Period	4th Report Period	MATHEMATICS SKILLS	1st Report Period	2nd Report Period	3rd Report Period	4th Report Period
Radical expressions (4 skills)									
Quadratic equations (4 skills)									

CLASSROOM SKILLS	1st Report Period	2nd Report Period	3rd Report Period	4th Report Period
Works well in group situation				
Works well independently				
Assumes responsibility				
Listens and follows directions				
Completes assignments on time				
Has necessary materials for work				
Achieves objectives				
Budgets time well				
Easily motivated				
Behavior is conducive to learning				

TEACHER COMMENTS;

Figure 10–2B. Supplemental Mathematics Assessment Report

Middle schools desiring to remodel effectively their reporting systems must keep the following recommendations in mind:

1. The items included should be stated in terms of the expressed beliefs, goals, and practices of the school.
2. The report card should communicate to parents and students the information the school wishes them to have.
3. The report card should make provision for reporting progress both in relation to a student's ability and in comparison with some sort of norm, preferably standardized test scores.
4. Completion of the report card should be relatively uncomplicated to avoid an unreasonable clerical burden.

A= Excellent
B= Above Average
C= Average
D= Below Average
U= Unsatisfactory

Materials above grade level (1)
blank — Materials on grade level
Materials below grade level (2)

UNION MIDDLE SCHOOL DISTRICT
Interim Profile of Student Participation and Performance for Students Grades 6. 7. 8

School

Report Period

1	2	3	4

Student ____ Grade/Section ____ Section/Teacher Advisor ____

____ School Year

LITERATURE READING. TEACHER ____
Materials being used ____

[ ] Drama [ ] Poetry [ ] Novel

[ ] Short Story [ ] Mythology [ ] ____

GENERAL ACHIEVEMENT	Yes	No
Shows evidence of comprehending		
Completes reading assignments		
Uses literary terms appropriately		
Pursues individual reading		

Comments:

SOCIAL CONDUCT		
Shows self-control		
Works well with others		
Observes property rights		
Shows respect for others		

LANGUAGE ARTS SKILLS: TEACHER ____

	Excellent	Satisfactory	Needs Improvement
1. Uses class time to full advantage			
2. Works constructively in small groups on cooperative assignments			
3. Completes majority of assignments on time			
4. Consistantly revises writing from original to rough draft			
5. Successfully revises rough draft from writing to final			
6. Consistently makes effort to note and eliminate his writing errors			
7. Consistently keeps up personal spelling chart and individual tests			
8. Other ____			

SPECIFIC COMMENTS:
Improvement noted:

Improvement needed:

MATHEMATICS: TEACHER ____
Skill or concept currently being emphasized: ____

One or more may be checked:
___ Understands processes but makes errors in drill or repetitive assignments
___ Understands processes and does repetitive assignments carefully and accurately.
___ Prefers not to do repetitive assignments after having mastered a process.
___ Seems to have difficulty in mastering ____
___ Other ____

SOCIAL CONDUCT	Yes	No
Shows self-control		
Works well with others		
Observes property rights		
Shows respect for others		

Comments:

Parents are to keep this copy of the report form. The school maintains a copy. Parent comments should be sent to the school addressed to the section advisor - written on a separate sheet of paper.

Figure 10–3A. Union Middle School Report Card

5. The report card should make some provision, consistent with goals and practices, for reporting performance in the areas of attitudes, citizenship, interpersonal relations, and study habits.
6. Performance should be reported in terms of behavior to a degree consistent with actual practice.

Student Grade Section

SCIENCE: TEACHER ______ | Yes | No | Comments

	Yes	No
Shows growth in developing solutions to problems independently		
Participates in seminars and discussion groups and projects		
Completes majority of assigned tasks on time		

SOCIAL CONDUCT

Shows self-control		
Works well with others		
Observes property rights		
Shows respect for others		

SOCIAL SCIENCE: TEACHER ______ Comments

Shows growth in developing solutions to problems independently		
Participates in seminars and discussion groups and projects		
Completes majority of assigned tasks on time		

SOCIAL CONDUCT

Shows self-control		
Works well with others		
Observes property rights		
Shows respect for others		

PHYSICAL EDUCATION

MUSIC

TYPING

ART

SPANISH

______

COMMUNICATIONS AND MINIMUM DAYS

Parent-Teacher Conference arrangements may be initiated by note or phone to provide time for teacher conferences and in-service activities - every Thursday - starting in October and continuing through May - students are dismissed at 2:10 rather than the regular 3:10 dismissal.

Grades are but one indication of how well both the student and the school are accomplishing their educational tasks.

Primary purposes of grades are:
To present an appraisal of accomplishments
To guide parents and students in planning realistically for the future
To maintain communication between home and school

All evaluation is based on the judgement of the teacher, who has sole responsibility for assignment of grades. Achievement is measured in terms of:
Tests and examinations
Preparation of assignments, including neatness and promtness
Ability to organize and present written or oral material
Contributions to class discussions and group participation
Application of facts and principals to new and unfamiliar situations
Initiation and originality in independent work
Conduct as a helpful influence in the class
Regular and punctual attendance

Evaluation and reporting pupil progress is an important, complex, and not always satisfying experience for pupil, parent, and teacher. Our intent is to be as objective and scientific as possible. By combining grades, parent-teacher conferences and periodical phone calls, we have a means to better understand student performance and adherence to standards of conduct. This combined reporting procedure provides information about the following questions:
How well do the teachers feel the student is performing in terms of what is expected in those classes in which he is enrolled? (This information is all that is included in this student report).
To what extent is my child able to perform his various school responsibilities successfully?
How does my child compare with the other children at the same grade level?
Various school personnel, including the administrative staff, are available to interpret the grading practices, but individual grades are the province of the teachers. Any concern about grades or school accomplishments should be discussed first with your child and then with the teacher. All teachers are available to amplify their evaluation of a student's progress.

Figure 10-3B. Union Middle School Report Card

CURRICULUM EVALUATION

Curriculum evaluation may be defined as the collecting and applying of information to the making of curricular decisions. It may also be described as a means for determining how effectively goals are being reached and for identifying those aspects of the program most needing improvement.

There are practical reasons for undertaking curriculum evaluation. First, the middle school may still be thought of as an innovation in many communities. Board of education members, teachers, students, parents, and taxpayers want to know how well this new unit is accomplishing its proclaimed ends. Secondly, decisions must be made concerning what is to be studied, how it is to be studied, who will study it, when it will be studied, and how outcomes will be determined. Only careful evaluation of the curriculum can produce substantiated answers to concerns expressed by interested persons and to questions raised during educational decision making.

Curriculum evaluation is a descriptive process that focuses on a particular program or some part of it and tells a story about it. To tell this story, it is necessary to gather information, to process it, and then to interpret it. The information gathered always includes data concerning the worth and value of the goals of instruction and the progress students are making toward the achievement of these goals. It may also include descriptions of ethnic balance and integration, school organization and services, school personnel and facilities, curricular content and arrangement, student growth in self-concept, compatibility of methods, curriculum materials, psychological climate, guidance, and student activities. The inclusion of any of these items as well as of others depends on what is to be evaluated. However, no single component of the curriculum can be accurately judged without taking into account related aspects of the whole picture.

Though the task of curriculum evaluation appears to be monumental, it is actually possible to undertake it in a middle school without imposing undue hardship on the staff. Evaluation can be limited to one aspect of the curriculum and the work spread over a fairly substantial period of time. Or the task can be reduced in size by collecting information on a sample basis. There is no need to measure the accomplishments of all students in a grade, a class, or a school in order to collect enough data to reach sound decisions. Sampling not only saves labor and time, but it is also reliable from a statistical point of view. Still another way to streamline the evaluative task lies in the handling of goals or objectives. Instead of searching for information about student progress toward a long list of objectives, it is far more efficient to limit scrutiny to four or five objectives chosen from those most widely recognized in each field of study. Those selected should be objectives that teachers are able and willing to measure in one way or another.

Successful curriculum assessment is a team effort requiring close cooperation among staff. It calls for an organizational design through which the load can be shared and direction provided. This arrangement often includes a steering committee to head and direct a series of subcommittees in areas related to the purposes of the investigation. For example, the steering committee might be composed of team leaders. Qualified teachers and specialists would serve on such subcommittees as mathematics, social studies, language arts, instructional resources, guidance, and physical facilities. Each of these subcommittees would be responsible for selecting data-gathering instruments and techniques, for analyzing collected information, and for drawing appropriate conclusions. The steering committee would define the work of the subcommittees, set up time schedules, provide needed materials and services, organize and edit the final report, and present the report to school authorities.

Frequently, a steering committee may be advised to good advantage by an outside consultant in planning an evaluative undertaking and in making pertinent decisions. It is also a good practice to invite laypersons to take part in the process after the decision to appraise a program has been made. Their involvement adds a diversity of experience, knowledge, and opinion to the project.

The procedures that one middle school took to assess the effectiveness of a new language arts program offer a concrete illustration of curriculum evaluation. Faced with a growing dissatisfaction among teachers regarding the effectiveness of certain aspects of the language arts program, the school formed a committee to study the problem and make recommendations. In addition to language arts teachers from the school, the committee included the language arts coordinator for the district and representatives from elementary and senior high schools in the district. After a detailed survey of staff concerns regarding the teaching of language arts and a review of the current literature on this topic, the committee pinpointed two questions that they felt were at the heart of the program's problem: How can the structure of the English language be taught more efficiently and effectively? How can the ability of students to express themselves in written language be improved?

After a thorough discussion, the committee's recommendation to pursue answers to these two questions was adopted by a majority of the middle school language arts teachers and approved by the district office.

The original committee was then asked to continue with the project. Their first step was to draw up specific instructional objectives for teaching the structure of language and its use in composition writing. Next, a program of studies to achieve these objectives had to be identified. The committee decided that the construction of such a program was an undertaking much too extensive for a teaching staff at the local school level, so they began to examine newly published language programs. They eventually chose a curricular program that was compatible with the instructional objectives that had been identified. The committee then initiated a three-year pilot study of these materials to compare their learning outcomes with those of the current language arts program.

The pilot program was instituted at the sixth-grade level. Two middle schools were involved; one set of matched experimental and control classes was established in each school. The chosen program was used in the experimental classes and the school's current language program was retained for the control groups. A consultant was hired to assist with the development of the experimental design and the application of statistical techniques. An outline of the activities comprising the pilot project for the first year follows.

1. Fall—collect baseline data.
   a. Collect 250-word writing samples from sixth-grade students.
   b. Analyze these compositions statistically.
2. Spring—collect data concerning program effects.
   a. Administer achievement tests compatible with programs presented in experimental and control classes. Analyze learning accomplishments against stated behavioral goals for each group.
   b. Collect 250-word writing samples from seventh-grade students.
   c. Analyze these compositions statistically. Run statistical analysis against baseline data to determine changes and their significance. All data to be analyzed by instruction method, by grade level, by class, by school, and by sex.
   d. Administer "opinionnaire" to assess student reactions to each program.
   e. Administer "opinionnaire" to assess teacher reactions to each program.

In the second and third years the same procedures were followed except that it was not necessary to collect baseline data in the fall. Since this was a longitudinal study, the educational outcomes were assessed against those prevailing in the year immediately preceding.

The committee made program appraisals at the end of each year and reported these to the staff. Subsequent program decisions were based on these reports. Although the process required time to complete, this project represented the admirable efforts of one staff to institute needed program changes on the basis of specific data regarding educational outcomes.

READINGS FOR TEACHERS

Bellack, Arno A., and Herbert M. Kliebard, eds., *Curriculum and Evaluation,* Readings in Educational Research, American Educational Research Association. Berkeley, Calif.: McCutchan Publishing Corporation, 1977. Probably the best book in this field.

Grobman, Hulda, *Evaluation Activities of Curriculum Projects: A Starting Point,* AERA Monograph Series on Curriculum Evaluation, No. 2. Chicago: Rand McNally & Co., 1968 (paperback). A good overview of problems and practices in curriculum evaluation.

Lewy, Arieh, *Handbook of Curriculum Evaluation,* UNESC. New York: Longman Inc., 1977. An excellent handbook for those planning programs of evaluation.

Selected Bibliography

Adams, James F., ed. *Understanding Adolescents: Current Developments in Adolescent Psychology.* Boston: Allyn and Bacon, Inc., 1976.

Alexander, W. M., and V. A. Hines. *Independent Study in Secondary Schools.* New York: Holt, Rinehart and Winston, Inc., 1967.

Alexander, W. M., et al. *The Emergent Middle School, 2nd ed.* New York: Holt, Rinehart and Winston, Inc., 1969.

Allen, D., and K. Ryan. *Microteaching.* Reading, Mass.: Addison-Wesley, 1969.

American Association of School Administrators. *Profiles of the Administrative Team.* Washington, D.C.: AASA, 1971.

Appel, Marilyn H., and Lois S. Goldberg. *Topics in Cognitive Development,* Vol. I, Jean Piaget Society. New York: Plenum Press, 1977.

Association for Supervision and Curriculum Development. *Feeling, Valuing and the Art of Growing,* 1977 Yearbook. Washington, D.C.: ASCD, 1977.

Association for Supervision and Curriculum Development. *Humanistic Education: Objectives and Assessment.* Washington, D.C.: ASCD, 1978.

Association for Supervision and Curriculum Development. *Individualizing Instruction,* 1964 Yearbook. Washington, D.C.: ASCD, 1964.

Association for Supervision and Curriculum Development. *Learning and the Teacher,* 1959 Yearbook. Washington, D.C.: ASCD, 1959.

Association for Supervision and Curriculum Development. *Life Skills in School and Society.* Washington, D.C.: ASCD, 1969.

Association for Supervision and Curriculum Development. *Middle School in the Making.* Washington, D.C.: ASCD, 1974.

Association for Supervision and Curriculum Development. *Perceiving, Behaving, Becoming,* 1962 Yearbook. Washington, D.C.: ASCD, 1962.

Association for Supervision and Curriculum Development. *Schools in Search of Meaning,* 1975 Yearbook. Washington, D.C.: ASCD, 1975.

Association for Supervision and Curriculum Development. *To Nurture Humaneness: Commitment for the 70's,* 1970 Yearbook. Washington, D.C.: ASCD, 1970.

Beggs, D. W., and E. G. Buffie. *Evaluation as Feedback Guide.* Washington, D.C.: Association for Supervision and Curriculum Development, 1967.

Beggs, D. W., and E. G. Buffie. *Nongraded Schools in Action.* Bloomington, Ind.: Indiana University Press, 1967.

Beggs, D. W., and E. G. Buffie. *Programmed Instruction,* National Society for the Study of Education, 66th Yearbook. Chicago: University of Chicago Press, 1967.

Block, J. H., ed. *Schools, Society, and Mastery Learning.* New York: Holt, Rinehart and Winston, Inc., 1974.

Block, J. H., and L. W. Anderson. *Mastery Learning in Classroom Instruction.* New York: Macmillan Publishing Co., Inc., 1975.

Bloom, Benjamin S. *Human Characteristics and School Learning.* New York: McGraw-Hill Book Co., 1976.

Bondi, Joseph. *Developing Middle Schools.* Belmont, Calif: Fearon Press, 1971.

Bondi, Joseph. *Developing Middle Schools: A Guidebook.* Wheeling, Ill.: Whitehall Company Publishers, 1977.

Borg, W. R., et al. *Improving Educational Assessment & An Inventory of Measures of Affective Behavior.* Washington, D.C.: ASCD, 1969.

Borg, W. R., et al. *The Minicourse.* Beverly Hills, Calif.: Macmillan Educational Services, Inc., 1970.

Cuff, W. A. "Can Middle Schools Cure a National Disgrace?" *American School Board Journal,* Vol. 157, November, 1969.

"Curriculum for the 70's," *Phi Delta Kappan,* Vol. 41, No. 7, March, 1970.

Curtis, Thomas E., and Wilma W. Bidwell. *Curriculum and Instruction for Emerging Adolescents.* Reading, Mass.: Addison-Wesley Publishing Co., 1977.

De Vita, Joseph, et al. *The Effective Middle School.* Englewood Cliffs, N.J.: Parker Publishing Co., 1970.

DiVirgilio, James. "Our Middle Schools Give the Kids a Break," *Today's Education,* Vol. 60, January, 1971.

Educational Leadership, Vol. 31, December, 1973. (Contains a series of fourteen articles on middle schools.)

Educational Leadership, Vol. 34, February, 1977. (Contains a series of eleven articles on individualized instruction.)

Educational Leadership, Vol. 36, January, 1979. (Contains a series of eight articles on learning styles.)

Eichhorn, Donald H. *The Middle School.* New York: The Center for Applied Research in Education, 1966.

Elkind, David. *Children and Adolescents,* 2nd. ed. New York: Oxford University Press, 1974.

Flavell, John H. *Developmental Psychology of Jean Piaget.* Princeton, N.J.: Van Nostrand-Reinhold, 1973.

Frank, John, Jr. *Complete Guide to Co-Curricular Programs and Activities for the Middle Grades.* West Nyack, N.Y.: Parker Publishing Co., 1976.

George, Paul S., ed. *The Middle School: A Look Ahead.* Fairborn, Ohio: National Middle School Association, 1977.

George, Paul S. "Unresolved Issues in Education for the Middle Years," *Clearing House,* Vol. 47, March, 1973.

Grooms, M. Ann. *Perspectives on the Middle School.* Columbus, Ohio: Charles E. Merrill Books, Inc., 1967.

Hansen, John, and Arthur Hearn. *The Middle School Program.* Chicago: Rand McNally & Company, 1971.

Havighurst, Robert J. *Human Development and Education.* New York: Longman, Inc., 1953.

Havighurst, Robert J., and Philip H. Dreyer. *Youth,* National Society for the Study of Education, 74th Yearbook. Chicago: University of Chicago Press, 1975.

Hertling, James E., and Howard G. Getz. *Education for the Middle School Years: Readings.* Glenview, Ill.: Scott, Foresman and Co., 1971.

Howard, Alvin W. *Teaching in Middle Schools.* Scranton, Pa.: Intext Educational Publishers, 1968.

Howard, Alvin W., and George C. Stoumbis. *The Junior High School and Middle School: Issues and Practices.* Scranton, Pa.: Intext Educational Publishers, 1970.

Hunt, J. M. *Intelligence and Experience.* New York: The Ronald Press, 1961.

Individually Guided Education in the Multi-Unit Elementary School. Madison, Wis.: Center for Cognitive Learning, University of Wisconsin, 1968.

Joyce, Bruce R. *Selecting Learning Experiences: Linking Theory and Practice.* Washington, D.C.: Association for Supervision and Curriculum Development, 1978.

Kealy, R. P., and H. T. Fillmer. "Preparing Middle School Teachers," *Peabody Journal of Education,* Vol. 47, March, 1970.

Kindred, Leslie W., ed. *The Intermediate Schools.* Englewood Cliffs, N.J.: Prentice-Hall, Inc., 1968.

Klingele, William E. *Teaching in Middle Schools.* Boston: Allyn and Bacon, Inc., 1979.

Kratzner, Roland, and Nancy Mannies. "Individualized Learning for Middle School Pupils," *Clearing House,* Vol. 47, March, 1973.

Maier, Henry W. *Three Theories of Child Development,* 2nd ed. New York: Harper & Row Publishers, Inc., 1969.

Manning, Duane. *Toward a Humanistic Curriculum.* New York: Harper & Row, Publishers, 1971.

McCarthy, Robert J. *How to Organize and Operate an Ungraded Middle School.* Englewood Cliffs, N.J.: Prentice-Hall, Inc., 1967.

Moss, Theodore C. *Middle School.* Boston: Houghton Mifflin Co., 1969.

Musgrave, G. Ray. *Individualized Instruction: Teaching Strategies Focusing on the Learner.* Boston: Allyn and Bacon, 1975.

National School Public Relations Association. *Differentiated Staffing in Schools.* Washington, D.C.: NPRA, 1970.

Overly, Donald E., John Rye Kinghorn, and Richard L. Preston. *Middle School: Humanizing Education for Youth.* Worthington, Ohio: Charles A. Jones Publishing Co., 1972.

Passow, A. Harry, and Robert P. Leeper, eds. *Intellectual Development: Another Look.* Washington, D.C.: Association for Supervision and Curriculum Development, 1964.

Piaget, Jean and Barbel Inhelder. *The Psychology of the Child.* New York: Basic Books, 1969.

Piaget, Jean. *To Understand Is To Invent.* New York: Grossman Publishers, 1973.

Piaget, Jean. *The Science of Education and the Psychology of the Child.* New York: Orion Press, 1970.

Popham, W. James, Elliot W. Eisner, Howard J. Sullivan, and Louise Tyler. *Instructional Objectives*, Educational Research Association Monograph No. 3. Chicago: Rand McNally & Co., 1969.

Pulaski, Mary Ann. *Understanding Piaget: An Introduction to Children's Cognitive Development.* New York: Harper & Row Publishers, Inc., 1971.

Pumerantz, Philip, and Ralph W. Galano. *Establishing Interdisciplinary Programs in the Middle School.* West Nyack, N.Y.: Parker Publishing Co., 1972.

Rennels, Max R. "Cerebral Symmetry: An Urgent Concern for Education." *Phi Delta Kappan*, Vol. 57, March, 1976, pp. 471–72.

Rogers, Carl R. *Freedom to Learn.* Columbus, Ohio: Charles E. Merrill Publishing Co., 1969.

Romano, Louis G., et al., eds. *The Middle School.* Chicago: Nelson-Hall Co., 1973.

Schein, Bernard, and Martha Pierce Schein. *Open Classrooms in the Middle School.* West Nyack, N.Y.: Parker Publishing Company, Inc., 1975.

Schoo, Philip H. "Optimum Setting for the Early Adolescent: Junior High or Middle School?" *North Central Association Quarterly*, Vol. 48, Spring, 1974.

Stoumbis, George C., and Alvin Howard, eds. *Schools for the Middle Years: Readings.* Scranton, Pa.: Intext Educational Publishers, 1969.

Stradley, William. *Practical Guide to the Middle School.* Englewood Cliffs, N.J.: Prentice-Hall, Inc., 1971.

Talmage, Harriet, ed. *Systems of Individualized Education.* Berkeley, Calif.: McCutchan Publishing Corp., 1975.

"Twenty-Eight Ways to Build Mistakes Out of Your Middle School," *American School Board Journal*, Vol. 158, July, 1970.

Vars, Gordon F., ed. *Common Learnings: Core and Interdisciplinary Team Approaches.* Scranton, Pa.: Intext Educational Publishers, 1961.

Weinstein, Gerald, and Mario D. Fantini. *Toward Humanistic Education.* New York: Praeger Publishers, 1970.

Index

D

E

F

G

H

I

N

O

P

Q

R

S